CLASSICAL COUNTY HISTORIES

GENERAL EDITOR: JACK SIMMONS

MAGNA BRITANNIA
BEDFORDSHIRE

MAGNA BRITANNIA
BEDFORDSHIRE

BY

DANIEL AND SAMUEL LYSONS

With a new Introduction by
JACK SIMMONS

This edition originally published 1806
Republished 1978 by EP Publishing Limited

PUBLISHER'S NOTES

This is a reprint of Vol. I, part i, of the Lysons brothers' *Magna Britannia*. Details of the issue of the whole series are given in the Introduction. The re-issue of 1813 contains the following supplementary items, all included in this reprint: the new title-page of 1813, the complete additions and corrections, including an extra plate, and the indexes, all specially paginated to follow the main text of part i. The revised List of Plates of 1813 is used here. The map is here reproduced in black and white.

The text and plates for this volume have been reproduced from Bedfordshire County Library copies nos. 130212 and 61877 in the Local Collections of Luton Central and Biggleswade Libraries. Full details of these are deposited with Bedfordshire County Library. The portraits of the authors have been reproduced by kind permission of the National Portrait Gallery.

The plates are inserted in the order given in the List of Plates; but Plate XIII, "Gravestone in Bromham Church", is numbered page 695 for inclusion in the page sequence of the Additions paginated for insertion at the end of the complete Volume I.

The plates have usually been reduced to 76% of original size, but occasionally the reduction has had to be increased to 70% of original size.

British Library Cataloguing in Publication Data
Lysons, Daniel
 Magna Britannia. – (Classical county histories).
 Bedfordshire
 1. Great Britain – History
 I. Title II. Lysons, Samuel III. Series
 942   DA30
 ISBN 0-7158-1312-9

ISBN 0 7158 1312 9

Printed in Great Britain by The Scolar Press Ilkley, West Yorkshire

THE LYSONS BROTHERS AND THEIR WORK

The study of topography and local history in England has been pursued with vigour since the sixteenth century.[1] Two main ideas can be discerned in it almost from the beginning: one, that local history forms an essential part of the history of England as a whole, and should be treated as such; the other, that a single tract of the country, a county or one town or parish, should be considered separately as an end in itself. The first may be called the "extensive" approach; the second the "intensive".

Both began to develop, from earlier origins, in the Elizabethan age. The extensive approach achieved a triumph in Camden's *Britannia*, published in 1586. This was a general survey, giving attention to Roman antiquities in particular but to many other things too, throughout the British Isles. It was the first comprehensive description ever written, not a study of antiquities alone nor resting solely on knowledge derived from books but a broad historical account based on reading and, in part at least, on the author's personal observation. The work had the full success it deserved. It ran through seven editions in England in Camden's life-time, besides two others issued at Frankfurt and Amsterdam; at least nine more were published down to 1806.

Camden's *Britannia* was the first monument of the extensive method, and it remains in many ways the noblest. It helped the growth of the intensive method too. Before the end of the sixteenth century a number of studies of individual counties had been written (not usually intended as part of a larger design), like Carew's *Survey of Cornwall*. None of these was primarily a work of history, though they all included a good deal of historical material. The first

---

[1] For a general survey of it, with separate accounts of eight individual writers, see *English County Historians*, ed. J. Simmons (1978).

county histories, properly so called, began to be undertaken not long afterwards. Again they had a distinguished prototype, which set the whole study on firm foundations, as Camden's had done. This was Dugdale's *Antiquities of Warwickshire,* published in 1656. The first book devoted solely to one English town, Somner's *Antiquities of Canterbury,* had appeared shortly before, in 1640; and the pioneer work in parish history, White Kennett's *Parochial Antiquities,* followed in 1695. By the end of the seventeenth century, therefore, it can be said that the intensive method had established itself firmly.

That method soon became popular, applied to the study of counties: units of English local government well adapted, in size and character, to treatment of this kind.[1] A classical pattern emerged, derived from Dugdale's example but sometimes extending its view further than he had done, and by the end of the eighteenth century about a third of the counties of England could point to competent histories of their own.

The progress made by the extensive method in these years was less remarkable. Thomas Cox and Anthony Hall produced, anonymously, their useful *Magna Britannia et Hibernia* in 1720-31, professedly based on Camden. A fine new edition of Camden's own work, very much enlarged, was published by Richard Gough in 1789. Some good illustrated works, surveying the antiquities of the country as a whole, came out (see p. xix). But nobody felt impelled to undertake an entirely new general survey. The nearest approach to it was perhaps represented by Daniel Lysons's big book *The Environs of London,* published in four volumes in 1792–7. It is a measure of the growth of the capital and its suburbs that a work such as this, which set out to treat every place within twelve miles of London, could be regarded as in any way comparable to studies of the nation as a whole. It is a young man's book – the first volume appeared when he was only thirty – and it evidently helped him to perceive the need for something more ambitious. Having produced a supplementary volume, on certain parishes in Middlesex, in 1800, he turned to assembling the materials for a larger work, in collaboration with his brother Samuel.

* * *

The Lysons family had been established in Gloucestershire at least since the sixteenth century. They had come to own substantial property in Hempsted,

---

[1] Cf. *ibid.,* 2.

just south of Gloucester itself, and they purchased the manor, with its house Hempsted Court, from the heirs of Sir Robert Atkyns, the historian of the county, after his death in 1711.[1] Later in the century they acquired the patronage of the living of Rodmarton, near Tetbury, and four generations of the family were rectors there in succession, from 1756 to 1893. Daniel Lysons, already mentioned, was the eldest son of the first of these four rectors, born in 1762; the second son, Samuel, followed a year later.

Both brothers were educated at Bath Grammar School, but then their paths diverged. Daniel went to St Mary Hall, Oxford, graduated in 1782, was ordained and became curate first of Mortlake in 1786, then of Putney in 1790. Shortly after he went to Mortlake he became acquainted with Horace Walpole, who lived at Strawberry Hill only four miles away and after his succession to the earldom of Orford in 1791 appointed him his chaplain.[2] This was valuable encouragement in the antiquarian studies on which he was now engaged, and Daniel requited it by the dedication of *The Environs of London*. His clerical duties cannot have been heavy, in what were then two quiet little riverside parishes.

Meanwhile, his brother Samuel had taken up the law. He served with a solicitor at Bath and was then entered at the Inner Temple, becoming a special pleader. He was called to the bar in 1798. By that time he was known to Sir Joseph Banks, an influential patron in almost every field of intellectual endeavour. Banks was President of the Royal Society, and both brothers were elected Fellows of that body in 1797. Next year Banks introduced Samuel to King George III and his family, who took a liking to him. Partly through their influence, he was appointed Keeper of the Records in the Tower of London (part of the national archives, which are in the Public Record Office today) in 1803.[3] He then ceased to practise the law, devoting himself to historical and antiquarian pursuits for the rest of his life. Both brothers were Fellows of the Society of Antiquaries. Samuel was its Director from 1798 to 1809 and one of its Vice-Presidents from 1812 to his death.

Daniel, as the eldest son, had inherited the family estate of Hempsted in 1800. In that year he began to collect materials with his brother for the *Magna Britannia*. Its plan, compilation, and publishing will be discussed shortly.

This enterprise was more than a life's work for both men, yet they both

---

[1] T. Fosbrooke, *Abstracts of Records . . . respecting the County of Gloucester* (1807), i. 275-6.
[2] His letters to Daniel and Samuel Lysons are printed in his *Correspondence*, ed. W. S. Lewis, xv (1952); they include a moving letter to Daniel of 29 October 1795 (xv. 271–3).
[3] For the friendly activity of Princess Elizabeth on his behalf, see L. Fleming, *Memoir and Select Letters of Samuel Lysons* (1934), 28–30.

pursued other historical interests while it was in preparation. Daniel published an account of the Three Choirs Festival in 1812, prefaced by an essay on the condition of the parish clergy in England. Samuel's interests were more specifically archaeological. He was a not unskilled draughtsman, and he produced three books on Gloucestershire antiquities, together with a very ambitious and elaborate work in two folio volumes: *Reliquiae Britannico-Romanae, containing Figures of Roman Antiquities discovered in England* (1801–17). The production of this book occupied his attention for twenty-five years of his life and is said to have cost him £6000.

Daniel succeeded his father as rector of Rodmarton in 1804 and continued there (living in the rectory, not at Hempsted) until 1833, when he resigned in favour of his eldest surviving son, Samuel. He died at Hempsted on 8 January 1834. He had been married twice and left six children. His eldest surviving son Samuel (1806–77) was more prominent as a clergyman than he had been himself, and was an author of a different kind. Besides several popular books on the history of Gloucestershire, he published a work on the identity of the Patriarch Job, one on Dick Whittington and his Cat, and an historical novel *Claudia and Pudens, or the Early Christians in Gloucester; a Tale of the First Century*. His youngest son, Daniel (1816–98), became a soldier and rose to be a General and Constable of the Tower. He produced a manual of drill and rifle practice for the Volunteers, which shot through ten editions in 1859–61; but he is better remembered for two volumes published at the very end of his long life, *The Crimean War from First to Last* (a series of his letters written home, 1895), and *Early Reminiscences* (1896). The Lysons were indeed a talented family.

* * *

Daniel Lysons was a man of method: evidently a hoarder, who was disinclined to throw papers away. Eight volumes of newspaper cuttings he assembled were presented by him to the British Museum. He made it another donation, more valuable: the correspondence and working papers he accumulated for *The Environs of London* and the *Magna Britannia*, sixty-four volumes of them in all, which he gave to the Museum in January 1833, shortly before his death.[1] Twelve of these volumes relate to *The Environs*[2] and can be ignored here. The rest throw a good deal of light on the preparation of

[1] Now British Library, Add. MSS. 9408–71.
[2] Add. MSS. 9431–6, 9451–7.

the second and larger work. They divide themselves into four groups: (1) correspondence concerned with the *Magna Britannia;*[1] (2) miscellaneous notes for the published volumes;[2] (3) illustrations, maps, and church notes, with many sketches by Samuel Lysons, in some cases to be engraved in the book;[3] (4) notes on the remaining counties of England never covered by the work as it was published.[4]

Unfortunately these papers tell us nothing about the genesis of the work itself. Doubtless it had been discussed between the brothers in conversation, perhaps for a long time before it was begun; but either nothing was ever put down on the matter in writing, or nothing was preserved. The project suddenly springs out, complete and under way, late in the summer of 1800. Daniel's succession to the Hempsted estate in the previous March, making him financially independent, must surely have had something to do with that.

At the outset the plan was for a work in a number of volumes composed of self-contained parts, each devoted to a single county, treated in alphabetical order. When Volume I appeared in 1806 it contained three parts, on Bedfordshire, Berkshire, and Buckinghamshire. Those were all, as it happened, small counties; but the volume in which they were combined together was large and cumbrous, in 750 pages quarto.[5] Volume II, containing Cambridgeshire and Cheshire, was still bigger, making 900 pages. Thereafter each county made a separate volume on its own – but, even so, Devonshire, the last to be published, had to be split into two parts.

The enterprise was launched with a visit paid by Daniel to Bedford in August 1800. We hear of this in letters written by him to Sir Joseph Banks, who was taking a kindly interest in what he was doing. He was visiting five parishes a day, he reported, and a number of the principal houses. The Duke of Bedford had been persuaded to allow him into Woburn Abbey (a jealously-guarded privilege then), but had signified his permission contemptuously to his agent, refusing to notice Daniel, who stood by, and indeed turning his back on him.[6] Such slights had to be put up with, and he did not make any fuss about them. They mattered little so long as he got what he wanted.

[1] Add. MSS. 9408–30.
[2] Add. MSS. 9437–50.
[3] Add. MSS. 9460–71.
[4] Add. MSS. 9458–9.
[5] It is seldom found today in a single volume, but there is a very fine copy of it in this form belonging to George III (to whom the work was dedicated) in the British Library: 192 e.3.
[6] *The Banks Letters,* ed. W. R. Dawson (1958), 559–60.

As others had done before him in similar inquiries, he sent out sets of questions to clergymen and such people. At first they were evidently individual, and written out in his own hand.[1] Later they took the form of a printed questionnaire concerning the parish, the living and the landowners.[2] We get an impression of a big enterprise on the move, acquiring a steady rhythm of its own. Some of the correspondence passes through the publishers, Cadell & Davies, in London; most of it to and from Daniel at Rodmarton. The whole undertaking had to pay its way on a commercial basis, and one problem that must have worried him considerably for a time was the cost of postage. That was largely solved in 1802, when the Post Office accepted an arrangement by which the replies to these questions from clergymen should be transmitted to Daniel Lysons without charge. He owed this valuable concession to Francis Freeling, who was not only a competent administrator (his work unjustly overshadowed by that of Rowland Hill in the next generation) but also a book-collector and a cultivated man. He had been elected a Fellow of the Society of Antiquaries in the preceding year, and was well able to recognise the standing of the Lysons brothers. They were, he told the Postmasters-General in making his liberal suggestion to them, "antiquaries of the first class".[3]

The financing of county histories and similar works is a matter of which we know too little.[4] Here is one instance of the contributions that could sometimes be made towards meeting the costs incurred in preparing them by an official body, where there was good will, and an influential friend to put the case forward. It shows the working of patronage in an enlightened form.

Although the whole task was begun in Bedfordshire, it was not confined to that county for long. Within two months it had been extended to Berkshire.[5] Much of the work on Buckinghamshire was carried through in 1802.[6] The

[1] For example those concerning Marston Mortayne, Beds. (Add. MS. 9408, f. 351), and East Garston, Berks. (Add MS. 9409, f. 237).

[2] Some examples of these, filled in with their replies, are among Daniel's papers: e.g. a Cornish one in Add. MS. 9416, f. 81.

[3] There is a copy of Freeling's minute of 17 June 1802, and of the approval given to it by the Postmasters-General, Lord Auckland and Lord Charles Spencer, in Add. MS. 9408, ff. 109–10. Freeling's helpful interest in the undertaking continued to the end: Add. MS. 9427, ff. 187–9.

[4] A few indications concerning the *Magna Britannia* emerge in Cadell's letters to Daniel in Add. MS. 9426, ff. 275–95.

[5] See the courteous letter from Shute Barrington, Bishop of Durham, to Daniel Lysons, 19 Oct. 1800: Add. MS. 9409, f. 193.

[6] See the letters in Add. MS. 9411.

DANIEL LYSONS, F.S.A., F.R.S., F.L.S.
Portrait sketch by George Dance
(Reproduced by courtesy of the National Portrait Gallery)

SAMUEL LYSONS, F.S.A., F.R.S.
Portrait sketch by George Dance
(Reproduced by courtesy of the National Portrait Gallery)

decision to proceed with the counties in alphabetical order, evidently made at the outset, was not the only possible one: a geographical scheme might have been adopted, by regions or by moving from south to north. But it had one great accidental advantage– how far did this enter into the calculations of the authors and publishers, one wonders? Seven counties stood first in the alphabet, beginning with the letters B and C; and of those seven only one, Cumberland, had a modern history that could be regarded as at all satisfactory.[1] There was indeed a good book on the antiquities of Cornwall, but that was a work of an earlier generation.[2] For the rest, there was little or nothing. By 1800 sound histories had been written of at least a dozen English counties; but with the exceptions just mentioned, none happened to exist for any of the first counties in the alphabet. So the Lysons had a clear field, to supply something that was evidently much desired, without having at first much competition to contend with.

They perceived just what was needed, in a series of histories executed to a standard pattern. The sub-title of their work was "A Concise Topographical Account of the Several Counties of Great Britain"; but in fact they aimed at providing something that extended well beyond topography to embrace antiquities and landholding, subjects that had exercised the classical historians of the past, as well as some things that had often been ignored or slighted. They showed an interest in economic history – fairs, markets, fisheries, manufactures – and in natural history too.

They declared their purpose, and their reasons for undertaking the work, plainly at the outset, in the Advertisement to Volume I:

> Although copious and well-executed histories of several counties have been published, and although the *Britannia* of the learned Camden has been universally and justly regarded as an excellent work relating to the kingdom at large; yet as the former, besides being for the most part very scarce, are moreover so bulky as to form of themselves a library of no inconsiderable extent; and as the *Britannia* gives only a general view of each county; it appeared to us that there was still room for a work, which should contain an account of each parish, in a compressed form, and arranged in an order convenient for reference.

The brothers divided the work regularly between them. Daniel bore the main brunt of it. He wrote the topographical accounts and the family history

---

[1] In fact, it had two: J. Nicholson and R. Burn, *The History and Antiquities of . . . Westmorland and Cumberland* (1777), and W. Hutchinson, *History of . . . Cumberland* (1794–7).

[2] W. Borlase, *Observations on the Antiquities, Historical and Monumental, of the County of Cornwall* (1754).

(which occupied more than half of each volume)[1] and organised the whole undertaking. He was less busy than Samuel, having only the small parish of Rodmarton on his hands, whilst Samuel was a man of affairs in London. Samuel attended to natural history, archaeology, and architecture, besides supervising the illustration of the work.

In the earlier phases of the undertaking it appears that the brothers travelled separately into the counties they were describing. Later they seem to have gone together: very few of Samuel's sharp and entertaining letters to his brother are to be found for any county after Cambridgeshire. It was still nevertheless their rule that every parish church must be visited,[2] and as there are rather more than 1600 parishes in their nine counties, that was itself no small undertaking.

No one could charge them with slackness in the prosecution of their task. At times indeed their friends seem to have thought they had too much energy, rather than too little. Horace Walpole referred to the young Daniel affectionately as "Stumpety Stump";[3] he may have been a little noisy for that sensitive old man's ears. Much the same seems to have been true of Samuel. His voice was loud, and he was inclined to be rather too blunt.[4] Yet these were the only faults of which their friends accused them, and they may be accounted good faults in two men who had taken on so big an undertaking, and were determined to press ahead with it to the limits of their powers. A certain impatience must even have been necessary, helping to spur them on. The drive, the speed of working, can be sensed from their own papers: Daniel's rapid drafts of letters, Samuel's reports of his doings, his sketches of scenes and antiquities – often made, as one feels, while a post-chaise was waiting, or his horse was tethered near by.

They assembled a mass of material, far beyond what they could publish. As often happens in such undertakings, their inquiries called forth enthusiastic help here and there, sometimes exceeding what they originally asked for, or required. Some of it was a mere nuisance. Samuel describes to his brother an exasperating day in west Berkshire:

I called this morning on Mr [named scored over] as you desired, and

---

[1] See Daniel to Villiers William Villiers, 11 Dec. [? 1806], Add. MS. 9411, f. 316, and to John Hawkins, c. 1 Aug. 1819: *The Letters of John Hawkins and Samuel and Daniel Lysons*, ed. F. W. Steer (1966), 49.

[2] "We have, as in other counties, visited all the parish churches": *Magna Britannia: Derbyshire*,

[3] *Correspondence*, xii (1944), 29.

[4] Fleming, *Memoir*, 3.

wished very soon that I had not. The man was very civil to be sure, but he bored and tired and hindered me an hour or two about nothing. He sent for a Mr Wise (a tradesman of the place), a very talkative man, and one was for carrying me east and the other west to see this and to see that, and at last both talked together and I was ready to run away from them, and they would not let me take a note quickly in the church of what I wanted but would come and drag me to see some confounded nonsense or other that hit their fancy . . . Mr S. made a great point of taking me to see an ancient inscription . . . It consists of the letters A.G. with a knot between, meaning as they wisely conjecture Alfred the Great.[1]

How well one recognises the experience: the kindly, ignorant chatterers, the inquirer fretting at the waste of his precious time!

On the other hand, again and again they struck unexpected oil, finding people who could not do too much to assist their work and understood very well what they were searching for: the excellent Dr Yeats in Bedford, for example; Mr Bond of East Looe, who drew up a list of the Volunteer companies in Cornwall as they were (ready to repel the French) in 1806 — twenty-eight of them in all, totalling 8362 men, with the strength of each unit shown and the name of its commanding officer. Again in Cornwall, Daniel was fortunate in J. T. Austen,[2] the remarkable man who succeeded to the estates of his mother's family, the Treffrys, and their beautiful house, Place at Fowey. He was tenaciously interested in their history, but no less in what was going on around him and the opportunities it afforded for the future — so that in the end he was largely responsible for the mineral and maritime development of the central part of the county, from Fowey across to Newquay. Twenty-six of his letters to Daniel are preserved, filled with antiquarian and genealogical matter, but also with such things as the current state of the pilchard fisheries, depressed owing to the Napoleonic wars, and the exact quantities of china-clay shipped from Charlestown in 1809–12.[3]

Their correspondents ranged widely over the social order. The majority of them — it was to be expected in any undertaking of the kind then — were country clergymen, some of whom took immense pains on the brothers' behalf: like the Rev. C. Cardew of St Erme in Cornwall, whose information extended well beyond his own parish, to embrace Truro and St Ives as well.[4]

[1] Letter dated "Wantage, Sat. evening": Add. MS. 9409, f. 378v.
[2] He took the surname Treffry in 1838.
[3] Add. MS. 9416, ff. 32–3, 37.
[4] *Ibid.*, ff. 176–232.

Bishops could be helpful too: Pretyman of Lincoln and Fisher of Exeter;[1] Douglas of Salisbury, who pressed his Registrar to investigate an historical query in the archives in his Muniment Room – though that, as the Bishop remarked, was no easy task, "the huge mass of manuscripts deposited not being, at all, arranged."[2] Their most generous episcopal correspondent, however, was Bishop Goodenough of Carlisle, who attended to their business and at the same time commented on the affairs of the day, revealing his own point of view:[3]

> I am quite surprised at the dilatoriness of my clergy in answering your letters. I wonder at nothing that the Evangelical part of them, Fawcett and Hartley etc., do but why Mr Lowry of Crosby, a rational good sort of man, should be behind hand I cannot account for. You had better write to him again and say that you have my full concurrence for your inquiries.[4]

Some peers gave valuable help: Lord Radnor, Lord de Dunstanville, Lord Lonsdale, Lord Fortescue;[5] and country gentlemen across the length of England, from Sir James Graham of Netherby close to the Scottish border to Joseph Pole Carew of Antony in Cornwall.[6]

The other chief correspondents were professional laymen, like Theed Pearse, solicitor and Clerk of the Peace in Bedfordshire; the Duke of Devonshire's agent at Chatsworth, Thomas Knowlton; and Robert Were Fox, shipping agent at Falmouth.[7] Henry Ellis, Keeper of Manuscripts at the British Museum, took pains on the brothers' behalf: his fine scholar's handwriting stands out in their papers still.[8] A whole range of miscellaneous people lies beyond. Richard Polwhele, who had already written histories of Devon and Cornwall himself, voluminous and ill-organised, wrote amiably;[9] Joseph Hunter, then Presbyterian minister at Bath but already collecting materials for his *Hallamshire*, to good purpose.[10] Like all students of topography, now just as much as then, the Lysons were greatly beholden to

---

[1] Add. MS. 9411, f. 171; 9417, ff. 127–8.
[2] Add. MS. 9410, ff. 115–7.
[3] Add. MS. 9421, ff. 91–101; 9423, ff. 198–9.
[4] 16 Feb. 1815: Add. MS. 9421, f. 93.
[5] Add. MS. 9410, ff. 58-66; 9417, ff. 11–97; 9422, ff. 8–44; 9427, ff. 154–73.
[6] Add. MS. 9421, ff. 216–23; 9415, ff. 234–85.
[7] Add. MS. 9408, ff. 248–75; 9424, ff. 176–96; 9417, ff. 143–51.
[8] See e.g. Add. MS. 9421, ff. 157–62.
[9] Add. MS. 9419, ff. 209–26.
[10] Add. MS. 9424, ff. 121–49.

local people who were passionately knowledgeable about their own place or district. Daniel received more than 100 letters from William Nicholls, of Chester and Charlton-on-Medlock,[1] and nearly as many from John Wallis of Bodmin.[2]

So, with the help of all these people and many more, the work was organised, shaped up, and at last printed and published, in this order:

Vol. I (1806, reissued 1813):

    Part i. Bedfordshire

    Part ii. Berkshire

    Part iii. Buckinghamshire

Vol. II:

    Part i. Cambridgeshire (1808)

    Part ii. Cheshire (1810)

Vol. III: Cornwall (1814)

Vol. IV: Cumberland (1816)

Vol. V: Derbyshire (1817)

Vol. VI: Devonshire (2 parts, 1822)

Considering the size of the task involved, in reading, travelling, and writing, the *Magna Britannia* made most creditable progress. Its reception was not uniformly favourable. The antiquarian world was full of critics, with sharp eyes and tongues, longing to pounce on errors, above all in an enterprise so generously bold as this one. Among the first was the ill-conditioned Samuel Egerton Brydges, who could seldom do justice to anyone with more constructive abilities than his own;[3] but he met his match instantly in Samuel Lysons. He wrote to correct a mistake he had found in the Lysons's account of Berkshire, adding with characteristic superciliousness: "I omit smaller errors, which must necessarily occur in works like yours". Samuel replied admitting the fault, and then continued: "Being on the subject of mistakes, I take the liberty of mentioning one which occurred to me some time since in your edition of Phillips's *Theatrum Poetarum* . . ."[4] Even Brydges seems then to have been silenced. His name occurs in the correspondence no more.

Errors and omissions were also pointed out more politely. William Belsham of Bedford, for example, wrote to the *Monthly Magazine* soon after the volume was published, drawing attention to some deficiencies in the

---

[1] Add. MS. 9415, ff. 1–220.

[2] Add. MS. 9420, ff. 180–372.

[3] Cf. his offensive remarks about Hasted, the historian of Kent: *English County Historians*, 219.

[4] Add. MS. 9409, ff. 111, 116.

description of his own county.[1] There may have been a little personal pique here, for the Lysons had not met Belsham's sensible request, put forward in a letter, that they should include a good plan of Bedford in their book.[2] One of his most interesting points arose from their statement that the town was growing. He denied this in terms of population, adducing some evidence; more convincingly, he observed that the extent of the built-up area was still almost the same as it had been when Speed produced his plan of Bedford in 1608. Rather surprisingly, Daniel fired up at these remarks, treating them as hostile and unfair, and he wrote to the *Gentleman's Magazine* (a periodical of more reputation) at length, admitting errors in part but showing his resentment clearly.[3] He was subsequently applauded by a correspondent signing himself S.D.D. for this "manly reply".[4]

The authors did not allow themselves to be discouraged by such criticism. Their volumes went on appearing, county by county, on average about every two years, down to 1817. The longest break occurred between 1810 and 1814, while *Cornwall* was in preparation; that county, when the work on it was finished, formed much the largest unit in the series so far. After the publication of *Derbyshire*, however, we can sense that things moved more slowly. Of the two brothers, Daniel appears to have retained his full vigour; but Samuel's energies were beginning to flag. Their work had been exhausting. They seem to have employed no assistants whatever, not even an amanuensis: Daniel is quite specific in stating that he transcribed the text for the printers himself.[5] It is fair to say that this doomed the enterprise, from the outset, to remain incomplete. The brothers themselves came to recognise that. Samuel thought at one time, optimistically, that they might get as far as their own county of Gloucester, the thirteenth in alphabetical order.[6] As it was, they reached only the ninth. Soon after he was fifty, his health began to fail. His heart troubled him, and evidently his work slowed up. One more agreeable distinction came to him. He was appointed Antiquarian to the Royal Academy, by the Academicians' unanimous vote, in January 1819.[7] Six months later he died, on 29 June: unmarried, at Cirencester, near his brother's home.

[1] *Monthly Magazine*, xxiii (1807), 6–9.
[2] Add. MS. 9408, f. 38.
[3] *Gentleman's Magazine*, lxxvii (1807), 405–8.
[4] *Ibid.*, 501–2.
[5] See e.g. Add. MS. 9417, f. 254 (*Cornwall*), and *Letters of John Hawkins*, 49 (*Devonshire*, 1819).
[6] *Ibid.*
[7] Fleming, *Memoir of Samuel Lysons*, 48.

Daniel decided almost at once that the *Magna Britannia* must be abandoned. "I cannot go on", he wrote to a friend, "without my fellow labourer. Our lives would not have sufficed to the completion had they been protracted even to old age. It is as well therefore to give it up now". But he felt nevertheless obliged to complete work on the next county, Devon: "it has been so long promised and so much expense has been incurred". His own part in it was nearly finished. The parochial descriptions and accounts of families were complete, and most of them ready for the printers. None of Samuel's part, on the other hand, had been written at all.[1] That points clearly to the decline of his powers; at least three years must have gone by before his death in which he wrote nothing whatever for the *Magna Britannia*. What was Daniel now to do, in the branches of the work that had been Samuel's, with which he was unfamiliar?

Fortunately he was well known and widely respected. He could rely on Robert Smirke to deal with architecture; he hoped for the assistance of Sir Richard Colt Hoare with archaeology. John Hawkins, of Trewithen in Cornwall, had immediately offered his help with the geology and mineralogy, and his work on those subjects for *Devonshire* was ultimately revised by William Buckland, the best English authority of the day.[2] With good assistance of this kind, Daniel struggled on. *Devonshire* came out in 1822: much the largest volume in the series, running to over 1000 pages. There the work came to an end. For the counties not treated in the *Magna Britannia*, from Dorset onwards, two volumes of scrappy notes are all that remain.[3]

* * *

It is sad that the ambitious undertaking should have been left unfinished. Yet we have reason to be grateful for what the Lysons achieved. The quality of their performance varies. It was bound to, given the conditions under which the work was compiled. They were dependent in large measure on the replies they received from their correspondents. Although, as we have seen, they travelled a good deal, they could not themselves visit all they described. Two of their nine counties, Cornwall and Cumberland, were very remote, whether from Gloucestershire or from London – though, by a happy dispensation,

[1] To John Hawkins, *c*.1 Aug. 1819: *Letters of John Hawkins*, 49.
[2] *Ibid.*, 57–63. Buckland's letters to Daniel are in Add. MS. 9426, ff. 223–43.
[3] Add. MSS. 9458–9. The publisher Thomas Cadell restrained Daniel from openly announcing, in the Advertisement to *Devonshire*, that the work had been abandoned. He evidently hoped that a continuator might be found: Add. MS. 9426, f. 294.

those two had been better treated by their predecessors than any of the other seven, so that more valuable information was assembled to hand there than anywhere else.

Samuel Lysons had at his disposal all the public libraries of London. As the Keeper of a large part of the national records he was well placed to secure access to historical documents of all kinds; repeated references appear to the patent rolls and to some of the other records in his care. But not everything was opened to the brothers easily. Daniel had a struggle at the outset of the undertaking to gain admittance to the important records in the Rolls Chapel.[1] For his part, no doubt he had a sound working library at Rodmarton, but it could comprise no more than a selection from the texts, works of reference, and histories that were available. In assessing the achievement the *Magna Britannia* represents, it is right to begin by considering briefly the literature at the authors' disposal.

They must have kept Gough's big edition of Camden constantly by them, and the later works that took off from Camden's, like the *Magna Britannia et Hibernia* of 1721–30. Sets of maps were available to them; the best covering the whole country when they began was John Cary's *New Map of England and Wales* of 1794.[2] There were guidebooks of the kind necessary to aid their own travelling, like the road-book of Paterson,[3] kept up to date through fifteen editions between 1771 and 1811, and Cary's similar *New Itinerary*.

Although gazetteers, known under that name, had been produced, none of them was worth very much. The first that could really have helped the Lysons substantially was Nicholas Carlisle's *Topographical Dictionary of England*, which was not published until 1808, when they had already covered the first four of their counties. Their interests extended to trade, but if they wanted even the simplest local information they had little more to go upon than the *Universal British Directory* of 1791–3. Nothing like a general bibliography of English topographical literature was available before Upcott's, which appeared only in 1818;[4] though Gough had produced an impressive and valuable guide to historical sources in his *British Topography* in 1780. Some of the prime texts were beginning to be published, notably Domesday Book, which had first been put into print in 1783. As for

[1] Add. MS. 9408, f. 62.
[2] The publication of the one-inch Ordnance Survey map began in 1805.
[3] D. Paterson, *A New and Accurate Description of all the Direct and Principal Cross-Roads in Great Britain*.
[4] W. Upcott, *A Bibliographical Account of the Principal Works relating to English Topography* (3 vols., 1818).

antiquities, important collections of engravings, covering the whole country, had been issued during the eighteenth century, by Grose and the Bucks for instance;[1] and John Carter was helping to show the way to increased precision in the study of Gothic architecture.[2] The cult of the picturesque had stimulated the production of books of views, like *The Beauties of England and Wales*.[3] Finally, there were the periodicals, in which discoveries were constantly being reported, theories advanced and discussed: *Archaeologia*, the annual volumes published by the Society of Antiquaries; the *Gentleman's Magazine*, which took a special interest in archaeology and matters of local history.

So knowledge was rapidly being enlarged and refined when the Lysons wrote. Their difficulty was that they were at once compilers, arrangers of known information according to a method strictly laid down at the outset, and also pioneers, making at least some attempt to explore the unknown. Once the work had begun, it had to observe some sort of timetable. In these conditions, they could not pursue much that we should call research. In spite of that, however, their work did really represent an important advance on what had gone before.

The advance was, above all, a matter of method. They drew up a sensible plan and applied it to each of their counties in turn. This procedure had one evident drawback. The English counties differ widely from one another, and no single pattern could be entirely suitable for them all. Yet, at this stage in the development of English county history, that deficiency was more than compensated by a great advantage. The progress that had so far been made in the study had been irregular, depending upon individual writers: a necessary result of the inward-looking, "intensive" method. It was high time that some effort should be made to put these studies into relation with one another, to supply useful cross-reference, above all to fill in the large and serious gaps appearing, for example, because no scholar happened to have addressed himself yet to any of the counties beginning with B. Once the Lysons had adopted their plan, they had necessarily to do all those things, to accept the discipline it imposed.

They could, however, vary the scale of their work and the proportion between its different parts. Perhaps it was a pity that their first effort, which

---

[1] F. Grose, *The Antiquities of England and Wales* (6 vols., 1773–87); S. and N. Buck, *Buck's Antiquities* (collected ed., 3 vols., 1774).

[2] In his *Views of Ancient Buildings in England* (6 vols., 1786–93) and *The Ancient Architecture of England* (2 vols., 1795–1814).

[3] By E. W. Brayley and J. Britton (18 vols., 1801–15).

was bound to be experimental in some ways, was directed to Bedfordshire, one of the very smallest counties in England; one that was not only small, moreover, but also contained no large town. Here they were evidently reining themselves in. They were too wise not to perceive the danger that if they spread themselves in treating a small county they would be obliged to make the volumes on the bigger counties, when they came to undertake them, impossibly large. Their sub-title promised a "concise" topographical account; and in writing about Bedfordshire they certainly pressed conciseness very far. Although their account of Bedford itself, and of some of the other more important places, is quite good, their treatment of most of the small country parishes is too brief to be satisfactory. Much the same is true of the two other counties that make up Volume I.

With Volume II the scale begins to change. The "parochial topography" tends to become larger absolutely, though at the same time smaller in proportion. Thus:

1 Volume	2 No. of pages (excl. corrigenda and index)	3 Parochial topography: no. of pages	4 3 as % of 2	5 No. of parishes	6 No. of pages per parish
I (Beds., Berks., Bucks.)	676	541	80	470	1.15
II (Cambs., Cheshire)	827	587	71	251	2.34
III (Cornwall)	593	341	58	203	1.68
IV (Cumberland)	385	175	45	104	1.68
V (Derbyshire)	553	311	56	117	2.66
VI (Devonshire)	936	581	62	471	1.23

The figures given here need some interpretation. In the three northern counties, Cheshire, Cumberland, and Derbyshire, the parishes were much larger than elsewhere, and that necessarily made many of the entries individually longer. Still, a marked difference appears in the table. Whereas in the first five counties the general historical description occupies only about a quarter of the whole volume, in the other four it takes up not much less than half – more than half in Cumberland. Serious students appreciated the value of this part of the work highly. One wrote from Cheshire as early as 1806 to ask that the general accounts should be published separately from the parochial topography;[1] but that policy was adopted only with the last volume, on Devonshire, and then on account of its bulk.

Nothing like this had been seen before. The *Magna Britannia et Hibernia* had indeed treated each county, but on a much smaller scale and

[1] Add. MS. 9414, f. 3v.

unsystematically. None of the older county histories had made any extended effort to deal with the county as a whole – though more recent works, from Hutchins's *Dorset* onwards, had done something valuable in this way. What the Lysons brothers provided for their nine counties was a general history and description to a uniform plan, under about two dozen headings, starting with origins and history, proceeding through political and ecclesiastical divisions to the landowning families; turning then to physical description, communications, and manufactures, and ending up with antiquities and architecture. No important deviation was made from this plan anywhere in the whole work, though occasionally sub-sections were inserted to deal with one county's special peculiarities – crosses and holy wells in Cornwall, the remarkable records of longevity in Cumberland. In the bigger counties these introductory discussions became the equivalent of a substantial book in itself: in the biggest of them all, *Devonshire*, it comprised a volume of something like 120,000 words.

It is easy to criticise these introductions. The general history is meagre and scrappy: entitled "Historical Events" and limited to them, which means that it is chiefly the record of battles and therefore stops, in most counties, at the Civil War in the seventeenth century. The account of the leading families is either too short or too long: too short to allow their descent to be traced adequately, whence a good deal of agitated protest from correspondents as the volumes were published, yet too long in proportion to the rest.[1]

The authors were unfortunate in trying to treat church architecture at that particular time, just before a sound analysis of its development had come to be accepted: Rickman's *Attempt to Discriminate the Styles of Architecture in England from the Conquest to the Reformation* was published only in 1817. As for archaeology, no one could have expected a scientific account of that subject then. But it must at least be remarked that Samuel Lysons was as well acquainted with the antiquities of Roman Britain, so far discovered, as any man of his time.

Something should be said here about the illustration of the work, for which Samuel was particularly responsible. In the first part, *Bedfordshire*, as it was originally issued, all the twelve plates (apart from the map) were engraved from his own drawings. The same is true of *Buckinghamshire;* but in *Berkshire* other artists appeared beside him. Samuel continued to supply some drawings to the end, but the proportion of these grew smaller. In *Cumberland* it

---

[1] In the final volume, *Devonshire*, the account of the nobility and gentry takes up nearly 40 per cent of the whole introduction.

was one-third; in *Devonshire* only two drawings out of twenty-seven were his. But if he drew less himself, he continued to direct what was done. He evidently chose the artists, and they became something like a regular team. There were four who undertook most of the work, in addition to Samuel himself: Robert Smirke, Frederick Nash, Joseph Farington, and C. A. Stothard.

Illustrations were provided sparely. None were paid for by private subscriptions. Only twenty-nine plates (apart from maps) are included with nearly 1000 pages of letterpress in *Devonshire*. The pictures were not intended to be a decoration to the text, as they had often been in county histories; they were included for the strict purpose of illustrating it, and on principles stated in the Advertisement to Volume II:

> Many of the subjects are expressed by little more than an outline, in order to show the several parts distinctly, which are often in a great measure lost in more laboured engravings . . . Our plates are intended to convey correct ideas of the forms of curious objects, for the purpose of information, and not to produce a picturesque effect.

Nevertheless Farington's drawings of landscape and buildings often have real charm — especially perhaps those of gates and old houses in Exeter. And Stothard's of monumental effigies and painted glass were prepared with meticulous care.[1]

Samuel deserves a good deal of credit for this element in the work. We can observe himself intent on the task himself once, at Ely in 1805,[2] and instructing Nash in what he wanted in Cheshire and Cumberland two years later.[3] If his own work is undistinguished, it is adequate; and it conforms exactly to the principles he had laid down.[4]

* * *

[1] Stothard may be said to have died in the service of the *Magna Britannia:* for he was killed by a fall from a ladder in the church of Bere Ferrers, Devon, when drawing the east window for the Lysons in May 1821. His work was completed, after some discussion, by his brother R. Stothard: cf. Add. MS. 9426, ff. 275–88; 9427, ff. 206–9.

[2] Add. MS. 9413, f. 37v.

[3] Add. MS. 9422, ff. 63–4.

[4] The very spare illustration of the work made it a most suitable subject for grangerising. Some notable extra-illustrated copies will be mentioned in the introduction to individual Parts, in this reprint.

Like most pioneer undertakings, the *Magna Britannia* will be judged most fairly by what it did, not by what it failed to do. Johnson's noble plea for his *Dictionary* should always be in one's mind: "In this work, when it shall be found that much is omitted, let it not be forgotten that much likewise is performed". Had the Lysons brothers been given to self-justification, they might have answered their critics in that way too. But they were not. For twenty years they were too busy with their huge task, and with other labours as well, to spend much time in defending themselves. They did something more useful. They never ignored criticism – indeed, in the Advertisement to Volume II they invited it; and they produced sets of corrections and additions (sometimes more than one for a volume) to rectify their errors. After Samuel's death Daniel's chief care was to keep faith by finishing *Devonshire*. When that was done he turned away from these studies altogether, and he never broke his silence about them.

Though the *Magna Britannia* is incomplete, it represents an impressive achievement: an achievement in collecting and ordering a great body of information, much of it never assembled in this way before, a signpost to those who might come after, pointing the way ahead very clearly to what was wanted. At the end of the nineteenth century the *Victoria County History* began to do – much more thoroughly and completely, and with the aid of a team of contributors – what the Lysons brothers had attempted at the beginning. For most of the counties it treated, the *Magna Britannia* supplied something entirely new, and it was admired for that in its own day. When Brougham heard that the work was likely to be given up after Samuel's death, he wrote to Daniel deprecating the abandonment of "the greatest topographical work ever attempted".[1]

The enterprise deserves to be valued by us still, for two reasons in particular. In the first place, it is a bold landmark in the writing of English local history. But it is something more than that too, more than a mere monument of learning, long superseded. The volumes are worth reading in their own right, as a concise account (the adjective in the sub-title of the book is fully justified) of the parts of England they treat, written by two intelligent and knowledgeable men. The work was based on extensive reading, in part on their own observation, and as their correspondence reveals on the copious assistance of others, afforded with good will and acknowledged generously. Those are the ingredients of the *Magna Britannia*. They make up a work that

---

[1] Add. MS. 9426, f. 214.

tells us not only a good deal about the past but also something of its own age, and – shyly concealed – a little of the character of the two brothers who wrote it.

JACK SIMMONS

MAGNA BRITANNIA: BEDFORDSHIRE

The Lysons brothers can claim to be the first historians of Bedfordshire. Before they wrote, nobody had published anything on the subject, apart from what appeared in general compilations such as the *Magna Britannia et Hibernia* of 1721–30 and *The Beauties of England and Wales* (see pp. xix, xx above), though some contributions had been made towards the history of Luton, Dunstable, and three rural parishes in 1783–7 in the *Bibliotheca Topographica Britannica* edited by John Nichols. The county was one of the very smallest in England – only Huntingdon, Middlesex, and Rutland were smaller – and it had as yet produced no native antiquary of consequence. In the field of natural history, however, it could already boast one of the earliest of all county floras.[1]

So the Lysons had to do much of the spadework themselves. The whole enterprise of the *Magna Britannia* may be said to have begun at Bedford, in August 1800 (see p. ix), and the brothers were hard at work on the county – as well as on Berkshire and Buckinghamshire, which were to join it in making up the first volume – over the next five years. Daniel found some useful correspondents, who helped him materially: in particular Theed Pearse, the Clerk of the Peace,[2] Dr G. Yeats,[3] and H. Wade-Gery of Bushmead Priory, close to the Huntingdonshire border.[4] Dr Yeats had a good deal to tell him about the contemporary affairs of the county town (which secured an Improvement Act in 1803, while the work was in progress) and the foundation of the Bedford Infirmary.

Both the general introduction and the topographical section are the

---

[1] C. Abbot, *Flora Bedfordiensis* (1798). Daniel Lysons was in touch with him (see British Library, Add. MS. 9408, f. 1).
[2] Two sets of letters: 1802–3, Add. MS. 9408, ff. 248–60; 1811–12, ff. 262–75.
[3] *Ibid.*, ff. 355–70.
[4] *Ibid.*, ff. 115–28.

shortest in the whole of the *Magna Britannia*, and they do not go very far beyond summarising the knowledge of the time. But that was a useful thing to attempt, and it remains useful to us still. Here is a clear and compendious statement of the facts as they were seen at the beginning of the nineteenth century, efficiently presented in a sensible arrangement.

The book was published in 1806, together with the other two parts of Volume I of the *Magna Britannia*. All three parts were reissued in 1813, with new preliminary pages and two sets of additions and corrections. The new title-pages do not indicate that the issue of 1813 was the second, and this has led to much confusion. Even such a careful bibliographer as J. P. Anderson fails to make it clear that the book was first published in 1806.[1]

The original issue included a map and twelve engravings, which had all been made from drawings by Samuel Lysons.[2] In the second issue a thirteenth plate was added, of the Wideville brass at Bromham, by Edward Blore; his superior skill, the refinement of his draughtsmanship, appear in it very plainly. There are some notable extra-illustrated copies of the work: for example, in the Luton Museum and Art Gallery and in the Library of the Inner Temple in London.

Before the second issue had been published Thomas Fisher (one of the many servants of the East India Company who distinguished themselves out of hours) began to produce a series of engravings of Bedfordshire antiquities under the title *Collections Historical, Genealogical, and Topographical for Bedfordshire;* but it consists of plates alone, without any text.[3] The Lysons's account held the field as the only general historical description of Bedfordshire throughout the nineteenth century.

In the twentieth century, however, things have changed notably. From being one of the most ill-equipped counties of England, in terms of historical scholarship, Bedfordshire has become one of the best. It was among the first to have a complete *Victoria County History* (1904–14). That is complemented by a full history in one volume by a single author, Joyce Godber (1968). It has an admirable bibliography, kept up to date in an exemplary manner with

[1] *The Book of British Topography* (1881), 48. He describes the whole work correctly, however, on p. 12.

[2] His notes and drawings are in Add. MS. 9460, ff. 3–28.

The publication of the whole work extended from 1812 to 1836. Fisher objected, on principle, to the requirement that eleven copies of printed books should be presented to the national libraries as a condition of securing copyright; hence his refusal to furnish the book with any letterpress.

supplements.[1] Its Historical Record Society has issued fifty-five volumes since 1915. The County Record Office established by Dr G. H. Fowler in 1913 was the second to be set up in the country, following only Middlesex. So in historical studies Bedfordshire today has cause for gratitude and pride. It ought still to be remembered that those studies were first put into order by the Lysons in their *Magna Britannia*.

J.S.

---

[1] L. R. Conisbee, *A Bedfordshire Bibliography* (1962); with supplements published in 1967 and 1971.

MAGNA BRITANNIA;

BEING

A CONCISE TOPOGRAPHICAL ACCOUNT

OF

THE SEVERAL COUNTIES

OF

GREAT BRITAIN.

By the Rev. DANIEL LYSONS, A.M. F.R.S. F.A. and L.S.
RECTOR OF RODMARTON IN GLOUCESTERSHIRE;

And SAMUEL LYSONS, Esq. F.R.S. and F.A.S.
KEEPER OF HIS MAJESTY'S RECORDS IN THE TOWER OF LONDON.

VOLUME THE FIRST,

CONTAINING

BEDFORDSHIRE, BERKSHIRE, AND BUCKINGHAMSHIRE.

LONDON:
PRINTED FOR T. CADELL AND W. DAVIES IN THE STRAND.
1806.

TO

HIS MOST SACRED MAJESTY

KING GEORGE THE THIRD,

THIS ATTEMPT TO ILLUSTRATE

THE TOPOGRAPHY OF GREAT BRITAIN,

IS,

WITH HIS MAJESTY'S GRACIOUS PERMISSION,

HUMBLY DEDICATED,

BY

HIS MAJESTY'S

MOST DUTIFUL SUBJECTS,

AND FAITHFUL SERVANTS,

DANIEL LYSONS.
SAMUEL LYSONS.

ADVERTISEMENT.

ALTHOUGH copious and well-executed Hiſtories of ſeveral
Counties have been publiſhed, and although the *Britannia*
of the learned Camden has been univerſally and juſtly regarded as
an excellent work relating to the kingdom at large; yet as the
former, beſides being for the moſt part very ſcarce, are moreover ſo
bulky, as to form of themſelves a library of no inconſiderable extent;
and as the *Britannia* gives only a general view of each county; it
appeared to us that there was ſtill room for a work, which ſhould
contain an account of each pariſh, in a compreſſed form, and arranged in an order convenient for reference.

Theſe conſiderations have given riſe to the following work, in
which all matters that would readily admit of ſuch an arrangement
are reduced under diſtinct heads; and the brief account of the
deſcent of property, and other local particulars in each pariſh,
are claſſed alphabetically; and we have endeavoured rather to
make ourſelves clearly underſtood, than to diſplay a more ornamented ſtyle, which we conceived leſs adapted to a work of this
kind. With reſpect to the plates, we have ſelected ſuch ſubjects as
preſented the greateſt variety, and appeared to us to be the moſt
intereſting; and we flatter ourſelves, that the manner in which
they are executed, will be found adequate to convey an accurate
idea of the objects intended to be repreſented *.

* A ſet of finiſhed engravings of views ſelected from the counties of Bedford, Berks, and Bucks,
executed by the late Mr. William Byrne, from drawings by the beſt maſters, are publiſhed by
Meſſrs. Cadell and Davies, at the ſame time with this volume.

The

The materials from which this work has been compiled, independently of thofe derived from the beft printed authorities, have been drawn from the following fources; 1ft, *Ancient Records and Manuscripts* preferved in the Britifh Mufeum, and in various publick offices; particularly from that inexhauftible treafure of antient hiftorical evidences, his Majefty's Records in the Tower of London, which we have had the advantage of confulting at all times, and the Records of the Augmentation office, to which we have had free accefs through the liberality of John Caley efq. which we have experienced on former occafions; our thanks are alfo due to the Right Hon. George Rofe, to Robert Gray efq. Richard Gray efq. and Robert Harper efq. for the permiffion they have given us to confult any of the records at the Chapter-houfe Weftminfter, the Duchy of Cornwall office, the Auditors of the Land-Revenue office, and the Duchy of Lancafter Office; and to Ralph Bigland efq. Norroy King at Arms, Francis Townfend efq. Windfor-Herald, and George Naylor efq. York-Herald, for the readinefs with which they have furnifhed us with fuch information as we ftood in need of from the College of Arms: and, 2dly, *Perfonal Surveys* in each county, where we have acquired much valuable information, particularly from the Clergy and the gentlemen of the profeffion of the Law, to whom our acknowledgments are due for their ready affiftance. We are alfo much indebted to the Lords Bifhops of Lincoln and Sarum, for their kind affiftance in their refpective diocefes, in which the three Counties contained in this volume are included; and to the Lord Bifhop of Cloyne for his valuable communications on the fubject of the Roman Roads and Stations in each county.

It was our intention to have given fome obfervations on the architecture of the middle ages in our General Introduction, but we conceived that they might be better introduced in the next volume, where we fhall have an opportunity of referring to fome excellent examples of different ftyles, taken from Ely Cathedral. In the mean time, it may be proper to obferve, that in the prefent volume we

have

have called the architecture of our ancient buildings, in which the circular arch is the moſt ſtriking characteriſtick, by the general name of *Saxon*, that being the appellation by which it is beſt underſtood, and not having hitherto diſcovered any difference ſufficiently ſtriking to conſtitute a diſtinct ſtyle: we have alſo in conformity to general uſage, called that ſtyle, of which the pointed arch is the leading feature, *Gothic;* as, however inappropriate the term may be if we regard its etymology, it is in our opinion better to employ it, ſanctioned as it is by common uſe, than to adopt either of thoſe which have been propoſed in its ſtead, and which are not ſo generally underſtood. In our General Introduction we have not enlarged on the early Hiſtory of Britain, that ſubject having been fully treated of by preceding writers; and, being in our opinion, more immediately connected with an hiſtorical than a topographical work.

A longer ſpace of time has been occupied in collecting materials for this volume than we had expected: this however will not occaſion much ſurpriſe when it is conſidered that there are no hiſtories either of Bedfordſhire, Berkſhire, or Buckinghamſhire; and that though the preſent work is much compreſſed, the collections made for it were nearly the ſame as for ſo many County-hiſtories. Various alterations in the ſtate of property, and other particulars, have doubtleſs occurred ſince its commencement: ſuch as have come to our knowledge are noticed at the end of the volume; and for the reſt, as well as for ſuch errors, as are almoſt inſeparable from a work of this kind, whatever care has been taken to avoid them, we rely on the candour and indulgence of the public.

LIST OF PLATES.

BEDFORDSHIRE.

GENERAL INTRODUCTION.

CAMDEN, ſpeaking of the Etymology of the word *Britain*, with great juſtice, ſeems to doubt the poſſibility of coming at the truth, " buried deep as it is in the obſcurity of ages." It is certain that no ſucceeding writer has given any ſatisfactory explanation of the word ; but it is the general opinion of the learned, that it is of Celtic origin.

The early hiſtory of Britain is involved in ſo much fabulous obſcurity, that there is nothing on which we can place any reliance as an hiſtorical fact, till the arrival of the Romans ; who found this iſland divided into 34 different tribes, ſeventeen of which occupying that part of it now called Scotland, according to Ptolemy were the *Caledonii, Cantæ, Careni, Carnonacæ, Cerones, Cornavii, Creones, Damnii, Epidii, Logi, Mertæ, Novantes, Selgovæ, Texali, Vacomagi, Venicontes,* and the *Gadeni,* whoſe territories ſeem to have extended into Northumberland.

According to Camden[a], the Engliſh counties were thus occupied by the remaining ſtates :

Attrebatii,	Berkſhire.
Belgæ, - -	{ Somerſetſhire. Wiltſhire. Hampſhire.
Brigantes, - -	{ Yorkſhire[b]. Lancaſhire. Durham. Weſtmorland. Cumberland.
Cantii, - -	Kent.

[a] Where later writers of good authority have differed in opinion from Camden, it will be noticed in the introduction to each county.

A people called the *Pariſi* are placed by Ptolemy about the Eaſt Riding of Yorkſhire.

7

Cattieuchlani,

Cattieuchlani, - -	{	Buckinghamſhire.
		Bedfordſhire.
		Hertfordſhire.
Coritani, - -	{	Lincolnſhire.
		Leiceſterſhire.
		Rutlandſhire.
		Derbyſhire.
		Nottinghamſhire.
		Northamptonſhire.
Cornavii, - -	{	Warwickſhire.
		Worceſterſhire.
		Staffordſhire.
		Shropſhire.
		Cheſhire.
Dimetæ, - -	{	Carmarthenſhire.
		Pembrokeſhire.
		Cardiganſhire.
Dobuni, - -	{	Glouceſterſhire.
		Oxfordſhire.
Danmonii, -	{	Devonſhire.
		Cornwall.
Durotriges, - -		Dorſetſhire.
Iceni, -	{	Norfolk.
		Suffolk.
		Cambridgeſhire.
		Huntingdonſhire.
Ordevices, -	{	Montgomeryſhire.
		Merionethſhire.
		Carnarvonſhire.
		Flintſhire.
		Denbighſhire.
Ottadini [c], -		Northumberland.
Regni, -	{	Suffex.
		Surrey.
Silures, -	{	Herefordſhire.
		Radnorſhire.
		Brecknockſhire.
		Monmouthſhire.
		Glamorganſhire.
Trinobantes, -	{	Effex.
		Middleſex.

[c] The *Ottadini* and the *Gadeni* are by ſome ſuppoſed to have been the ſame people.

The

The firſt diviſion of Britain, or more properly of England and Wales, made by the Romans, was into *Britannia inferior*, and *Britannia ſuperior*: a ſtill more ancient diviſion mentioned by Ptolemy into *Britannia magna* and *parva*, is underſtood by Camden to refer to Great-Britain and Ireland, and by ſome other writers to England and Scotland. *Britannia inferior* is ſuppoſed to have compriſed the northern part of England, and *Britannia Superior*, the more ſouthern part and Wales. This diviſion is ſuppoſed by Camden to have been made by Severus, who according to Herodian, divided the government of the province of Britain into two *præfecturæ*: Scotland they had long before this time abandoned as unprofitable.

The Romans afterwards divided the province of Britain into three parts, *Maxima Cæſarienſis*, *Britannia Prima*, and *Britannia Secunda*: Camden ſuppoſes theſe to correſpond with the three archbiſhoprics which anciently exiſted in Britain, London, (afterwards removed to Canterbury,) York, and Caerleon which included Wales; his reaſon is, that Pope Lucius inſinuates that the Chriſtians eſtabliſhed their eccleſiaſtical juriſdictions in imitation of thoſe of the Roman magiſtrates, and that the archbiſhops fixed their ſees in the cities where the Roman Governors had their reſidence; the province of London, as being nearer Rome, he ſuppoſes to have been *Britannia Prima*, it having been cuſtomary to give the name of *Prima* to that part of their foreign colonies which was ſo ſituated; Wales, which was ſubject to the Biſhop of Caerleon, *Britannia Secunda*; and the province of York, *Maxima Cæſarienſis*. In the next age they divided Britain into five parts, retaining the three former names, and adding thoſe of *Valentia*, and *Flavia Cæſarienſis*. *Valentia* was doubtleſs the northern part of *Maxima Cæſarienſis*, recovered by Theodoſius from the Picts and Scots, and called in honor of his maſter the Emperor Valens, *Valentia*: from this time it was conſidered as a ſeparate diſtrict, and had a governor of its own. *Flavia Cæſarienſis* is ſuppoſed by Camden, following the opinion of Giraldus Cambrenſis, to have been in the centre of England, probably taken partly from *Britannia Prima*, and partly from the ſouthern part of *Maxima Cæſarienſis*; and called *Flavia*, as Camden with great probability ſuppoſes, in honour of *Flavius Theodoſius*, the Emperor, ſon of the above-mentioned *Theodoſius*. When the Romans had abandoned Britain, and the Saxons invited to aſſiſt the haraſſed inhabitants againſt the Scots and Picts, had turned their arms againſt thoſe whom they came to aid, and after many bloody conflicts had made themſelves maſters of their country, they divided the whole Roman province, excepting Wales where the remains of the Britons had retired, into ſeven kingdoms, known by the name of the Saxon Heptarchy, viz. Kent, Suſſex, Eaſt-Anglia, Weſſex, Northumberland, Eſſex, and Mercia.

Under the Saxon heptarchy, England was not divided into counties properly

ſo

so called, but into certain districts, thirty-four in number, containing each a definite number of hides. They are enumerated by Camden from an ancient MS. but their names are in general so different from those of any of our modern counties, or districts, that it would be very difficult, and perhaps impossible, to ascertain their positions. The situation of a few, as *Ciltern-setna*, *Cant-Warena*, and *Suth-Sexena*, are obvious. Although England was not divided into counties, before the whole kingdom was united into one monarchy under Alfred; yet it is sufficiently ascertained, from the testimony of ancient historians, that the present counties were divided among the seven kingdoms of the Heptarchy, according to the following table.

The Kingdom of Kent comprehended the county of Kent only; Sussex, or the Kingdom of the South Saxons, Sussex and Surrey;

The Kingdom of the East-Angles,	*The Counties of*	Norfolk. Suffolk. Cambridge, with the Isle of Ely.
Wessex, or the Kingdom of the West Saxons.		Cornwall. Devon. Dorset. Somerset. Wilts. Hants. Berks.
The Kingdom of Northumberland,		Lancaster. York. Durham. Cumberland. Westmorland. Northumberland, and the more southern parts of Scotland.
Essex, or the Kingdom of the East Saxons,		Essex. Middlesex, and Part of Hertford.
The Kingdom of Mercia,		Gloucester. Hereford. Warwick. Worcester. Leicester. Rutland. Northampton. Lincoln. Huntingdon. Bedford.

Buckingham.

Buckingham.
Oxford.
Stafford.
Salop.
Derby.
Nottingham.
Chester and Part of Hertford.

The counties are also called shires, from the Saxon word *Scyre*, signifying to divide. At the first distribution of them there were only 32, as may be collected from a passage in William of Malmsbury [d]. " At this time, says Camden, the counties were divided according to the diversity of laws. For the laws of England were of three sorts, those of the West Saxons, called *West Saxonlage*, of the Danes called *Danelage*, and of the Mercians, called *Merchenlage*: The West Saxon laws obtained in nine counties, Kent, Surrey, Sussex, Berks, Hants, Wilts, Somerset, Dorset, and Devon : those of the Danes in fifteen ; York, Derby, Nottingham, Leicester, Lincoln, Northampton, Bedford, Bucks, Herts, Essex, Middlesex, Norfolk, Suffolk, Cambridge and Huntingdon. The other counties, Gloucester, Worcester, Hereford, Warwick, Oxford, Chester, Salop and Stafford, were governed by the Mercian laws." This opinion of a diversity of laws, obtaining in the three districts, was generally received among antiquaries, till Bishop Nicholson's time ; who has ably refuted it in his preface to Wilkins's edition of the Saxon laws, and shewn that the word *lage*, mistaken by the Norman writers for their *ley* or *loi*, in reality signifies *ditio*, or jurisdiction ; and that there was not such a diversity of laws, although there were so many governments. In the survey of Domesday 34 counties are described : Northumberland, Westmorland, and Cumberland, then belonged to the Scots ; Durham and Lancashire are omitted : these make up the number 39 : Monmouth, which was made an English county in the reign of Charles II. completes the present number of 40. Camden says that the Welch counties were six in number in the reign of Edward I. and that the others were formed by act of parliament in the reign of Henry VIII. : but it appears by the act itself, that there had been eight shires of ancient and long time, viz. Glamorgan, Carmarthen, Pembroke, Cardigan, Flint, Carnarvon, Anglesey, and Merioneth ; Monmouth, (afterwards made, as before-mentioned, an English county) Radnor, Brecknock, Montgomery, and Denbigh, were then added.

[d] At this time (Anno 1016) the Danes over-run 16 out of the 32 counties in England.

King Alfred, for the more convenient adminiſtration of juſtice, divided each county into hundreds and tithings; the hundreds in the north of England being called Wapentakes, and in Suſſex, Rapes. The ridings of Yorkſhire compriſe many hundreds; the Leathes in Kent are ſmaller, and compriſe three or four hundreds. A hundred has been defined as conſiſting of ten tithings, and every tithing of ten houſeholds; but if ſo, the number of hundreds muſt have been in ancient times much greater, or the population very ſmall.

In the time of King Alfred, a deputy or lieutenant was appointed, as guardian of each county; King Henry III. in the latter part of his reign, reſtored this officer by the name of Captain, to keep the peace with the aſſiſtance of the ſheriff: it is probable that he was alſo called *Comes.* The office became hereditary in many noble families, who had by Royal Grant, as a kind of ſalary attached to it, the *third penny* of the county over which they preſided. *Comes* is by ſome ſuppoſed to be derived from *Comitatus,* by others *Comitatus* from *Comes:* this is the origin of the third rank among our nobility, that of earls. It is certain that the ſheriff, who was the deputy of this principal officer, was invariably ſtyled *Vice-comes,* and was one of the principal gentry in each county; and it was not till the reign of Henry VI. that the title of *Vice-comes* or Viſcount, was made a title of honour unconnected with office: it now forms the fourth in rank of the nobility, being next to that of earl.

It may not be amiſs to ſpeak here very briefly of the other degrees. The higheſt rank, that of duke, was not granted to any ſubject in England before the reign of King Edward III. Robert Vere, Duke of Ireland, being the firſt perſon, unconnected with the blood royal, who had that honour conferred on him: he was at the ſame time (1385) created Marquis of Dublin, being the firſt inſtance of the introduction of that title, now the ſecond in rank in our peerage.

The firſt mention of the title of baron amongſt us, is as early as the reign of Canute, when the word ſeems to have been uſed ſynonymouſly with Thane; though it ſeems the general opinion of antiquaries, that the Thane and Vavaſor, orders, long ſince extinct, were of a rank inferior to barons: it is certain that under the firſt Norman kings, barons were ſuch perſons as were poſſeſſed of an entire barony, that is thirteen knights-fees and one third, being lands of the yearly value of 400 marks. Theſe claimed a right of being ſummoned to parliament. K. Henry III. firſt made a ſelection of the barons, who in his time were become very numerous, and admitted thoſe only to parliament whom he ſummoned to it by writ. K. Richard II. firſt made it a title of honour, and created barons by patent:

the

the firſt ſo created was John Lord Beauchamp of Holt, made Baron Kiderminſter in 1387.

The diviſion of diſtricts into pariſhes was an eccleſiaſtical inſtitution, which aroſe from the Pope's aſſigning particular churches to each prieſt; and firſt took place in England about the year 636, by order of Honorius, Archbiſhop of Canterbury.

The whole of England, as far as relates to its eccleſiaſtical juriſdiction, is divided into two provinces, and 25 dioceſes. The provinces or archbiſhoprics are Canterbury and York. The Archbiſhop of Canterbury is primate and metropolitan of all England; he has a dioceſe of his own, conſiſting of part of Kent, and ſeveral pariſhes in other counties, which are in his immediate juriſdiction: the biſhops ſubject to him are 21 in number;

Rocheſter, *whoſe dioceſe compriſes*	Part of Kent.
London, - - - -	Eſſex, Middleſex, and Part of Hertfordſhire.
Chicheſter, - - -	Suſſex.
Wincheſter, - - -	Hampſhire (including the Iſle of Wight,) Surrey, and the Iſlands of Guernſey and Jerſey.
Saliſbury, - - - -	Wiltſhire, and Berkſhire.
Exeter, - - - -	Devonſhire, and Cornwall.
Bath and Wells, - - -	Somerſetſhire.
Worceſter, - - -	Worceſterſhire, and Part of Warwickſhire.
Hereford, - - - -	Herefordſhire, and Part of Shropſhire.
Litchfield and Coventry, - -	Staffordſhire, Derbyſhire, Part of Warwick- ſhire, and Part of Shropſhire.
Lincoln, - - - -	Lincolnſhire, Leiceſterſhire, Huntingdonſhire, Bedfordſhire, Buckinghamſhire, and Part of Hertfordſhire.
Ely, - - - - -	Cambridgeſhire (including the Iſle of Ely.)
Norwich, - - - -	Norfolk, and Suffolk.
Oxford, - - - -	Oxfordſhire.
Peterborough, - - -	Northamptonſhire, and Rutlandſhire.
Glouceſter, - - -	Glouceſterſhire (excepting a few Pariſhes.)
Briſtol, - - - -	The city of Briſtol, Dorſetſhire, and a few Pariſhes in Glouceſterſhire.
St. Davids - - - -	Pembrokeſhire, Carmarthenſhire, Breck- nockſhire, the greater Part of Radnorſhire, and ſome Pariſhes in Monmouthſhire, Here- fordſhire, Montgomeryſhire, and Glamor- ganſhire.

Llandaff,

Llandaff, *whose diocese comprises*	The greater Part of Monmouthshire and Glamorganshire.
Bangor, - - - -	Carnarvonshire (excepting three Parishes,) Anglesea, and Part of Denbighshire, Merionethshire, and Montgomeryshire.
St. Asaph, - - - -	Flintshire, Part of Denbighshire, Montgomeryshire, and Merionethshire, and a small Part of Shropshire.

The sees continue as they were some time before the conquest; excepting that Bristol, Gloucester, and Oxford, were created Bishoprics by King Henry VIII. before whose time Dorsetshire was in the diocese of Salisbury, Gloucestershire in the diocese of Worcester, and Oxfordshire in the diocese of Lincoln.

The archbishop of York has within his immediate jurisdiction the counties of York and Nottingham; and has subject to him three bishoprics, viz.

Carlisle, *whose diocese comprises*	The greater part of Westmorland and Cumberland.
Chester, - - - -	Cheshire, Lancashire, and part of Westmorland, Cumberland, and Yorkshire.
Durham, - - - -	Durham, and Northumberland.

Chester was created a bishopric by K. Henry VIII. and was anciently part of the diocese of Litchfield. Each bishopric, unless of very small jurisdiction, is divided into two or more archdeaconries, and into several smaller districts called deaneries, each containing an indefinite number of parishes. The total number of parish churches in England, according to the list made out by Cardinal Wolsey in 1520, was 9407; the Catalogue presented to King James, as mentioned by Camden, makes them only 9284; Camden accounts for the difference by the supposition that some churches had in the interval been destroyed; that parochial chapels were omitted in one list, and in the other, those which were only chapels, accounted parish churches. The number of parishes subjoined by Camden to each county, correspond with the number of parish churches in Wolsey's list. It will not be found exactly to agree with the present number of parishes, which will be ascertained with as much accuracy as possible in each county, in the course of the following work. Some small parishes have long since Camden's time been united, and the churches in some instances taken down; whilst other large ones have been divided, and new parishes created by act of parliament. It is sometimes difficult to determine which chapelries are, and which are not, parochial.

The

The extent of South Britain has been fo differently ftated that fome writers on that fubject have fuppofed its area to contain no more than twenty-eight millions of acres, whilft others have eftimated it at forty-feven millions ; no one appears to have written fo fatisfactorily on this head as the prefent Profeffor of Modern Hiftory at Oxford[a], who fays that the true number is between thirty-eight and thirty-nine millions ; the Profeffor obferves, that " Our prefent maps differ indeed confiderably from one another, according as they have been more or lefs corrected, by adopting modern aftronomical obfervations ; but none of the older maps, which are of any credit, give more than forty millions, and fome of the *modern* ones fcarcely give thirty-eight millions of acres. It is true that the exact number cannot be afcertained with mathematical precifion, till the prefent very excellent trigonometrical furvey has been completed ; but fince that furvey has already corrected more than one-third of the whole outline, and verified the breadth of the fouthern part of England, fince in the latitude, and confequently in the diftance from north to fouth, there cannot be any error worth noticing ; and fince many other points, which are material to this inquiry, have already been fatisfactorily determined by good aftronomical obfer-vations, the poffibility of error is, in fact, reduced within very narrow limits, and there is no chance that the number of ftatute acres in South Britain can greatly exceed thirty-eight millions five hundred thoufand. Scotland, with its adjacent iflands, contains about twenty-one millions."

[a] In his Obfervations on the Income-Tax, publifhed in 1800.

BEDFORDSHIRE.

INTRODUCTION.

Ancient Inhabitants and Government.

THIS County, when the Romans invaded Britain, was inhabited by a people called the *Caſſii*, or *Catieuchlani*. During the government of the Romans, it formed part of *Britannia Superior*, afterwards of *Britannia Prima ;* and upon the laſt Roman diviſion of the iſland, it was included in the diſtrict of *Flavia*. After the eſtabliſhment of the Saxon Heptarchy, it became part of the kingdom of Mercia. When two kingdoms of the Heptarchy were aboliſhed, as related by Bromton, the kings of Mercia retained one moiety of Bedfordſhire ; the kings of Eſſex became poſſeſſed of the other [a]. After the whole of England was united into one monarchy, this county was compriſed within the diſtrict which was called *Denelege*, or the Daniſh Juriſdiction.

Hiſtorical Events.

THE firſt hiſtorical event which we find relating to this county, is the battle fought at Bedford between Cutha, or Cuthwulf, brother of Ceauline, king of the Weſt-Saxons, and the Britiſh army, in the year 571, or as ſome ſay 580. The Saxons proved ſucceſsful ; and the conſequence of the defeat to the Britons was the loſs of four of their principal towns, Lygeanburgh, Egleſburgh, Bennington, and Egeneſham [b]. The firſt has, by ſome antiquaries, been ſuppoſed to be Loughborough in Leiceſterſhire ; by others, with more probability, Leighton in Bedfordſhire ; that town and Egleſburgh (which all agree to have been Ayleſbury) lying in a direct line under the Chiltern to Benſington and Enſham. One of the moſt ancient Britiſh roads is ſuppoſed to have paſſed under the Chiltern. No particular mention of this county appears in hiſtory after this period till the reign of Edward the Elder (ſon to king Alfred) when it became frequently the ſcene of ac-

[a] Decem Scrip. i. 800, 801.   [b] Sax. Chron. p. 22.

tion in the wars between that victorious monarch and the Danes. About the year 907, according to Bromton, or as the Saxon Chronicle, with greater appearance of accuracy, informs us, in 919[c], this monarch came to Bedford, ftaid there four weeks, received the fubmiffion of all the neighbouring country, and built a fortrefs on the South fide of the river. In 921, the Danes, coming from Huntingdonfhire into Bedfordfhire, fortified Temesford (now Tempsford) and ftationed themfelves there. In an excurfion from thence they attacked Bedford, but the men of that town made a fally, and put them to flight with great flaughter[d]. The fame fummer King Edward, collecting a great force, befieged the Danes at Tempsford, took that city, as it is called in the Saxon Chronicle, deftroyed their fortrefs, and put their king to death, together with a great number of his nobles[e]. In 1009, the Danes made an excurfion through a part of this county by the Chiltern to Oxford[f]. In 1010, the Danifh army burnt Bedford and Tempsford[g]. The next year this county fubmitted to the dominion of King Ethelred[h].

Bedford caftle, built by the Beauchamps on the fite, it is probable, of King Edward's fortrefs, was efteemed a garrifon of fuch importance, that, as Camden obferves, there was fcarcely a ftorm of civil fury, whilft it ftood, that did not burft on it. It was held by the Beauchamps againft Stephen, and taken by him in 1138[i]. The fame family held this caftle againft King John, who fent his favourite, Fulk de Brent, to befiege it; and when he had taken it, gave it to him as a reward for his good fervices[k]. This fame Fulk having committed a moft violent outrage on Henry Braybroke, one of the King's juftices itinerant, whom he imprifoned in open defiance of the law in his caftle at Bedford, King Henry III. went in perfon with his nobles to befiege it. After a fiege of two months, it was taken by ftorm, and the King caufed it to be difmantled[l]. It is probable that all the baronial caftles in this county, of any confequence, excepting Bedford, had been before demolifhed when King John in his march to the northward burnt and deftroyed, as Matthew Paris informs us[m], all the caftles which lay in his route; and this perhaps is the reafon why we read of no remarkable occurrences in this county during the wars between the houfes of York and Lancafter.

During the war between Charles the Firft and his Parliament, Bedfordfhire was one of the firft counties that affociated againft the King, being within that diftrict known by the name of the Eaftern affociates[n]. A fpecial licence for this affociation paffed the Houfe Nov. 30th, 1642. The Earl of Manchefter was commander in chief of the Eaftern affociates: Cromwell commanded the horfe under him[o]. Lord Clarendon obferves, that Bedfordfhire was one of the counties

[c] Sax. Chron. p. 106.   [d] Ibid. p. 107.   [e] Ibid. p. 108.   [f] Ibid. p. 139.   [g] Ibid. p. 140.
[h] Ibid.   [i] Hift. Angl. Scrip. ii. p. 153.   [k] Dugdale's Baronage.   [l] Chron. Dunft.
[m] P. 230.   [n] Heath's Chronicle, p. 59.   [o] Lord Clarendon's Hiftory of the Rebellion.

in

in which the King had not any vifible party, nor one fixed quarter. The fame author informs us, that in October 1643, the King fent Prince Rupert with a ftrong party of horfe and foot into Bedfordfhire : that he took the town of Bedford, which was occupied as a ftrong quarter by the enemy, and that this expedition was principally defigned to countenance Sir Lewis Dyve, whilft he fortified Newport-Pagnell, at which place he hoped to fix a garrifon. Heath fays, that it was Sir Lewis Dyve himfelf who had the command of this expedition ; and that, being fent into Bedfordfhire with 2000 or 3000 horfe, he came firft to Ampthill, then to Bedford, which town he entered, and took Sir John Norris, and other parliamentary officers, prifoners. From thence he went to Sir Samuel Luke's houfe [p], and ferved *that* as Sir Lewis Dyve himfelf was ferved in the fame county [q] by the fequeftrators. Soon after this, Col. Montague, with fome of the parliamentary troops, entered Bedford by a feint, under a pretence of their being the Royal army, under Sir Lewis Dyve, and took away fome money and horfes intended for the King's ufe [r]. None of the fubfequent tranfactions of the war appear to have been in any way connected with this county.

Ancient and modern Divifion of BEDFORDSHIRE.

WHEN the Norman furvey was taken, this county was divided into nine hundreds and three half hundreds. The town of Bedford was affeffed as half a hundred. Leighton-Bufard, Luton, Houghton-Regis, and the adjoining manor of Sewell, feem to have been affeffed feparately. The hundreds were as follows :

Manfheve,	-	- now	Manfhead ;	Bereford,	- - now	Barford ;
Flictham,	-	- —	Flit ;	Bichelefwade,	- —	Bigglefwade ;
Wilga,	-	- —	Willey ;	Clifton, or Clifton,	—	Clifton ;
Wicheftanftou,	-	—	Wixamtree;	Radburneftoc, or Radborgeftoch,	—	Redbornftoke.
Stodene,	-	- —	Stodden ;			

The half hundred of Bochelai, or Buchelai, contained the manors of Biddenham, Bletfoe, Bromham, Stagfden, and Steventon, now included in the hundred of Willey, and Renhold and Goldington, now in the hundred of Barford.

The half hundred of Stanburge, or Stanbridge, comprifed the manors of Eaton-Bray, Toternhoe, Tilfworth, Studham, and the Bedfordfhire part of Edlefborough, which are all now in the hundred of Manfhead.

The half hundred of Weneflai contained only the three manors of Hatley, Potton, and Sandy, now in the Hundred of Bigglefwade.

The following is a lift of the manors noticed in the furvey of Domefday, with their modern names, as far as they could be afcertained.

[p] Either Hawnes, or Woodend, near Bedford.   [q] At Bromham, then the feat of the Dyve's.
[r] Pamphlet in the Britifh Mufeum.

Aieworde, or Aiffe-worde	Eyworth	Eitone	Eaton-Bray, and Eaton-Socon
Acheleia	Oakley	Elneftou	Elftow
Alricefeia	Arlefey	Elvendone	
Ammetelle	Ampthill	Efeltone and Effelton	Shelton
Afpleia	Afpley	Eftodham	Studham
Badlefdone	Battlefden	Eftone	
Bedeford	Bedford	Eftwiche	Aftwick
Bereford	Barford	Eurefhot	Everfholt
Berton	Barton	Fernadis	Farndifh
Bichelfwade	Bigglefwade	Falmerfham, or Flam-merfham	Felmerfham
Bideham	Biddenham	Flicteham	Flitton
Biffoppefcote	Bifcot, in Luton	Flictewicke	Flitwick
Biftone	Beefton, in Sandy	Giveldone	Yieldon
Blechefhou	Bletfoe	Gledlai	Gledley
Blunham	Blunham	Goldentone	Goldington
Bolehestre, or Bulehes-tre	Bolnhurft	Hagenes	Hawnes, or Haynes
Bruneham	Bromham	Hanefelde	
Cadendone	Caddington	Haneflau	Henlow
Caiffot, or Chaifot	Keyfoe	Harewelle	Harold
Cameftone, or Cham-belton	Campton	Hatlei	Cockayne-Hatley
Carlentone	Cardington	Henewich	Hinwick, in Puddington
Celgrave	Chalgrave	Herghetone	Harrowden, in Cardington
Chainhall	Renhold	Herlingdon	Harlington
Chainhou	Cainhoe, in Clophill	Hockleia	Hockliffe
Chalveftorne	Chalvefton, in Roxton	Holewelle	Holwell
Chenotinga	Knotting	Holme	Holme, in Bigglefwade
Chernetone		Houftone	Houghton-Conqueft, and Houghton-Regis
Chichefana	Chickfand	Lalega	
Cliftone	Clifton	Langeford	Langford
Clopeham	Clapham	Leftone	Leighton-Bufard
Clopelle	Clophill	Litingletone	Litlington
Cochepol, or Chochepol	Cople	Loitone	Luton
Colmeworde	Colmworth	Malperteffelle	Mepperfhall
Cranfelle	Cranfield	Meleburne	Melchbourn
Cravenheft	Gravenhurft, (upper and lower)	Meldone	Maulden
Crawelai	Hufborn-Crawley	Melebroc	Milbrook
Cudeffane		Melehou	Milnho, in Dunton
Daintone, or Domtone	Dunton	Mereftone	Marfton-Morteyne
Dena	Dean	Middletone, or Mil-denton	Milton Bryant, and Milton-Erneft
Dodingtone	Toddington	Newentone	
Echam	Higham-Gobion	Northgivil	Northill
Edworde	Edworth	Otone	Wotton

Pabeneham

Pabeneham	- Pavingham	Stanedone -	- Stondon
Pechefdone	-	Stanewiga -	-
Pileworde	- Tilfworth	Stanford -	- Stanford, in Southill
Podíntone	- Puddington	Stepigelai -	- Stepingley
Polocheffelle	- Pulloxhill	Stiventone -	- Steventon
Potefgrave	- Potefgrave	Stotfalt -	- Stotfold
Potone	- Potton	Stradli, or Straillei	- Stretley
Preftley	- Preftley, in Flitwick	Stratone -	- Stratton in Bigglefwade
Putenhou	- Puttenhoe, in Goldington	Sudgivele -	- Southill
Radwelle	- Radwell, in Felmerfham	Sudtone, or Suttone	- Sutton
Rifeden	- Probably Ravenfden	Tamifeford -	- Tempsford
Riflai	- Rifeley	Tilebroc -	- Tilbrook
Rochefdone, or } Roxton		Tingrei -	- Tingrith
Rocheftone -		Torvei -	- Turvey
Salchou	-	Totenhou -	- Toternhoe
Saleford	- Salford	Wadelle, or Wadhulle Odell	
Sandeia	- Sandy	Wardone -	- Warden
Segenhou	- Segenhoe, in Ridgmont	Welitone -	- Willington
Segrefdon	-	Weftcote -	-
Sernebroc	- Sharnbrook	Wiledene -	- Wilden
Sethlingdone	- Shitlington	Wimentone -	- Wimington
Sewelle	- Sewell, in Houghton Regis	Wineffameftede	- Wilhamfted
Sewileffou	- Silfoe, in Flitton	Woburne -	- Woburn
Sonedone	- Sundon	Wyboldeftone - { Wybofton, in Bigglef- wade.	
Stachedene	- Stagfden		

The parifhes of Dunftaple, Hulcot, Kempfton, Pertenhall, Ridgmont, Soul-drop, Little Staughton, Thurleigh, Weftoning, Whipfnade, Wreftlingworth, and feveral confiderable hamlets and manors, are not mentioned in the furvey.

Ecclefiaftical Divifion of BEDFORDSHIRE.

THIS County, which lies within the diocefe of Lincoln, is under the jurifdiction of an Archdeacon, and is divided into fix Deaneries, viz. Bedford, Clopham, Dunftaple, Eaton, Fleete, and Shefford. Wolfey's lift, quoted by Camden, makes the number of parifhes 116; the prefent number is 121. Several of the be-nefices are confolidated, as Afpley-Guife, with Hufborn-Crawley; Aftwick with Arlefey; Barford with Roxton; Battlefden with Potefgrave; Carlton with Chil-lington; Chalgrave with Hockliffe; Felmerfham with Pavingham; Hulcot with Salford; Knotting with Souldrop; and Southill with Old-Warden. The parifhes, neverthelefs, remain diftinct: fome of the confolidations are of recent date[s]. Shef-ford is a chapel of eafe to Campton; Silfoe to Flitton. Billington, Egginton, Heath and Reach, and Stanbridge, are all chapels to Leighton-Bufard. Of the

---

[s] See the dates under the refpective parifhes.

121 parifhes, 63 are vicarages : the great tithes of thefe, with very few exceptions, were appropriated formerly to religious houfes, and are now in lay hands.

Monafteries and Hofpitals.

THE Benedictine Nuns had an Abbey at Elftow; the Ciftercian Monks, Abbeys at Warden and Woburn; the Auftin Canons, Priories at Dunftaple, Biffemede, or Bufhmead, Caldwell and Newenham; the Auftin Nuns a Priory at Harold; the Gilbertines a Priory at Chickfand; the Grey Friers a houfe at Bedford; the Black Friers at Dunftaple; the Knights Hofpitallers a preceptory at Melchbourn. At Grovebury, in the parifh of Leighton-Bufard, was an alien Priory, fubject to the Abbey of Fontevralt in Normandy; at Milbrook and Clophill were cells to the Benedictine Abbey of St. Alban's. At Ruxox in Flitwick, a cell to the Priory of Dunftaple, and at Leighton-Bufard a cell to Woburn-Abbey. Thefe cells feem to have been all removed at an early period. At Northill was a college of Priefts. There were ancient hofpitals at Dunftaple, Farleigh, Hockliffe, and Toddington, and two at Bedford, dedicated to St. John and St. Leonard.

Market and Borough Towns.

THIS county fends two members to parliament. Bedford, the county-town, which is the only parliamentary borough, fends alfo two members. Dunftaple, which was made a royal borough by Henry I., never fent reprefentatives to parliament. Browne Willis, in his *Notitia Parliamentaria*, ftates the number of market-towns to be ten; the editors of the *Magna Britannia*, and moft modern writers, mention the fame number. In the laft edition of Camden, they are faid to be eleven, which was correct at the time of that publication, the markets at Shefford and Toddington having been fince difcontinued. The market-houfe at Toddington was pulled down in 1799 : a century ago this town had one of the moft confiderable markets in the county. The prefent number of market-towns is nine, Ampthill, Bedford, Bigglefwade, Dunftaple, Harold, Leighton-Bufard, Luton, Potton, and Woburn. Harold, which has been omitted by moft writers who have enumerated the Bedfordfhire towns, ftill keeps up the name of a market on Tuefdays, though it is attended only by one or two butchers, who open fhambles on that day. Bedford, Bigglefwade, and Luton, are the principal markets for corn. Potton has declined within thefe few years. Leighton is noted for its abundant fupply of fuckling calves. Arlefey, Afpley Guife, Blunham, Silfoe in the parifh of Flitton, Marfton-Morteyne, Melchbourn, Odell, Sundon, Warden and Weftoning, had formerly markets, as appears by their refpective charters among the records in the Tower. They have all been long fince difcontinued, not one of them being enumerated in Leland's lift. Arlefey is mentioned as a market town in the furvey of Doomfday.

Population.

Population.

IN the year 1377, the number of perfons in this county who were charged to a poll-tax, from which the clergy, children, and paupers, were exempted, amounted to 20,239. This poll-tax took place not long after a very fatal peftilence.

The number of inhabited houfes in this county in 1801, according to the returns made to Parliament, purfuant to the act for afcertaining the population of the kingdom, was 11,888; of uninhabited houfes 185; the number of inhabitants 63,393. Of thefe 30,523 were males; 32,870 females.

The following account of the number of houfes, families, and perfons in each parifh, is taken from the above-mentioned return, and arranged alphabetically:

	Inhabited Houfes.	Uninhabited Houfes.	Families,	Perfons.
Ampthill - - - -	237	3	266	1234
Arlefey - - - -	69	1	79	404
Afpley Guife - - - -	100	3	114	679
Aftwick - - - -	12	0	16	81
Great Barford - - - -	83	4	83	431
Little Barford - - - -	18	0	18	80
Barton - - - -	71	5	88	448
Battlefden - - - -	21	0	28	133
Bedford, St. Paul's - - -	444	9	554	2150
——— St. Cuthbert's - - -	82	4	107	351
——— St. Peter's - - -	87	4	98	577
——— St. John's - - -	54	0	62	254
——— St. Mary's - - -	116	0	154	616
Biddenham - - - -	57	1	61	252
Bigglefwade - - - -	298	3	241	1650
——— Holme } in the Parifh of {	11	2	12	80
——— Stratton } Bigglefwade {	8	0	9	64
Bletfoe - - - -	56	1	70	321
Blunham - - - -	73	0	83	376
——— Muggerhanger, in the Parifh of Blunham	43	0	76	345
Bolnhurft - - - -	35	0	42	225
Bromham - - - -	43	0	58	297
Caddington - - - -	54	0	67	319
——— Market Street (partly in Caddington, and partly in Studham) - }	28	1	43	235
Campton - - - -	45	1	47	316
——— Shefford Townfhip, in the Parifh of Campton	90	0	107	474
Cardington - - - -	92	0	100	509
——— Cotton-End } in the Parifh of {	43	0	48	190
——— Harrowden and Fenlake } Cardington {	51	0	59	314
Carlton - - - -	87	6	89	376

Chalgrave

	Inhabited Houses.	Uninhabited Houses.	Families.	Persons.
Chalgrave	73	1	114	534
Chickfand (Extra-parochial)	6	0	6	42
Chillington	24	1	26	112
Clapham	30	0	36	157
Clifton	62	1	75	329
Clophill	142	1	148	706
Colmworth	56	0	63	347
Cople	41	0	53	403
Cranfield	202	3	241	961
Dean	82	0	84	385
Dunstaple	243	2	296	1296
Dunton	61	0	61	336
Eaton Bray	104	0	122	583
Eaton Socon	332	12	461	1625
Edworth	16	1	16	90
Elstow	96	2	116	475
Eversholt	143	3	160	715
Everton (Bedfordshire part of)	26	0	31	141
Eyworth	13	1	19	86
Farndish	11	1	14	68
Felmersham	40	0	48	201
———— Radwell (in Felmersham)	23	2	30	128
Flitton	49	0	61	292
———— Silfoe (in Flitton)	73	0	95	447
Flitwick	80	1	101	436
Goldington	60	1	74	339
Upper Gravenhurst	31	2	44	201
Lower Gravenhurst	9	1	9	48
Harlington	63	2	70	344
Harold	155	0	166	763
Hatley Cockayne	18	1	20	102
Hawnes	82	0	121	588
Henlow	99	1	114	552
Higham Gobion	15	1	17	91
Hockliffe	52	1	53	256
Holwell	20	0	20	113
Houghton Conquest	100	5	120	507
Houghton Regis	139	1	165	784
Hulcot	10	0	10	65
Hufborn Crawley	101	5	125	543
Kempston	180	2	206	1035
Keyfoe	158	0	175	370
Knotting	22	0	22	105
Langford	73	3	98	458

Leighton

				Inhabited Houfes.	Uninhabited Houfes.	Families.	Perfons.
Leighton Bufard	-		-	376	11	392	1963
———— Billington			-	39	1	48	200
———— Egginton		in the Parifh of Leighton	-	44	0	46	206
———— Heath and Reach			-	111	0	111	541
———— Stanbridge			-	57	0	*	262
Litlington	-	-	-	106	4	145	559
Luton	-	-	-	612	0	656	3095
Marfton Morteyne		-	-	130	3	161	709
Maulden	-	-	-	125	0	173	738
Melchbourn	-	-		40	0	40	229
Mepperfhall	-	-		51	4	56	309
Milbrook	-	-		67	0	71	327
Milton Bryant	-	-		64	1	76	333
Milton Erneft	-	-		59	6	69	300
Northill	-	-	-	122	0	149	715
Oakley	-	-	-	68	0	72	265
Odell	-	-	-	63	0	69	361
Pavingham	-	-	-	57	1	86	447
Pertenhall	-	-	-	38	0	44	190
Potefgrave	-	-	-	29	0	35	157
Potton	-	-	-	239	2	255	1103
Puddington	-	-	-	70	0	92	415
Pulloxhill	-	-	-	52	4	92	317
Ravenfden	-	-	-	33	0	46	218
Renhold	-	-	-	34	0	54	245
Ridgmont	-	-	-	113	2	132	581
Rifely	-	-	-	108	1	128	576
Roxton	-	-	-	66	1	80	465
Salford	-	-	-	46	1	46	210
Sandy	-	-	-	108	1	119	615
——— Beefton	in the Parifh of Sandy		-	28	0	35	180
——— Girtford			-	54	0	86	320
Sharnbrook	-	-	-	101	0	122	585
Shelton	-	-	-	18	1	19	100
Shitlington	-	-	-	80	1	85	420
Souldrop	-	-	-	30	0	47	188
Southill	-	-	-	107	3	129	621
——— Broom	in the Parifh of Southill		-	30	0	36	187
——— Stanford			-	36	0	38	177
Stagfden	-	-	-	84	0	114	492
Little Staughton	-	-	-	54	0	58	272
Stepingley	-	-	-	46	1	46	264

* No return of families.

	Inhabited Houses.	Uninhabited Houses.	Families.	Persons.
Stevington - - -	78	0	99	415
Stondon - - -	5	0	5	29
Stotfold - - - -	92	1	101	495
Stretly - - - -	42	4	46	209
Studham - - - -	22	0	22	99
Sundon - - - -	61	1	61	315
Sutton - - -	68	0	71	301
Tempsford - - -	78	2	91	409
Thurleigh - - -	69	1	91	411
Tilbrook - - -	40	2	49	219
Tilsworth - - -	38	2	36	195
Tingrith - - - -	23	0	26	116
Toddington - - -	360	5	360	1143
Toternhoe - - -	65	0	65	332
Turvey - - -	151	0	168	758
Warden - - -	63	0	92	455
Weston-ing - - -	76	1	89	410
Whipsnade - - -	28	0	30	140
Wilden - - -	53	0	70	300
Wilhamsted - - -	84	1	90	477
Willington - - -	36	0	44	229
Wimington - - -	36	0	39	226
Woburn - - - -	277	6	336	1563
Wotton - - - -	139	1	148	732
Wrestlingworth - - -	56	3	74	330
Yielden - - -	41	1	45	209

Principal Land-owners at various Periods, and principal extinct Families.

AT the time of the Norman survey, the principal land-owners of this county were Hugh de Beauchamp, who possessed no less than 20 manors; Nigel de Albini (ancestor of the Mowbrays), who had 12 manors [1]; William Spech, or Espec, and Walter Giffard, who had 6 manors each; Walter Flandrensis (ancestor of the barons Wahul), who had 5 manors; and Judith, Countess of Northumberland, who had 7. Ten manors belonged to religious houses. The Beauchamps had the chief seat of their Barony at Bedford: a younger branch of the family had a castle at Eaton Socon. Their large property was divided among female heirs. The greater part of their lands in this county fell to the share of the Mowbrays. The principal part of Nigel de Albini's estates in Bedfordshire went to a younger son, who had a castle at Cainhoe, in the parish of Clophill, and passed by a female heir

[1] Dugdale enumerates 23; it appears that he had that number of estates, but eleven of them are not described as manors.

to the St. Amands, who were confiderable land-owners in this county in the 13th and 14th centuries. The Wahuls, or Wodhuls, defcended from Walter Flandrenfis, were barons, and continued in the male line till about the year 1550. Agnes, only child of the laft male heir, married Richard Chetwode efq. and died in 1575. The chief feat of the Wahuls was at Wodhul, or Odell Caftle, which paffed, with other eftates, to the Chetwodes. The Wahuls had feats alfo at Shortgrave and Segenhoe. Segenhoe caftle is mentioned in the chronicle of Dunftaple priory under the year 1276. It feems to have been afterwards the feat of lord Grey of Ridgmont.

Among the earlieft extinct families which are known, by records fubfequent to the Norman furvey, to have poffeffed property in this county, may be reckoned the Barons Trally, Patfhull, and Cantilupe, the families of Hoo, Firmband, Pabenham, Pavely and Morteyne. The Trallys were not fummoned to parliament after the reign of king John, but the family was not extinct till about the year 1350. Their chief feat was at Yielden, anciently called Giveldune. The Patfhulls, who had their feat at Bletfoe, were extinct in the male line about the year 1368; their Bedfordfhire eftates paffed by a coheirefs to the family of Beauchamp, and from them to the St. Johns, who had before inherited confiderable eftates by a female heir from the Pavelys. The Cantilupes became extinct in the year 1272, when their eftates in this county devolved by a coheir to the Zouches, and paffed from them by purchafe, about the year 1480, to the Brays, an ancient family, who gave name to the village of Eaton-Bray. They were ennobled in the 21ft year of king Henry VIIIth's reign; and became extinct in the principal branch by the death of John lord Bray, without iffue, in 1557.

The noble family of Grey of Ruthin, was fettled at Wreft in this county before the year 1324. Their eftates are now poffeffed by their reprefentative Lady Lucas, grand-daughter of Henry the laft earl of Kent, who in 1710 was advanced to a dukedom, and died without leaving any male iffue.

The Hoos, though not mentioned in the record of Doomfday, are faid to have been fettled at Luton-Hoo before the conqueft[u]. Sir Thomas Hoo was created lord Hoo and Haftings in 1447, and dying without iffue male, his Bedfordfhire eftate went to his eldeft daughter, who married fir Geoffrey Boleyne. Paulinus Peyvre, a man who from a mean origin was raifed to the high ftation of Steward of the houfehold to Henry III., having amaffed great wealth, became the founder of a family, who had their chief feat at Toddington, and poffeffed confiderable eftates in the county, which, after a fucceffion of feveral generations, paffed, by an heir fe-

[u] See Chauncy's hiftory of Hertfordfhire, p. 510.

male,

male, to the Broughtons.   The Goftwicks became poffeffed of a large landed property in this county, about the end of the 15th and the beginning of the 16th centuries, principally by purchafe from the Mowbrays.   Their feat was at Willington.
William Goftwick, of that place, was created a baronet in 1612.   The title and
family are extinct.   Moft of their eftates were purchafed by Sarah duchefs of Marlborough, and are now, by fubfequent purchafes, in the Bedford family.   The Charnocks, who fettled in this county about the year 1500, had their chief feat at Hulcot.   St. John Charnock efq. was created a baronet in 1661.   The male line of
this family became extinct by the death of Sir Villiers Charnock, the laft baronet, in
1779, when the eftates paffed to the family of Hervey of Chilton in Buckinghamfhire, as heirs in the female line.   The Cockaynes, who gave name to the village
of Cockayne-Hatley, were defcended from chief baron Cockayne, who purchafed
an eftate there, and died in 1427.   This family has not long been extinct.   They
are reprefented in the female line by the Cufts.   The Conquefts, who gave name to
Houghton-Conqueft, were fettled in that village as early as the 13th century.   The
family became extinct by the death of Benedict Conqueft efq. father of lady Arundel of Wardour.

Fuller, who wrote in the reign of Charles II., after giving, from an ancient
record, a catalogue of the principal gentry of Bedfordfhire in the time of Henry
VI., fays, " Hungry Time has made a glutton's meal on this catalogue of gentry,
and hath left but a little morfel, for manners, remaining ; fo few of thefe are
found extant in this fhire, and fewer continuing in genteel equipage ; among whom
I muft not forget the family of the Blundells, whereof fir Edward Blundell behaved himfelf right valiantly in the unfortunate expedition to the ifle of Roe [x]."   The
only family in this catalogue that is not now extinct, is that of Mordaunt, fince
ennobled, and no longer connected with the county.   The Blundells, the Hafel-
dens of Goldington, and the Conquefts, have become extinct fince Fuller's time.
The Wingates of Harlington are extinct alfo in the male line, being reprefented
by the family of Jennings.

A few families which fettled in the county at a later period have alfo become extinct.
The Fitzjefferys of Creakers in Barford, were fettled there not long after the reign
of Henry VI., and became extinct in the 17th century.   The Aftreys came
into Bedfordfhire in the early part of the 16th century.   The late Dr. Aftrey was
the laft heir male of this family, whofe eftates have paffed, by inheritance in the
female line, to the Penyftons of Cornwell in Oxfordfhire.   The Bechers, who were
of Howbury in Renhold, as early as the reign of Henry VIII., have not long

------

[x] The expedition to the ifle of Rhée, under the duke of Buckingham.

been

been extinct. They possessed considerable estates in that neighbourhood, which were sold about the year 1780. The Gerys, who settled at Bushmead priory soon after the dissolution of Monasteries, became extinct in the male line by the death of the late William Gery esq. in 1802. The Rev. Hugh Wade, who married one of his daughters and co-heirs, and some years ago took the name of Gery at the request of his father-in-law, in addition to his own, resides at Bushmead. The Caters, who had a seat at Kempston, and possessed considerable estates there for nearly two centuries, have not long been extinct. Their estates have since been sold. The Bromsalls of Blunham, who had large estates in that, and some of the neighbouring parishes, during the 17th century, are supposed to be extinct. Some of their estates were sold in the reign of queen Anne.

Nobility of the County, and Places which have given Titles to any Ranks or Branches of the Peerage.

BEDFORD, the county-town, has given title to several noble families. Ingram de Coucy, constable of France, and earl of Soissons, was created earl of Bedford by Edward III. in 1365. John Plantagenet, third son of Henry IV., was created duke of Bedford, and was afterwards Regent of France. George Plantagenet, youngest son of king Edward IV., who died in his infancy, had the title of duke of Bedford. George Neville was created duke of Bedford in 1470, and degraded in 1478. Jasper Tudor, (uncle of Henry VII.) was created duke of Bedford in 1485 ; the title became again extinct at his death. The lady Mary, daughter to Henry VIII., (afterwards queen of England,) was created countess of Bedford by her father, in 1537[y]. In 1549 the earldom was revived in the person of John lord Russell, whose descendant was, in 1694, advanced to the dukedom. In this family the title still continues. Cranfield, a village on the borders of Buckinghamshire, gives the title of baron to the duke of Dorset, whose ancestor Charles Sackville, was in 1675 created baron Cranfield, and earl of Middlesex. When Henry earl of Kent was in 1706 advanced to the rank of a marquis, he was at the same time created earl of Harold in Bedfordshire, which title was borne by his only son, who died in his father's life-time. Milbrook near Ampthill gave the title of baron in 1442 to sir John Cornwall, who was also lord Fanhope, by which title he was generally known. William Clayton esq. being possessed of the manor of Sundon, in this county, was in 1735 created an Irish peer by the title of lord Sundon, which became extinct at his death. These are the only places in the county which have given titles to any orders of the peerage.

[y] See Gough's Camden.

The

The following peers, upon their fummons or creation, were defcribed as of places in this county. Lord Beauchamp of Bletfoe; lord Grey of Ridgmont; lord Bray of Eaton-Bray; and lord Cheney of Toddington, all extinct; lord Mordaunt of Turvey (now earl of Peterborough); lord St. John of Bletfoe; Vifc. Bruce of Ampthill (now earl of Aylefbury); lord Bathurft of Battlefden; lord Carteret of Hawnes; and lord Byng of Southill (now Vifc. Torrington). When lord Ongley was created an Irifh peer he was defcribed as of Old-Warden, which, by a fic- tion in ufe upon fuch occafions, is faid to be in the kingdom of Ireland. The earls of Peterborough and Aylefbury, lord Bathurft and lord Torrington are not now connected with this county.

Noblemen's Seats.

FULLER tells us, that in his time Toddington, Ampthill (by which he means Houghton Park, the feat of the earls of Aylefbury, partly in Ampthill parifh), and Woburn, carried away the credit among the houfes of the nobility. Toddington houfe, which after the Cheneys, became a feat of the noble family of Wentworth, has been nearly pulled down. Houghton Park is in ruins. Woburn, with in- creafed magnificence, is ftill the chief feat of the noble family of Ruffell, who firft fettled in this county in the reign of Henry VIII. That monarch granted to their anceftor John lord Ruffell the fcite of Woburn abbey, and feveral manors which had belonged to the abbot and convent. Their eftates have been from time to time augmented by various purchafes, particularly by the grandfather of the prefent duke; and now form what may be confidered as by far the largeft landed property in the county. The duke of Bedford has a pretty villa at Oakley, which was his chief refidence before he fucceeded to the title. The marquis of Bute, the earl of Upper-Offory, lady Lucas, lord St. John, lord Carteret, and lord Ongley, have feats in this county. The earl of Afhburnham has no feat at Clapham, as erro- neoufly ftated in fome of the Peerages, and other works. He inherited the manor in confequence of his anceftor's marriage with the heirefs of Mr. Taylor of that place; but the manor-houfe is an inconfiderable building, and has long been occu- pied as a farm. Lord Hampden has a fmall villa at Bromham, on the banks of the Oufe, which he feldom vifits. It was a favourite refidence of the late lord.

The Marquis of Bute's father, the late Earl, purchafed Luton-Hoo in 1763, and began a magnificent manfion which is not yet completed. The Earl of Offory's family fettled in this county in 1736, when Ampthill park was purchafed by his grandmother, Lady Gowran. Lady Lucas, as before mentioned, inherits Wreft Park, as reprefentative of the ancient and noble family of Grey, who were fettled there before the year 1324. The St. Johns became poffeffed of confider-

able

able eſtates in Bedfordſhire in the 14th century, by marriages with the Pavelys and Patſhulls. They were ennobled in 1559. Bletſoe, then the family ſeat, is now a farm houſe. Melchbourn, their preſent reſidence, came into the family by purchaſe; exactly at what time cannot be learned. It had been in the Ruſſell family, by grant from the crown, after the diſſolution of Monaſteries. Lord Carteret's anceſtors ſettled in this county by the purchaſe of Hawnes Park, in the year 1667. Lord Hampden inherits Bromham from Lord Trevor, who purchaſed that and other eſtates about a century ago. Lord Ongley inherits his ſeat at Warden from Sir Samuel Ongley, an opulent merchant, who purchaſed it about 1690. His father changed his name from Henley.

Earl Spencer, although he has no reſidence in this county, has conſiderable eſtates, the greater part of which have been in his family for nearly two centuries. Others were purchaſed by the Ducheſs of Marlborough, and by her bequeathed to his grandfather, the Honourable John Spencer.

Baronets extinct and exiſting.

THE extinct baronets of this county are, Napier of Luton-Hoo, created in 1612, and extinct in 1747; Goſtwick of Willington, created in 1612, extinct about 20 years ago; Winch of Hawnes, created in 1660; Charnock of Hulcot, created in 1661, extinct in 1779; Anderſon of Eyworth, created in 1664, and extinct in 1773; Sabine of Eyne, or Ion, created in 1671; and Corniſh of Sharnbrook, created in 1765, and extinct in 1770.

The preſent baronets who have ſeats in the county are Sir Montague Burgoyne of Sutton; Sir Philip Monnoux of Sandy; Sir George Oſborn of Chickſand; and Sir Hugh Inglis of Milton-Bryant.

The Burgoynes are one of the moſt ancient families in this county, where they appear to have been ſettled as early as the latter end of the 15th century. Sir Montague Burgoyne's anceſtor was created a baronet in 1641. The Monnouxes were originally a Worceſterſhire family. Humphrey Monnoux, grandfather of Humphrey, who was created a baronet in 1660, was the firſt who ſettled in Bedfordſhire, at Wotton, the ancient family ſeat, now occupied by a tenant. Sandy, their preſent reſidence, appears to have been a ſubſequent purchaſe. The Oſborns were an Eſſex family. Sir John Oſborn, treaſurer's remembrancer of the Exchequer, ſettled at Chickſand about the year 1600; his grandſon, Sir John Oſborn knt. was created a baronet in 1661. Sir Hugh Inglis, who married the heir of the Johnſons of Milton-Bryant, was created a baronet in 1801.

The anceſtor of the Langleys of Sheriffs-Hutton Park, in Yorkſhire, advanced to the degree of baronet in 1641, was then of Higham-Gobion, in Bedfordſhire, which

not

not long afterwards paffed out of the family. The prefent baronet, of the Alfton family, which was raifed to that degree in 1641, refides wholly in Cambridgefhire: he has no male iffue, nor is there any prefumptive heir to the title. Odell caftle, and the Bedfordfhire eftates of this family are, by fettlement or bequeft, the property of Thomas Alfton efq. Lord Torrington's anceftor, when he was created a baronet, was defcribed as of Southill, now the feat of Mr. Whitbread. Lord vifcount Newhaven having fome property, though no refidence at Marfton-Morteyne, in this county, was, when created a baronet in 1763, (by the name of Sir William Mayne) defcribed as of that place.

Sir Gregory Page Turner bart. of Ambrofden, in Oxfordfhire, has a feat in this county at Battlefden, by inheritance from the Pages. The late Sir Gillias Payne bart. had a feat at Tempsford, which he purchafed in 1772, now the property of his grandfon, a minor.

Principal Gentry, and their Seats.

THE moft diftinguifhed feats of the gentry are, Odell Caftle, Mr. Alfton's; Southill, the feat of Samuel Whitbread efq. M. P.; and Colworth houfe, the feat of William Lee Antonie efq. M. P.; befides which may be enumerated:

Place	the feat of	Place	the feat of
Arlefey, - -	——— Edwards	Houghton Regis,	Henry Brandreth, efq.
Blunham, - -	Mrs. Campbell	Howberry,	J. Polhill, efq.
Bufhmead, - -	Rev. H. W. Gery	Ickwell-bury, -	John Harvey, efq.
Egginton, -	Fr. Moore, efq.	Ickwell, - -	C. Fyfhe Palmer, efq.
Fenlake Barns,	A villa of Mr. Whitbread,	Kempfton, -	Robert Dennis, efq.
Flitwick, - -	Geo. Brooks, efq. in the occupation of the Rt. Hon. John Trevor	Leighton Bufard,	Hon. Mrs. Leigh, in the occupation of Mr. Dickinfon.
		Muggerhanger, -	Godfrey Thornton, efq.
		Ridgmont, - -	Dr. Macqueen
Harold, - -	Robert Garftin, efq.	Stockwood, -	John Crawley, efq.
Henlow, - -	George Edwards, efq.	Tingrith, - -	C. D. Willaume, efq.
Hinwick, -	Richard Orlebar, efq.	Turvey, - - -	John Higgins, efq.
Hockliffe, - -	Richard Gilpin, efq.	Turvey Abbey, -	John Higgins, jun. efq.

The Whitbreads are faid, by family tradition, as appears by an infcription on the monument of the prefent Mr. Whitbread's grandfather in Cardington church, to have been of great antiquity in this county; but their name does not occur in the lift of gentry of the reign of Henry VI.; nor is there any pedigree of the family in the Heralds' vifitations. It is certain, neverthelefs, that Ion houfe in Gravenhurft, which, in the infcription above alluded to, is faid to have been the ancient feat of the family, was fold by William Whitbread gent. in 1639, as appears by

the

the title-deeds of the prefent poffeffor[x]. The Crawleys were fettled in the parifh of Luton foon after the year 1600, if not before. The Brandreths were fettled at Houghton-Regis before the year 1672. The Edwards's have been fettled at Arlefey, and the Harveys, at Ickwell-bury, more than a century. The Willaumes of Tingrith fettled there in 1710.

Non-refident Families.

A FEW families, which are no longer refident, ftill retain their anceftors' eftates in this county, as the Leighs, the Franklins, and Sadleirs. The Leighs of Stoneleigh have held the manor of Leighton-Bufard, under the church of Windfor, above 200 years; and fome of the family formerly refided in the manor-houfe. The Franklins were of Maverns, in Bolnhurft, as early as the year 1600; they afterwards removed to Great Barford: it is a confiderable time fince they quitted the county. Mr. Franklin, the prefent reprefentative, poffeffes the family eftates at both places. Mr. Sadleir's collateral anceftor, from whom he inherits the manor of Afpley-Guife, was created a baronet in 1661; and appears to have had a feat in that parifh, although in his patent he was defcribed of Temple-Dinefley, in Hertfordfhire: feveral of the family are interred at Afpley.

Geographical and Geological Defcription of the County.

THE county of Bedford is bounded on the North and North-Eaft by Northamptonfhire; on the Eaft by Huntingdonfhire, Cambridgefhire, and Hertfordfhire; and on the Weft by Buckinghamfhire and part of Northamptonfhire.

The author of the General View of the Agriculture of this county, publifhed by the Board of Agriculture, calculates it to be 145 miles in circuit, inclofing an area of 307,200 acres[y]: of thefe he computes 217,200 to be in open or common fields, common meadows, commons and waftes; 68,100 in inclofed meadows, pafture, and arable; and 21,900 of woodland. A great proportion of the woodland has been planted within a few years: the chief planters have been the Duke of Bedford, the Earl of Upper-Offory, Lord Carteret, and Fr. Moore, efq. There are fome woods of confiderable extent in the neighbourhood of Southill, Warden, Chickfand, and Hawnes. Woburn park is well wooded with oak and other timber trees. In Lord Offory's park at Ampthill, fome aged oaks, of a remarkable fize, are a great embellifhment to the fcenery; and, combined with the natural inequality of the ground, render it very picturefque: few fituations in the county have a claim to that defcription. There is fome pleafing fcenery

---

[x] See the account of Gravenhurft.

[y] Dr. Beke calculates the number of acres at 293,059. See his Obfervations on the Income Tax.

about Aſpley-Guiſe, Ridgmont, and Warden. The view from Ridgmont rove Buckinghamſhire is very extenſive. The view from Milbrook church-yard over the vale of Bedford, that from Toternhoe Caſtle over a great part of Bedfordſhire and Buckinghamſhire, and the ride along the downs from Stretley to Barton, looking over Wreſt park and towards Hertfordſhire, claim particular notice.

The ſcenery of Bedfordſhire is conſiderably enlivened by the ſteeples of churches, although not ſo much as in ſome other counties. Towards the borders of Northamptonſhire are ſeveral handſome ſpires; of theſe Keyſoe and Souldrop are moſt conſpicuous in the ſcenery. In the Southern parts of the county, the churches of Toddington and Shitlington are among the moſt remarkable, as diſtant objects. In this part of the county the Buckinghamſhire churches of Bow-Brickhill, and Edleſborough are ſtriking objects. The beautiful ſpire of Hanſlape, lately deſtroyed by lightning, was ſeen to much advantage from the neighbourhood of Ridgmont.

Fuller, ſpeaking in general terms of the ſoil of this county, gives a pretty juſt deſcription of it by ſaying, that it is a deep clay, with a belt or girdle of ſand about, or rather athwart, the body of it, from Woburn to Potton. The author of the agricultural report ſays, that there is every ſoil, and every mixture of ſoil, in this county. He deſcribes the prevailing ſoil of the North and Weſt parts to be clay and ſtrong loam; that of the South and Eaſt parts, light loam, ſand, gravel, and chalk. The chalk hills extend acroſs the county from Hertfordſhire to Buckinghamſhire, including the whole range of Luton and Dunſtaple downs.

Produce.

THIS county has been long noted for its abundant produce of fine wheat and barley. The vale of Bedford is one of the moſt extenſive corn diſtricts. The cultivation of woad, mentioned by former writers as carried on to a conſiderable extent in Bedfordſhire, has long been wholly laid aſide. Three hundred acres were lately let for this purpoſe at 7l. per acre at Tyringham and Lathbury, in the neighbouring county of Buckingham; but at the expiration of two years, the term for which this land was taken, the perſons concerned in the culture took ſome land in Northamptonſhire, for the ſame purpoſe, at a lower rent. In ſome parts of Bedfordſhire, particularly in the pariſh of Sandy, garden vegetables are raiſed in conſiderable quantities for the ſupply of the neighbouring towns. In the Southern part of the county are many large dairy farms, the produce of which, being chiefly butter, is conveyed in carts to the London markets.

NATURAL

NATURAL HISTORY.

Foſſils.

THIS county does not abound in foſſils either native or extraneous. It has been ſaid indeed that gold ore was formerly diſcovered at Pollux-hill, and that an attempt was made to work a mine there : but it is probable that this idea originated in miſtake. Woodward mentions " a maſs of yellow ſhining talc, with a yellow earthy matter mixt with it," as found at this place : probably a ſimilar ſubſtance was miſtaken for gold, by perſons not ſkilled in mineralogy.

The greater part of the extraneous foſſils which occur in this county, are found in the ſtratum of lime-ſtone, which follows the courſe of the river Ouſe. This ſtratum abounds with the different kinds of ſhells, and other marine productions, which are commonly found imbedded in the yellow lime-ſtone. *Cornua Ammonis,* and other kinds of ſhells, are found in the ſtratum of ſtone in the Toternhoe quarries, which lies above that which is uſed for building ; and great abundance of petrified wood, together with *gryphites, belemnites,* &c. under the ſtratum of fuller's-earth, at Aſpley. Petrified wood has alſo been found in other parts of this county, where the ſoil is ſandy. The petrifying ſpring ſpoken of by Fuller and other writers does not exiſt.

Woodward mentions *nautili,* and other ſhells, as found in a chalk-pit at Cad-dington [z]; ſhark's teeth, *ammonites, belemnites,* &c. in a light coloured clay near Leighton [a]; and *echini* in the fields near Eaton-bray [b].

Rare Plants.

THE botanical hiſtory of this county has been induſtriouſly inveſtigated by the Rev. Dr. Abbot, of Bedford, who has publiſhed a very ample Flora of its indigenous plants. Among the moſt rare are *Lythrum hyſſopifolium,* which grows plentifully in the fields between Oakley and Clapham ; *Malaxis paludoſa,* which grows in the neighbourhood of Potton ; *Campanula latifolia* and *Eriophoron poly-ſtachion,* near Dunſtaple ; *Geranium Phæum,* near Everſholt ; *Hyoſeris minima,* near Aſpley and Ampthill ; *Centunculus minimus,* near Ampthill ; *Ornithogalum Pyrenai-cum,* near Eaton-Socon ; *Hypochæris glabra ; Salix rubra ; Melampyrum criſta-tum ; Aliſma ranunculoides ; Inula Helenium ; Trifolium ochroleucum ; Carex ſtrigoſa,* and *Phlæum paniculatum.* One ſhould be almoſt inclined to ſuppoſe that the ſeeds of the *Draba muralis* and *Erodium moſchatum,* two Northern plants

---

[z] Catalogue, vol. II. p. 93. b. 6.   [a] Ibid. b. 10, and p. 104. i. 2.   [b] Ibid. p. 67, h. 49, and p. 72. h. 162.

found

found by Dr. Abbot in Bedfordſhire ſince the publication of his Flora, had been introduced into this county by ſome botaniſt. Many rare plants have thus become
naturalized, at places very remote from that of their original growth. Dr. Abbot
found the *Euphorbia Cypariſſias*, conſidered as a doubtful native plant, growing
wild in Barton-Leet woods.

Mineral Waters.

SEVERAL ſprings in this county are known to be impregnated with various
minerals, but none of them have acquired much celebrity. The ingenious Dr.
Yeats, phyſician to the Infirmary at Bedford, who has beſtowed conſiderable attention on this ſubject, has favoured us with a liſt of the places where mineral ſprings
have been pointed out to him, and the reſult of his analyſis of a few of them. The
ſprings enumerated are at Barton; Bedford (near the Friars); Cupwell at Bletſoe
(near the Falcon); Poplar well at Blunham (near Barford bridge); Bromham (near
Webb's lane); Buſhmead; Clapham; Cranfield; Hulcot; Milton-Erneſt; two at
Odell; Chadwell at Pertenhall; a well called Ochres at Riſely; Silſoe (at a farm
called New Inn); Turvey (in Dovehouſe Cloſe); and the ſpring which ſupplies the
cold bath in Wreſt-gardens. Dr. Yeats has analyſed the water from Clapham,
Wreſt-gardens, Bromham, Oakley, and Turvey. " The two firſt evidently con-
" tain iron. In the Wreſt-garden water, iron appears to be held in ſolution by
" the carbonic acid; in the Clapham water, by the vitriolic acid forming the *fer-*
" *rum vitriolatum*. They both of them contain alſo the *ſulphat* and *muriat* of
" lime, as likewiſe the *ſulphat* of magneſia, or Epſom ſalts. The Bromham water
" contains no iron, but holds in ſolution the different ſalts juſt mentioned; the
" *muriat* of lime being in conſiderable quantity." The ſpring at Oakley contains
the ſame ſalts in ſmall quantities, except that it is not ferruginous: it is remarkably
clear and tranſparent. The ſpring at Turvey contains " a very large proportion of
" lime, held in ſolution by a ſuperabundance of carbonic acid." Of the waters
which have not been analyſed, one of the ſprings at Odell is known to be mildly
cathartic; and Chadwell at Pertenhall, ſomewhat ferruginous.

Rivers.

THE principal rivers in this county are the Ouſe and the Ivel. The circuitous
courſe of the Ouſe ſeems to have been much exaggerated. Fuller ſays that its
courſe through this county (which is only 18 miles in width) is no leſs than 80
miles; and the editors of the *Magna Britannia* ſtate it to be 90 miles: but as it is
deſcribed on Jeffries's map, which was made by a trigonometrical ſurvey, its courſe
does not appear to be more than forty-five miles.

The

The Ouſe enters this county, on its courſe from Buckinghamſhire, in the pariſh of Turvey; from whence it paſſes between Carlton and Harold; between Odell and Chillington, near Felmerſham, Sharnbrook, Bletſoe, Milton-Erneſt, and Oakley; between Bromham and Biddenham to Bedford, where it becomes navigable; thence near Goldington, Willington, Barford, Tempsford, Roxton, Little Barford, and Eaton-Socon: between the laſt mentioned place and St. Neots, it quits the county, and enters Huntingdonſhire. The principal bridges over the Ouſe are Carlton, Radwell, Stafford bridge near Oakley, Bromham, Bedford, Barford, and Tempsford. Over the laſt mentioned bridge paſſes the great road from London to Glaſgow.

The fiſh of the Ouſe are pike, perch, bream, chub, bleak, cray-fiſh, fine eels, dace, roach, and gudgeon. Bleak abound particularly about Bedford bridge. Eels are found in the greateſt abundance, and of the largeſt ſize, at Stoke mill. The Ouſe is eſteemed a good river for trolling [y]. The average depth of the Ouſe is conſidered to be about 10 feet; at Sharnbrook it is not leſs than 25 feet, in few places leſs than 4: there are, notwithſtanding, ſeveral fords; as at Odell, Pinchmill in the pariſh of Sharnbrook, Radwell, Oakley, Clapham, Kempſton, Tempsford, &c.

The river Ouſe is ſubject at all ſeaſons of the year to ſudden inundations, which are not only deſtructive to the produce of the rich meadows on its banks, but have in ſome inſtances been the cauſe of more extenſive calamities, particularly at the town of Bedford in the year 1256, as recorded by Matthew Paris; and in 1570, as related in two pamphlets bearing that date. The effects of a dreadful ſtorm, which happened Auguſt 19, 1672, are related alſo in two pamphlets. The Cambridgeſhire proverb of " the bailiff of Bedford is coming," mentioned by Fuller, alludes to the inundations of the Ouſe, a moſt rapacious diſtrainer of hay and cattle.

The Ivel riſes near Baldock in Hertfordſhire, and enters Bedfordſhire near Stotfold, not far from Arleſey; it is augmented by a ſmall ſtream called the Hiz: paſſing near Henlow to Langford, it is there joined by a rivulet, which conveys to it the waters of two ſmaller ſtreams, which unite near Shefford. One of theſe ſtreams paſſes through ſir George Oſborn's grounds at Chickſand. At Biggleſwade, the Ivel becomes navigable, and paſſes thence near Sandy and Blunham to Tempsford, where it falls into the Ouſe. The only conſiderable bridges over the Ivel are at Girtford (a hamlet of Sandy) and at Bigglefwade. The bridge at Girtford was rebuilt with ſtone from the quarry at Sandy in 1781, that at Bigglefwade in 1796, both under the inſpection of ſir Philip Monnoux. The fiſh of the Ivel are for the moſt part the ſame as thoſe of the Ouſe: it is particularly famous for gudgeon. An act of parliament paſſed in 1757, for making the Ivel and its branches

[y] Daniel's Book of Sports.

navigable,

navigable, from the Ouſe at Tempsford to Shotling *alias* Burntmill, in the pariſh of Hitchin, and Blackhorſe mill in the pariſh of Bygrave, Herts, and to the North and South bridges in Shefford. Under this act the Ivel was in 1758 made navigable to Bigglefwade, but the navigation has not as yet been extended any farther.

The river Lea, whoſe courſe is principally through Hertfordſhire, riſes near Houghton-Regis in this county, and runs through the whole extent of Luton pariſh, feeding a fine piece of water in the marquis of Bute's park.

The river Ouzel riſes not far from Whipſnade, and leaving Eaton-Bray on the right, ſeparates this county from Buckinghamſhire in its courſe to Leighton-Buſard.

No navigable canal paſſes through this county; but the Grand Junction Canal touches on its borders in the neighbourhood of Leighton-Buſard, and comes up to that town. It has been in contemplation to make a canal from Leighton to join the Ouſe at Bedford.

Roads.

THE great northern road to Glaſgow, &c. enters Bedfordſhire about the 41 mile-ſtone, and paſſes between Aſtwick and Edworth to Bigglefwade; thence through the hamlets of Lower Caldecot and Beeſton-croſs to Girtford, where it croſſes the Ivel, and leaving Blunham on the left, proceeds to Tempsford: here a turnpike road to St. Neots branches off, and goes about two miles through this county, paſſing through Little Barford. The Glaſgow road croſſes the Ouſe at Tempsford, and leaving Roxton on the left, paſſes through the hamlet of Wyboſton to Eaton Socon, about two miles beyond which it quits the county.

The great road to Cheſter and Holyhead enters this county about the thirty-three mile-ſtone, a mile before you come to Dunſtaple: from that town, leaving Houghton-Regis on the right, and Tilſworth and Stanbridge on the left, it paſſes to Hockliffe, commonly called Hockley-in-the-hole: after which leaving Battleſden and Poteſgrave on the right, it quits the county about the 42 mile-ſtone. The great road to Liverpool branches off from the laſt-mentioned road near Hockliffe, and paſſing through Woburn quits the county about two miles on the other ſide of that town, and enters Buckinghamſhire.

The road from London to Higham-Ferrars and Kettering enters this county from Hertfordſhire about the 36 mile-ſtone; leaving Holwell and Stondon on the left, it proceeds to Shefford; thence to Bedford, without paſſing through any village, leaving Southill, Warden, Cardington, and Cople on the right, and Hawnes, Wilhamſted, and Elſtow, on the left. From Bedford it paſſes through Clapham, Milton-Erneſt, and Bletſoe; and leaving Sharnbrook, Souldrop, and Wimmington on the left, quits the county about 11 miles beyond Bedford, and enters Northamptonfhire; its courfe through this county being about 26 miles.

In 1802, an act paffed for making a new turnpike-road from Browne's lane in Great Staughton to the Bedford turnpike road in the parifh of Lavendon in Buckinghamfhire. A confiderable part of this road has been completed: it croffes the laft-mentioned road at Stokemill, and is intended to pafs through Sharnbrook, Odell, and Harold.

Another road, from London to Bedford, enters the county at the 27 mile-ftone from London, and paffes through Luton, over Luton downs to Barton-in-the-clay and Silfoe; from thence through Clophill, leaving Hawnes on the right, and through Wilhamfted and Elftow to Bedford.

Befides thefe principal roads, there is a very good turnpike road from Ampthill to Bedford; a turnpike road from Ampthill to Woburn, and from Bedford to Eaton-Socon, on either fide of the Oufe; the two roads joining at Barford bridge. The road from Baldock to Shefford enters this county near Stotfold, and paffes through Arlefey, Henlow, and Clifton.

A turnpike road from Bedford to Olney, of late much out of repair, paffes over Biddenham bridge through Bromham to Turvey, where it leaves the county.

The old road, which was formerly the route of the judges on their circuit from Bedford to Buckingham, and paffed through Stagfden towards Newport-Pagnel, is become by difufe quite impaffable for carriages.

A turnpike road from Bedford to Kimbolton was began fome years ago, and nearly completed as far as Bolnhurft, but is ftill unfinifhed.

It is remarkable that there is no carriage road from Dunftaple to Luton, though both are confiderable towns, and the diftance only five miles.

The private roads in general are bad, excepting in the immediate vicinity of Bedford. In the neighbourhood of Cardington and Elftow, the public have been much indebted for the improvement of the roads to the exertions of the late Mr. Whitbread.

Manufactures.

THE principal manufacture of this county is thread-lace, formerly known by the name of bone-lace; a term now grown obfolete, but ftill retained as fynonymous in the ftatute-books. Lace is made in every part of the county, excepting in a few villages, where it has been fuperfeded by the ftraw manufacture. The texture is not fo fine as that of the lace made in fome parts of Buckinghamfhire, nor are the earnings of the perfons employed in it fo large; the average day's work of an

adult

adult producing about a shilling only; and children earning from two-pence to five-pence. The trade is neverthelefs flourishing, and the demand for the manufacture increafing. Lace-making has been generally efteemed particularly prejudicial to health, and perfons travelling through the counties where this manufacture prevails, have been ftruck with the fickly appearance of the women and children employed in it; which, exclufively of the pernicious effects attributed by fome to the pofture of the manufacturers, might be fufficiently accounted for by the fedentary nature of their employment, and their habit of working together in fmall crouded rooms.

The ftraw manufacture prevails, and has of late much increafed, in the neighbourhood of Dunftaple and Toddington, and on the borders of Hertfordfhire. The employment is not neceffarily fo fedentary as lace-making, for the ftraw may be platted by perfons ftanding or walking. The earnings, even of thofe who make the coarfe plat, are higher than thofe of the lace-makers, and the profit of making the fine plat is very confiderable.

According to the returns made to parliament, of the population of this county in 1801, the number of perfons employed in agriculture was then 18,766; of thofe employed in trade, manufactures, and handicrafts, 13,816.

ANTIQUITIES.

Roman Remains.

THE Roman antiquities, which have been difcovered in this county, are not numerous, or of much importance. They confift chiefly of earthen veffels, fragments of pottery, and coins. Several urns of various forms were dug up about twenty years ago, in the parifh of Sandy, at a place called Chefterfield, with many Roman coins, a fmall mirror of metal, a fibula, and fome fragments of the beautiful red pottery, ornamented with figures, commonly fuppofed to be the ancient Samian ware[c].

An *amphora* was found about the year 1798, in the peat on Maulden Moor, together with feveral urns of different forms and fizes, containing bones and afhes, and fragments of the red pottery enriched with figures and other ornaments; they lay about three feet below the furface of the moor, which is quite level.

Roman coins have been found alfo near Dunftaple, and at Market-ftreet.

[c] Archæolog. vol. VIII. p. 378.

Roman

Fig. 1.2.3. ROMAN URNS, *found at Sandy Bedfordshire* 4 *An Amphora found on Wavendon heath. Bucks.*

Published 1.ˢᵗ June 1805, by T. Cadell & W. Davies.

Roman Roads and Stations [d].

" THIS county is croffed by three roads of undoubted antiquity : the Ikening-ſtreet, the Watling-ſtreet, and a confiderable Roman road, which came from Hertford-ſhire to the ſtation near Sandy, and paffed from thence to the Ermin-ſtreet, at Godmancheſter. The firſt of theſe differs in ſome refpeɕs from the others : it is by no means ſo direɕ in its line as Roman roads generally are ; it ſhews no tendency (where it remains in its primitive ſtate) to paſs through Roman towns ; nor are ſuch towns found on it at diſtances ſuited to travelling ; it does not appear to have been ever raiſed or paved (the peculiar and infallible mark of the roads conſtruɕed by the Romans) ; and in many parts of its progreſs it divides itſelf into ſeveral branches, but all nearly parallel to its original courſe. Theſe reaſons, added to its name, which is Britiſh, give great countenance to the opinion that it was a track-way of the ancient inhabitants, before the conqueſt of the country by the Romans, in its courſe from the Iceni (the inhabitants of the eaſtern counties of England), from whom it took its name. After paſſing through Cambridgeſhire and a part of Hertfordſhire, it enters this county on its ſouth-weſterly borders, and croſſes the turnpike-road from Luton to Bedford, about the 16th mile ſtone ; here a branch ſeems to bear to the right, through Great Bramingham and Houghton, to the Britiſh town of Maiden Bower ; while the principal road continues on the ſide of the hills between Great Bramingham and Limberly, over Seagrave marſh, through the preſent town of Dunſtaple, where it croſſes the Watling-ſtreet, and ſoon after enters Buckinghamſhire. In the whole of its paſſage through this and the neighbouring counties, it continues on the top or ſides of the Chalk hills, and is known to every inhabitant by the name of the Ikeneld or Ikening-ſtreet.

A ſecond great military way paſſes through Bedfordſhire, under the name of the Watling-ſtreet ; this alſo I have no doubt was another Britiſh track-way, traverſing the iſland from the Kentiſh coaſt to the country of the Guetheli ; and it is a curious circumſtance, that an ancient track-way, under the very ſame name, tends from the eaſtern extremity of Scotland to the ſame country. Theſe Guetheli were the remains of the old Celtic inhabitants of England, who had been driven, by powerful and ſucceſſive invaders, to the extremity of Wales, and to the oppoſite ſhores of Ireland ; and the communication with their country muſt have been of the utmoſt

---

[d] We have been favoured with an account of the Roman roads and ſtations in Bedfordſhire, and other counties, [by the Lord Biſhop of Cloyne ; who has taken great pains in the inveſtigation of this branch of antiquarian ſcience ; and has viſited every part of the iſland for the purpoſe of local obſer-vation. He has been ſo obliging as to arrange his materials, and draw up a brief ſtatement of the reſult of his inquiries in each county for the uſe of this work.

VOL. I.   E   importance

importance in thofe early times, as providing a paffage for cattle and other articles of trade, from the extreme coafts of the weft, to the great marts for foreign merchants in the eaftern ports of Britain. Thus the Watling-ftreet, (Via Guethelinga, as Richard of Cirencefter exprefsly calls it) would be the road of the Guetheli, as the Ikening-ftreet was the road of the Iceni. Nor let fuch perfons as have not much directed their minds to thefe ftudies, be ftartled at the idea of Britifh ways. As the Britons, even in Cæfar's time, made ufe of chariots, it is not very probable they could have been without fome fort of roads, efpecially as their country abounded with moraffes and forefts. Now, as the Romans would of courfe adopt fuch parts of thefe roads as fuited their own convenience, and as they carried on a trade of the fame nature with this people, they made ufe of the whole of the road, from the coaft of Kent to Wroxeter, with little variation. It is carried through well-known Roman towns at regular diftances, bears fteadily and directly to its point, and wherever it is deferted by the modern turnpike-road, (as between Weedon, in Northamptonfhire, and Wall, in Staffordfhire,) fhews ftill a very elevated creft; the original pavement is alfo found in many places, though fometimes, where it has paffed over a moffy foil, fuch pavement is beneath the prefent furface; it enters this county at the 33d mile-ftone, in its way from St. Albans to Stony Stratford, keeping nearly in the track of the modern Irifh road, and is not to be diftinguifhed from it; with this road alfo it leaves the county a little beyond the 42d mile-ftone, having paffed through one itinerary ftation on it, which is generally agreed to have been at Dun-ftaple. Roman coins have been found near this town; its prefent ftreets are at right angles with each other, and coincide with the four points of the compafs, corroborat-ing proofs of its having been the work of that people. The name of *Forum Dianæ*, given to it by Richard, fhews it to have been a confiderable mart of trade, for which its fituation, at the interfection of the Ikening and Watling-ftreets, was par-ticularly convenient; and it is indeed not improbable, that the fcite was fixed upon by the Romans for their new town on this very account, in preference to that of the neighbouring Britifh town at Maiden Bower.

But, though all our antiquaries (except Mr. Salmon, whofe fancies are fo extra-vagant as to make him at all times an incompetent guide) agree in the exiftence of a ftation at Dunftaple, there is a difference of opinion refpecting its name. As long as the world fuffered itfelf to be mifled in thefe purfuits by a fondnefs for etymology, it left the fafe and pofitive direction of the itineraries, to attend to the ingenious dreams of Baxter, who, finding that Maes Gwyn fignified a white field, fixed here the ftation of *Magiovintum*, becaufe it in fome degree correfponded with the chalkinefs of the foil; but the numbers are all in Antoninus's 2d, 6th, and 8th iters fo exprefs, that *Magiovintum* was 24 miles from *Verulam*; and the affertion is fo ftrongly confirmed by the firft iter of Richard (in neither of which iters do the

numbers

numbers permit us to fuppofe the ftation to have been out of the road,) that I fubfcribe to the opinion of the learned and accurate Horfley, and arrange with him the Roman ftations in this part of the Watling-ftreet in the following manner :

Antonine's Names.	Richard's Names.	Modern Names.	Roman Miles.	Modern Miles.
1. Sulloniacæ.	Sulloniagis.	Brockley-hill.	12.	12.
2. Verolamium.	Verolamium Municip.	St. Albans.	9.	9.
3. Durocobrivæ.	Forum Dianæ.	Dunftaple.	12.	12.
4. Magiovintum.	Magiovinium.	Fenny Stratford.	12.	12.
5. Lactodorum.	Lactodorum.	Towcefter.	17.	17.

After obferving this coincidence of numbers in the ancient and modern miles, we muft either agree that the town called by Antonine *Durocobriva*, and by Richard *Forum Dianæ*, was at Dunftaple; or adopt the opinion of Mr. Ward, that *Magiovintum* and *Durocobrivæ* have changed places by the miftake of fome tranfcriber.

The third ancient road that traverfed any part of Bedfordfhire was the Roman military way, which enters the county near Baldock, in the line of the prefent north road, with which it continues as far as *Stretton*, between the 44th and 45th mile-ftone, where the modern turnpike-road (as is often the cafe) turns off to the left to pafs through Bigglefwade, while the Roman road preferves its old ftraight line directly forward to Chefterfield. The Roman ftation near the village of Sandy, on the hill above this village, is a large camp called Cæfar's camp (once poffibly the Britifh poft) but the coins and every fpecies of remains decidedly point out the Roman town in the valley beneath it; and, although the road is not travelled, or the name of the town mentioned in any of the iters, it is univerfally and juftly allowed to be the Σαληναι of Ptolemy, and the *Salinæ* of Ravennas. From the N. E. part of the ftation, near the banks of the Ivel, this road is continued through a fmall valley, leaving the Britifh camp before-mentioned on the left hand, and another hill which has been dug up for a ftone quarry, on the right, ftraight to a hedge-row which runs down through a piece of land to a fmall copfe in the bottom, from whence it continues equally ftraight, firft as a boundary between Mr. Pym's land and Sandy-field, and then entering fome inclofures, croffes the road from Everton to Tempsford; then paffes through a farm yard (leaving the houfe on the left) belonging to Governor Pownal; and through fome more inclofures to a farm houfe, belonging to General Parker, which ftands upon it; then through another inclofure to Tempsford marfh (or as it is called the cow-common); after paffing which, it afcends the hill clofe by a barrow or tumulus, (almoft the invariable attendant on Roman roads,) which is planted with trees, and known by the name of the Hen and Chickens; then ftraight by the fide of the hedge-row, leaving Hardwick on the right, and croffing the road from Gamlingay, and that from Cambridge to St. Neot's, proceeds not far from

E 2

Tofeland,

Tofeland, leaving the Offords on one fide, and Papworth and Yelling on the other, to the village of Godmanchefter, allowed to be a Roman town, and fuppofed by many antiquaries to be the fcite of the ancient *Durolipons*.

A very confiderable military way has been alfo obferved, coming from the Ifle of Ely to Cambridge, and vifibly tending to the borders of Bedfordfhire in a direct line for Sandy: this road, though in fome parts obfcure, is fuppofed, with great probability, to have paffed through Hatley and Potton to our poft at Chefterfield; and Dr. Mafon (our moft intelligent tracer of Roman roads) has continued it on the weftern fide of the ftation, in a line bearing towards Fenny Stratford; the country is fo deep that no perfon, except he is well acquainted with the neighbourhood, and has an eye accuftomed to thefe purfuits, would have any chance of following it with fuccefs; but I am clearly of opinion, from the general bearing of this road, where it is ftill vifible, that it formed a part of a great Roman way, leading from the eaftern coaft of England towards Wales, between the two Britifh ways, the Ikening and Rykning; but of this I mean to fpeak more at large when I come to treat of the courfe of the Akeman-ftreet, in the counties of Bucks, Oxford, and Gloucefter.

That there were connecting roads between the ftations of Chefterfield and Dun-ftaple, Chefterfield and Chefterford in Effex, and Chefterfield and Chefter near Wellingborough, in the fame manner as between Chefterfield and Godmanchefter, there is little reafon to doubt; although at prefent, from the conftant cultivation of the whole face of the country, much of which alfo is old inclofure, and very deep land, the traces of them may be entirely defaced."

Church Architecture.

The moft ancient remains of ecclefiaftical architecture in Bedfordfhire are to be feen in Elftow church; the chancel of which has plain femicircular arches fpringing from fquare maffive piers, unqueftionably part of the original church of the monaftery, which was founded in this place foon after the Norman conqueft. The north door of this church has a femicircular arch, with zig-zag mouldings.

The parifh church of Dunftaple, which was formerly that of the convent, founded by Henry the Firft in 1131, exhibits confiderable remains of the original ftructure. The columns are maffive and cluftered, with femicircular arches, and a fingle zig-zag moulding: the eaft end of the fouth aifle has the original groined roof of ftone.

There are no other remains of this early architecture in Bedfordfhire of any importance. In Puddington church the arches of the nave are circular, and have zig-zag mouldings. Door-ways with circular arches, having the zig-zag and other

mouldings

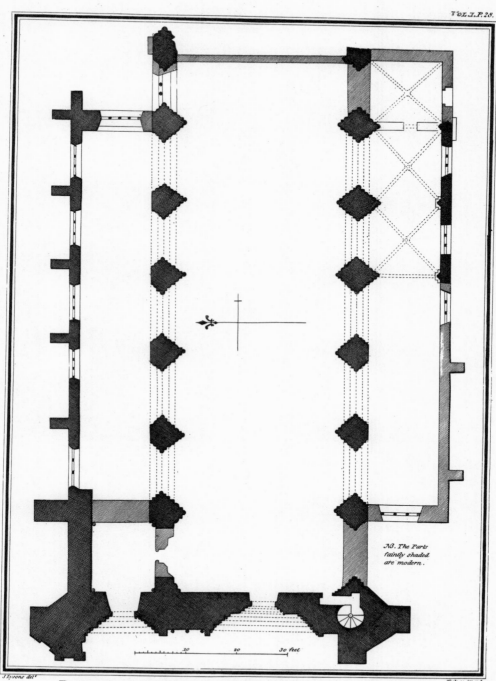

NB. The Parts
faintly shaded
are modern.

S. Lysons delt.

20   20   30 feet

Scole se. Strand.

PLAN OF THE REMAINS OF THE PRIORY CHURCH AT DUNSTAPLE.

mouldings of Saxon architecture, occur in St. Peter's church at Bedford, and in the churches of Little Barford, Caddington, and Thurleigh ; over the laſt of which are rude figures of Adam and Eve in bas relief.

Remains of the earlieſt ſtyle of Gothic architecture are to be ſeen in the nave of Elſtow church, ſome of the columns of which are large and octangular, with foliage round the capitals ; the arches are pointed, and have plain deep mouldings ; over the arches are ſmall lancet-ſhaped windows. The weſt door has been very elegant ; the pillars on each ſide are ſlender, having capitals richly ornamented with foliage, now much mutilated.

The weſt front of Felmerſham church affords another example of this ſtyle of architecture, exhibiting a variety of pointed arches, ſlender columns with plain capitals and baſes, and long lancet-ſhaped windows. The other parts of the church are very plain, and appear, by the ſhape of the windows, to be of the ſame age.

The weſt end of Dunſtaple church exhibits alſo a rich diſplay of this early Gothic architecture, engrafted upon part of the original fabric, a ſemicircular arch of which appears in the great weſtern door-way, formerly enriched with a profuſion of ornaments, conſiſting of highly-relieved foliage and figures, executed in Toternhoe ſtone, the greater part of which has been deſtroyed or mutilated. Over this door are three tiers of pointed arches ; the central one forms a gallery, leading to the tower. On the inſide of the church this ſtyle of architecture is ſeen only in a ſtone gallery leading to the tower, formerly open, but now hid by the organ-loft ; it has lofty pointed arches, ſeparated by cluſtered pillars with capitals of foliage. The windows of this church are of a much later date.

Studham church, which was dedicated in 1220 (5th of Hen. 3.) retains its original architecture in the pillars of the nave, which are octagonal, with capitals variouſly ornamented.

The church of Eaton-Bray is nearly of the ſame age, and has both cluſtered and octagonal columns, the capitals of which are richly adorned with foliage.

Of the ſucceeding ſtyle of Gothic architecture, which prevailed during the fourteenth century, few examples exiſt in this county : Wimmington church, however, though ſmall, is an elegant ſpecimen of it, and appears never to have been altered. This edifice was rebuilt by John Curteys, mayor of the ſtaple at Calais, who died in 1391, and Albrena his wife. It has two octangular turrets at the eaſt, and a very elegant ſpire at the weſt end, ornamented with crockets, riſing from an embattled tower, which has tracery of quatrefoils, and other ornaments. The upper parts of the windows of this church are ramified in various forms ; a ſtriking characteriſtic of the ſtyle of architecture which prevailed during the period above mentioned.

Several

Several of the Bedfordſhire churches are in the latter ſtyle of Gothic architecture, which prevailed during the fifteenth and the beginning of the ſixteenth century. Northill is large and handſome, having cluſtered columns and pointed
arches : it was made collegiate in 1405, and probably erected at that time.
Willington church is a handſome building in the ſame ſtyle. Marſton church is a
light uniform ſtructure, with ſide-aiſles ſeparated from the nave by cluſtered
columns. Eaton-Socon church is in the ſame ſtyle ; the nave is eighty feet long
and fifty-ſix wide. The windows of the nave were formerly richly ornamented
with ſtained glaſs. The greater part of the church of Leighton-Buſard, which is a
large handſome building, with ſide-aiſles and tranſepts, having a lofty plain ſpire in
the centre, is in this latter ſtyle of Gothic architecture ; as are alſo the churches of
Odell, Biggleſwade, and St. Paul's at Bedford.

The ſouth end of the Wenlock chapel in Luton church, erected in the reign of
Edward the IVth, has a lofty double arch opening to the chancel, reſting on cluſtered pillars, and enriched with Gothic tracery ; as is alſo the whole of that end
of the chapel.

Stained Glaſs.

THE remains of ancient ſtained glaſs in the windows of Bedfordſhire churches
are very few, and, for the moſt part, in a mutilated ſtate. The moſt perfect are to
be ſeen in Eaton-Socon church, all the windows of which appear to have been
originally filled with theſe ſplendid ornaments : only a few fragments remain in
the windows on the ſouth ſide of the church, which appear to have been decorated
with deſigns taken from the New Teſtament ; but in the range of windows along
the north aiſle, a conſiderable number are preſerved, the moſt entire of which
repreſent deſigns taken from the legends of St. Nicholas and St. Etheldreda. Theſe
remains have little to recommend them, except the brilliancy of their colours : by
the form of ſome of the dreſſes, they ſeem to have been executed during the reign of
Edward the IVth.

From ſome fragments in the ſouth tranſept of Luton church, that building alſo appears to have been richly ornamented with ſtained glaſs. In the windows of the Wenlock chapel in the ſame church, erected in the reign of Edward the IVth, there are
ſufficient remains to ſhew the ſtyle of the original decorations, which were not of
the richeſt kind, but conſiſted of ſingle figures and coats of arms on a ground of
plain glaſs, charged with various ſmall devices, among which the broom-pod and a
rudder, accompanied with the word *Hola*, are the moſt conſpicuous. The figure
of St. George on foot, and the arms of John Lord Wenlock the founder, within
the garter, are ſtill to be ſeen ; but the portrait of this Lord, with a rhyming
inſcription under it, formerly in the eaſt window, has been long ſince deſtroyed or
removed.

Leighton-Busard.

Studham.

Puddington.

Elstow.

ANTIENT FONTS IN BEDFORDSHIRE.

Published by T. Cadell & W. Davies, 1st May, 1803.

BAPTISTERY AT LUTON.

J. Lysons delin et fecit.

Published 1 March, 1805, by T.Cadell & W.Davies.

removed. The upper compartments of the windows of this chapel are filled with small figures of faints and angels.

In a north window of the nave of Warden church, among other remains, is the figure of an abbot praying under a turretted and embattled canopy. Single figures of faints, &c. occur in feveral other churches, but none of them fufficiently remarkable to entitle them to particular notice.

Rood-Lofts, Screens, &c.

In Tilbrook church is a rich Gothic fcreen of wood, between the nave and chancel. At Marfton is a fimilar fcreen, richly ornamented with gilding and tracery; on the lower part are figures of faints and prophets under Gothic canopies, with infcriptions on fcrolls. In Felmerfham church is a light Gothic fcreen, the central arch of which is ornamented with figures of angels, inftead of crockets: over it is a rood-loft remaining entire.

Gothic niches, fome of them richly ornamented with fculpture and tracery, occur in feveral of the Bedfordfhire churches; the moft remarkable are at Arlefey, Tingrith, Sundon, Pavingham, Flitwick, and Harlington.

Fonts.

The greater part of the fonts in this county are either circular or octagonal, and without any ornament; the following, which are octagonal, and for the moft part of Toternhoe ftone, are varioufly decorated. Edworth font is enriched with quatrefoils, rofes, and fhields; Barton with quatrefoils and rofes; Clifton has on each fide two plain arches; Caddington has rofes, leopards' heads, &c.; Houghton-Conqueft rich Gothic tabernacle work; Pertenhall, Kempfton, and Stagfden, ftand on clufters of pillars, on the fides of the two laft are figures under Gothic canopies; Oakley has Gothic tracery; Sundon ftands on a circular fhaft, and has two pointed arches on each fide; Stretley has ornaments of foliage, and zig-zag mouldings on the pedeftal; Stepingly has fhields of arms; Shitlington has quatrefoils on the fides; Sharnbrook and Wimmington have Gothic tracery; Arlefey has figures of Adam and Eve, the crucifixion, &c. in compartments, fome of which appear never to have been finifhed, and others have been much mutilated; Wilden has fhields and quatrefoils; Luton ftands on five pillars, and is ornamented with Gothic arches; this font is inclofed within a baptiftry of ftone at the weft end of the nave, enriched with pinnacles, quatrefoils, and foliage, in the ftyle of the fourteenth century.

Some of the circular fonts alfo are varioufly ornamented; Flitwick has the upper part fcallopped; Houghton-Regis has various mouldings and foliage; Eaton Bray, Leighton-Bufard, and Holwell, are in the fhape of a bafon ftanding on five pillars,

some

some of which have capitals of foliage; Puddington has zig-zag mouldings; Studham is ornamented with dragons and foliage; Battlesden has crosses patées, and fleurs de lys.

Mepershall and Warden fonts are dodecagon; Gravenhurst and Tingrith decagon, the latter on a cluster of columns; Eaton-Socon is square, standing on four short pillars, with tracery of intersecting arches on the side; Southill is square, and has its sides ornamented with pointed arches.

Stone Stalls and Piscinæ.

MANY of the Bedfordshire churches have stone stalls in the south wall of the chancel, but few of them are remarkable for their ornaments. In Turvey and Luton churches, they are four in number; those at Luton, which were erected by Abbot Wheatenhurst, are ornamented with several coats of arms, and the Abbot's motto as on his tomb at St. Albans. Blunham and Caddington churches have three in each. Dunton, Higham-Gobion, Cranfield, Barton, Bigglefwade, Sandy, and Sutton churches, have also three stone stalls with a *piscina* to each, and in some of them a double one; those of Sutton are richly ornamented with trefoils, crockets, pinnacles, &c. Tempsford and Sharnbrook churches have two; Hockliffe and St. Mary's church in Bedford two of unequal height without canopies, the former has a *piscina*; in Lower-Gravenhurst and Wimmington churches are two with *piscinæ*, those of Wimmington are richly ornamented with crockets, &c. In Clifton church are two stone stalls with pointed arches, and a double *piscina*, all richly ornamented with crockets and pinnacles; at Chalgrave is a *piscina* with rich Gothic niches in the chancel, and another in the south aisle; a single *piscina* occurs in several other churches.

Ancient Tombs.

IN Salford church are two antient stone coffins, with crosses and shields of arms on the lid. At Tilsworth is one for Adam de Tullesworth, with a French inscription in Gothic capitals. In Sutton church is a slab with a cross florée; and another in Oakley church-yard. In St. Paul's church at Bedford is a slab, with a French inscription in Gothic capitals, for Muriel Calt. At Lower Gravenhurst is the tomb of Sir Robert de Bilhemore, founder of the church, with a similar French inscription.

In Salford church is the tomb of a crusader, under a low arch richly ornamented; at the feet of the figure are two lions, and an angel at the head; on his shield is a plain chevron. In the south chancel of Pertenhall church is the figure of a crusader under a pointed arch ornamented with foliage. In the south aisle of Toddington

church,

STONE STALLS IN LUTON CHURCH.

Published 1 March 1819, by Kendall & W. Davies.

church, among the tombs of the Cheneys, is one of the Peyvre family as a crufader. At Chalgrave are two altar tombs, with the effigies of knights in armour,
with mail gorgets, faid to be fome of the Loring family; but the arms do not
correfpond.

In the north wall of the chancel in Blunham and Little Staughton churches are
altar tombs, under Gothic arches ornamented with quatrefoils. In Oakley church
is an ancient tomb on the fouth fide of the nave, under a large trefoil arch, for one
of the family of Reynes, fuppofed to have been the founder of that church. In
the nave of Tilfworth church, under a Gothic arch with pinnacles, is a recumbent
figure of an ecclefiaftic on an altar tomb. At Luton, under the arch which
divides the Wenlock chapel from the chancel, is an altar tomb, with the effigies of
an ecclefiaftic, fuppofed to be that of William de Wenlock, great uncle of Lord
Wenlock.

At Yielden, againft the fouth wall of the nave, is a richly-ornamented tomb,
without any figure.

In Wimmington church, under an arch on the fouth fide of the chancel, is an
altar tomb, ornamented with Gothic tracery, on which is a black marble flab, with
the figures on brafs of John Curteys, mayor of the ftaple at Calais, who died in
1391, and his Lady, under Gothic canopies. In the fame church are braffes,
with the figures of Sir Thomas Bromflet, cup-bearer to Henry the Vth, in armour,
with a lion at his feet, and Margaret his wife.

In Elftow church is a brafs plate, with the effigies of Elizabeth Harvey, the laft
abbefs of Elftow.

The moft remarkable monuments of the fixteenth century are thofe of the Mordaunt family, at Turvey; Sir John Goftwick, at Willington; Sir Michael Fifher, at
Clifton; Sir Edmund Anderfon, at Eyworth; and the mutilated remains of thofe of
the Cheneys, at Toddington. Thofe of the Kent family at Flitton are, for the moft
part, of the following century; as is the Countefs of Elgin's maufoleum at
Maulden.

Monaftic Remains.

THERE are very few monaftic remains of any confequence in Bedfordfhire,
except thofe of Dunftaple Priory and Elftow Abbey. Befides the church at Dunftaple, which has been already fpoken of, part of the buildings of the monaftery
are to be feen in the houfe of Colonel Maddifon, confifting of fome rooms with
groined roofs of ftone.

At Elftow, the conventual church remains as already defcribed: and adjoining
to it, at the fouth-weft corner, is a fmall building, having a low groined roof refting

on

on a fingle pillar, with a plain capital and bafe, in the ftyle of the earlieft Gothic architecture.

There are fome flight remains of the Grey-Friars at Bedford, confifting of a part of the cloifters, and what is fuppofed to have been the refectory, now a barn.

Chickfand Priory, it is probable, was converted into a manfion-houfe foon after the diffolution. It is now the feat of Sir George Ofborn. The eaft, and part of the fouth fide of the cloifters, remain entire, with rich Gothic windows. On the weft fide, even with the ground, is a range of rooms with ftone roofs, vaulted and groined.

No part of the buildings of Woburn Abbey, or of the Priories of Newenham and Caldwell, now exift. The fite of the two laft may be traced. The refectory of Bufhmead Priory is converted into a ftable and offices ; that of Harold Priory, now a barn, has the original wooden roof. The fmall remains of Warden Abbey confift of a brick building, being only a part of what is reprefented in Buck's View.

Sites of Caftles and Caftellated Manfions.

ALL the caftles in this county have been demolifhed ; but confiderable earthworks remain on their fites. The only traces now exifting of Bedford Caftle, formerly the chief feat of the Beauchamps, barons of Bedford, confift of a large circular mount, with a flat fpace on the top, now ufed as a bowling-green, and fome earth-works adjoining.

Extenfive veftiges of Eaton-Socon Caftle, which belonged to a younger branch of the Beauchamps of Bedford, are to be feen in a field near the church. In the centre is a high mount, furrounded by a moat, communicating with the river : about twenty-four yards beyond the moat is a vallum furrounding the whole, except on the river fide.

The traces of Yielden Caftle, the feat of the ancient barons of Trally, are extenfive. The principal works form a fquare of about eighty paces ; in the centre is a large mount called the Caftle-hill, with a vallum on the weft fide of it, including a fpace 90 paces long and 45 wide ; round thefe works is a moat, in fome parts of which the water ftill remains ; and beyond the moat appear traces of walls for a confiderable fpace.

The elevated keeps of Rifinghoe and Cainhoe Caftles remain, with extenfive earth-works. At Bletfoe and Ridgmont are alfo traces of caftles. In a field near Toddington church is the keep of a caftle, and fome flight earth-works, called Conger-hill. At Mepperfhall, Puddington, and Thurleigh, are veftiges of caftles, or at leaft caftellated manfions. At Sutton is a moated fite, in the park, commonly called

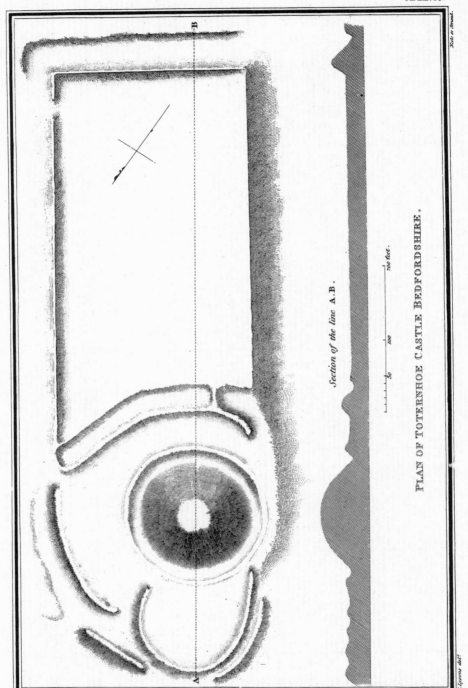

Section of the line A.B.

50 100 200 Feet.

PLAN OF TOTERNHOE CASTLE BEDFORDSHIRE.

S. Lyons del.

Neele et Strand.

called John of Gaunt's Castle. At Odell, a mansion-house, now the seat of Thomas Alston Esq. has been erected on the site of the Castle, the ancient seat of the Barons Wahull, which was a ruin in Leland's time. At Arlesey are considerable earth-works, called Etonbury.

Camps and Earth-works.

THE most remarkable object of this kind in Bedfordshire is called Toternhoe Castle; a work of great strength, situated on the brow of a hill about two miles north-west of Dunstaple. It consists of a lofty circular mount, with a slight vallum round its base, and a larger one of an irregular form at some distance from it. On the south-east side is a camp in the form of a parallelogram, about 500 feet long and 250 in width, three sides of which are secured by a vallum and ditch, very entire on the south-east side; the south-west side, being on the edge of a precipice, has no vallum. It is probable that the irregular fortress first mentioned was British, and that the adjoining works were added by the Romans, whose station of Durocobrivæ is supposed to have been at Dunstaple. The view from the mount is very extensive, commanding a long range of the Chiltern Hills, the vale of Aylesbury, and the central part of Bedfordshire.

A little more than a mile from Dunstaple is a circular earth-work, about 2500 feet in circumference, commonly called Maiden-Bower, consisting of a single vallum and ditch.

On a hill near Sandy is a camp of large dimensions, and of an irregular oblong form, overlooking the site of a Roman station, now called Chesterfield. This camp was unquestionably occupied by the Romans, if not originally made by them.

Near Leighton-Busard on the heath is an inclosure nearly circular, containing several fields surrounded by a ditch, which in many parts is deep, and has a good deal the appearance of having been a camp.

About four miles from Bedford, adjoining the road which leads to Eaton-Socon, on the north side of the river, is a circular vallum of considerable height, with openings on the north and south sides. The area is 112 feet in diameter.

The spot near Bushmead, which is called a camp in the late maps of the county, is merely the site of a moated mansion.

PAROCHIAL TOPOGRAPHY,

(ALPHABETICALLY ARRANGED.)

VERY little has been done towards elucidating the topography of this county. In the Bibliotheca Topographica Britannica are hiſtorical accounts of the pariſhes of Luton, Dunſtaple, Wimmington, and Odell, and ſome anſwers to queries reſpecting Puddington. The late Rev. Mr. Cooper, who wrote the accounts of Wimmington and Odell, had made collections for ſeveral other pariſhes in the county; but they conſiſt chiefly of church notes and compilations from Dugdale's Monaſticon, and other printed works. They are now the property of the Rev. Mr. Marſh, Vicar of Steventon, who has been many years collecting materials for a natural hiſtory of the county. The following brief account of the ſeveral pariſhes is collected from records in the public offices, aided by a variety of information obligingly communicated by the owners of landed property or their agents, and by the clergy. Every pariſh has been perſonally viſited by the Editors, who deſire to return their acknowledgments to all who have favoured them with their aſſiſtance, particularly to the Earl of Upper-Oſſory, Dr. Yeats, and Mr. Theed Pearſe of Bedford, the Rev. Hugh Wade Gery of Buſhmead, Dr. Abbot, and Mr. Marſh. The diſtances of each village from the neighbouring towns are taken from Jeffries's map, made by actual ſurvey.

———————

AMPTHILL, anciently *Ametulle*, in the hundred of Redbornſtoke, and deanery of Flitt, is a ſmall neat town, pleaſantly ſituated, but in a ſandy ſoil. Its earlieſt charter for a market bears date 1219[f]; it was then held, as it ſtill is, on Thurſdays. It was confirmed by a ſubſequent charter in 1242[g], with the grant of a fair on the feſtival of St. Mary Magdalen. The only fair now held is on the 4th of May. The market is not conſiderable. The town has been much improved by the removal of ſome old houſes which ſtood very incommodiouſly in the market-place, where there is now a pump with an obeliſk, erected by the Earl of Oſſory in 1785. There is no town-hall or other public building; the court of the honour is held in a mean old room called the Moot-houſe, which, although ſmall, may have been uſed occaſionally as a court of

[f] Fin. Rot. 3 Hen. III.   [g] C. 26 Hen. III.

juſtice.

juftice. The affizes are faid to have been held there in 1684, having been removed thither, as it is faid, through the intereft of the Earl of Aylefbury : the Epiphany feffions were certainly held there that year [h]. The number of inhabited houfes within the parifh of Ampthill in 1801, according to the returns made under the Population Act, was 237; of inhabitants 1234. The manor of Ampthill, at the time of the Norman furvey, belonged to the baronial family of Albini, from whom it paffed by female heirs to the St. Amands, and Beauchamps [i]. William Beauchamp, who in right of his wife enjoyed the barony of St. Amand, conveyed Ampthill, in 1441, to Sir John Cornwall [k], a diftinguifhed military character in the reigns of Henry IV. and Henry V. By his gallant behaviour in a tournament at York, in 1401, he won the heart of Elizabeth, the King's fifter, then the widow of John Holland, Earl of Huntingdon and Duke of Exeter. In the glorious battle of Agincourt he was one of the chofen officers who had the poft of honour with the Duke of York in the van [l]. Leland fays, that he " builded the " caftelle of Antehill of fuch fpoils as it is faid he won in France." It was not till 1432 that he was created Lord Fanhope, and in 1433 Baron of Milbrook. The account which the learned antiquary above mentioned gives from hearfay, of the manner in which Lord Fanhope's lands came to the crown, and of their being granted by Edward IV. to Lord Grey of Ruthin, as a reward for the part which he took in the battle of Northampton, appears to be wholly erroneous, as Lord Fanhope died in peace feventeen years before that battle, at Ampthill caftle [m], whither he had retired after the death of his only legitimate fon, who was flain in France. In 1453, ten years after the death of Lord Fanhope, Henry Duke of Exeter, his wife's fon, entered into a bond of 6000 marks to abide by the arbitration of Sir Thomas Bourchier refpecting the manor of Ampthill and other eftates [n]. What became of it immediately after, is uncertain. The Duke of Exeter died in extreme poverty. The manor is next to be traced to the noble family of Grey, but whether they became poffeffed of it by grant or purchafe does not appear. Reginald Grey, Earl of Kent, was poffeffed of it in 1524. Not long after this it came into the King's hands, probably by an exchange, and was made an honour by act of Parliament. Queen Catherine of Arragon refided at Ampthill whilft the bufinefs of the divorce was pending, and was cited thence to attend the commiffioners at Dunftaple, but refufed to obey their fummons [o]. No accounts of Ampthill Caftle, or its inhabitants, are to be difcovered during the fubfequent reigns; and it is moft probable that it

[h] Biograph. Brit. laft Edition, vol. i. p. 607, *notes.* [i] Bedfordfhire Efcheats, and Dugdale's Baronage.
[k] Clauf. Rot. 19 Hen. VI.   [l] Dugdale.   [m] Efcheat, 22 Hen. VI.   [n] Cl. 31 Hen. IV.
[o] Holinfhed.

was fuffered to go to decay. The furvey made by order of Parliament in
1649, fpeaks of it as having been long ago totally demolifhed. When Fuller,
in his "Worthies," mentions Ampthill as one of thofe three which carried
away the credit among the houfes of the nobility in Bedfordfhire, he meant
Houghton Park, then (1662) the feat of the Earl of Aylefbury, and fituated partly
in Ampthill parifh. We are told by Ofborn, in his Memoirs of King James's
reign, that the honour of Ampthill, no fmall prefent to be made at one time, as the
writer obferves, was given by that monarch to the Earl of Kelly. It foon reverted
to the crown. In 1612, Thomas Lord Fenton, and Elizabeth his wife, refigned the
office of high fteward of the honour of Ampthill to the king. The following year the
cuftody of the great park was granted to Lord Bruce, whofe family became leffees
of the honour [p]. The leafe continued in that noble family till 1738, when it was
purchafed by the Duke of Bedford. In the 17th century the Nicolls's were for
many years leffees of Ampthill Great Park, under the Bruce's, who referved to
themfelves the office of mafter of the game. The Nicolls's refided at the Great
Lodge, or capital Manfion, as it is called in the furvey of 1649. After the
reftoration, Ampthill Great Park was granted by Charles II. to Mr. John Afhburnham, as a reward for the faithful fervices which he had rendered to that monarch
and his father [q]. In 1720 it was purchafed of the Afhburnham family by Lord Vifcount Fitzwilliam, who fold it in 1736 to Lady Gowran, grandmother of the prefent
noble owner, John, Earl of Upper Offory, who, in 1800, became poffeffed of the
leafe of the honour of Ampthill, by exchange with the late Duke of Bedford. The
fite of Ampthill caftle, which Leland defcribes as " ftanding ftately on a hill, with
" a four or five faire towers of ftone in the inner warde, befides the baffe courte,"
has been denoted by a Gothic column, erected in 1770, by the Earl of Offory. It is
infcribed with the following lines, from the pen of the late Earl of Orford :

> " In days of yore here Ampthill's towers were feen,
> The mournful refuge of an injur'd queen ;
> Here flow'd her pure but unavailing tears,
> Here blinded zeal fuftain'd her finking years :
> Yet Freedom hence her radiant banner wav'd,
> And love aveng'd a realm by priefts enflav'd.
> From Catherine's wrongs a nation's blifs was fpread,
> And Luther's light from Henry's lawlefs bed."

The prefent manfion at Ampthill is fituated near the foot of the hill, yet fufficiently
elevated to command a profpect over the vale of Bedford, broken by the fine trees
in the park. It was built about the year 1694, by the firft Lord Afhburnham. The

[p] Duke of Bedford's Records.　　　[q] Lord Offory's Papers.

Earl

Earl of Ossory has a small collection of pictures at Ampthill; amongst which may be noticed an original portrait of Sterne, by Sir Joshua Reynolds. This mansion felt very severely the effects of the dreadful storm on the 19th of August 1800: not less than 700 panes of glass were broken in the west front by the hail-stones; which, by persons of the strictest veracity, were affirmed to have been seven inches in circumference, and of a flat form. The town of Ampthill, and many of the neighbouring villages, were in an equal degree sufferers; scarcely a window, which was exposed to the storm, escaped being broken.

The grounds of Ampthill, which are disposed on a steep natural bank behind the house, afford some very beautiful scenery. A survey of Ampthill Park, taken by order of Parliament in 1653, describes 287 trees as being hollow, and too much decayed for the use of the navy. These oaks, thus saved from the axe by the Commissioners' report, remain to the present day; and, by their picturesque appearance, contribute much to the ornament of the place.

The church of Ampthill contains little that is remarkable. The figures of Lord Fanhope and the Dutchess of Exeter, mentioned by Sandford, have been removed from the east window of the aisle. The only monument of note is that of Robert Nicolls, of Ampthill Park, Governor of Long Island, who, being in attendance on the Duke of York, was slain on board his ship in 1672. A cannon-ball, said to have been that which occasioned his death, is inlaid in the marble within the pediment; and on the moulding is this inscription:

" Instrumentum mortis et immortalitatis."

The benefice is a rectory in the patronage of Lord Ossory.

In the year 1654, the name of Colonel Okey, the regicide, occurs in the parish register, attesting the celebration of marriages as a justice of peace. About that time he purchased the honour of Ampthill, as part of the confiscated property of the crown[r], and resided, it is probable, at the Park. The signature of Edmund Wingate the arithmetician, occurs also as a justice the same year. He resided at Woodend, in Harlington.

About a mile from the town of Ampthill is a hospital, founded in 1690, by Mr. John Cross, for twelve poor men and a reader, and for four poor women. The reader has fifteen pounds per annum, the others ten pounds. They must be unmarried. The Vice Chancellor of the University of Oxford, and the Bishop of that Diocese, are visitors.

ARLESEY, anciently Alricheseye or Alnericheseye, about three miles south east of Shefford, in the hundred of Clifton, was formerly a market town. Its market, which was on Wednesday, is mentioned in the record of Doomsday. The tolls were

[r] Browne Willis's Papers in the Bodleian Library.

then valued at 10s. per annum. It was confirmed in 1270 to Stephen Edworth, then lord of the manor, with a fair to be held at the festival of St. Peter and St. Paul. Both the market and fair have been long disused.

In the reign of Edward III. the De la Poles had the manor[s]. In the reign of Henry VIII. the manor of Arlesey, alias Etonbury, was held by the Tanfields under the Earl of Shrewsbury[t]. It is now the property of Richard Edwards, a minor, in whose family it has been for many years. It is probable that the ancient entrenchment near the road to Baldock, called Etonbury, was the original site of this manor. It appears to have been a place of considerable strength.

In the church are monuments of Sir Samuel Browne, a barrister, who died in 1665, and several of the families of Vigerous and Edwards. Richard Edwards, who died in 1691, is called in his epitaph the last grand reader of the temple. The great tithes of this parish, which were appropriated to the Abbey of Waltham, were the property of the late Mrs. Schutz, daughter and heir of Dr. Browne, in whose family they have been vested for many years. Michael Angelo Taylor esq. is patron of the vicarage, which is united to Astwick, and lies in the deanery of Shefford.

ASPLEY GUISE, in the hundred of Manshead and deanery of Flitt, about two miles north of Woburn, received its additional name from the ancient family of Gyse, or Guise. It had formerly a market; a charter for which was granted to Anselm de Gyse in 1267[u], with a fair at St. Botolph's tide. The market, which was on Fridays, has been long disused, but it continues to be a populous village, and is very pleasantly situated.

The manor was anciently vested in the Beauchamps, as parcel of the Barony of Bedford. Simon de Beauchamp surrendered it by way of a composition to Guy de St. Walery, who had laid claim to his whole barony[w]. Reginald de St. Walery gave it to Hubert de Burgh, Earl of Kent, and Grand Justiciar of England, whose widow Margaret, daughter of the King of Scots, died seised of it, as her dower, in 1259[x]. After this, Aspley became the property and chief seat of the Gyses or Guises, ancestors of the Gloucestershire family of that name. Anselm de Gyse had this manor in marriage with a daughter of Hubert de Burgh above-mentioned. John de Gyse was one of the knights of this shire in 1328. In 1540 John Guise esq. gave the manor of Aspley to king Henry VIII. in exchange for lands in Gloucestershire[y]. It is probable that the king granted it to Sir Ralph Sadler[z], one of his chief favourites, whose descendants are still possessed of it. Edwin Sadleir, of Aspley, was created a baronet in 1661. Sir Edwin Sadleir, his son, the last baronet, died in 1719, bequeathing

---

[s] Cl. Rot.   [t] Escheats.   [u] Cart. 51 Hen. III.   [w] Dugdale's Baronage.   [x] Escheats.
[y] Records in the Augmentation Office.   [z] So the name has of late been spelt.

the

the manor of Afpley to his kinfman George Sadleir efq. from whom it has defcended to the prefent proprietor Richard Vernon Sadleir efq.

In the church is the effigies in brafs of one of the Guife family in armour, a tomb of Sir Edwin Sadleir, the laft baronet of that name, and an ancient altar tomb, with the effigies of a man in chain armour. The advowfon of the rectory was given to the priory of Newenham by Simon de Beauchamp the founder. It has been in the Duke of Bedford's family fince the year 1752. An Act of Parliament for inclofing this parifh was paffed in 1759, and a fecond Act in 1793. The rectory was confolidated with that of Hufborn Crawley in 1796.

ASTWICK, in the hundred of Bigglefwade, and the deanery of Shefford, is a fmall village on the borders of Hertfordfhire, about five miles from Shefford, a little north of the road to Baldock. The manor was formerly in the Beauchamps and Nevills [z], of late years in the family of Browne, and now the property of Michael Angelo Taylor efq. In the church are memorials of the family of Cockayne. The benefice is a rectory united to Arlefey, and is in the patronage of Mr. Taylor. The advowfon was formerly in the priory of Chickfand. In the founder's charter it is called the *Chapel* of Eftwick.

GREAT BARFORD gives name to a hundred, and is in the deanery of Eaton. It is a village about fix miles N. E. of Bedford, on the road to St. Neots. The principal manor was formerly in the St. Johns [a]. It is now the property of John Franklyn efq. in whofe family it has been for feveral generations. Creakers, in this parifh, was in the 15th, 16th, and 17th centuries a feat and manor of the Fitzjeffreys, one of whom has a memorial in the church. It is now the property of Mr. Pedley, whofe father purchafed it of the Halfeys. The old manfion, of which a fmall part only remains, ftood within a moated fite. The manor of Netherbury, which belonged to the Mordaunts, is now the property of Charles James Metcalf, a minor, in whofe family it has been for a confiderable time. The manor of Birchfield, called anciently Brytvills, Burtfield, or Burdefleys, was formerly in the Spencer family [b], and is now the property of J. Polhill efq. In 1481 the Fitzjeffreys had a moiety of this manor [c]. The benefice is a vicarage in the patronage of the Mafter and Fellows of Trinity College, Cambridge, to whom the great tithes are appropriated. Mr. Franklyn is leffee under the college. At this place is a bridge over the Oufe, built in the early part of the 15th century [d].

---

[z] Efcheats, Ric. II.   [a] Collins's Peerage.   [b] Cole's Efcheats.   [c] Efcheats in the Tower.
[d] See the Charter of 25 Hen. VI. to the Town of Bedford.

LITTLE BARFORD, or BERKFORD, in the hundred of Bigglefwade and deanery of Shefford, is a fmall village on the borders of Huntingdonfhire, about two miles and a half from St. Neots. The manor has of late years been in the families of Lee and Browne, and is now the property of Mr. Williamfon of Baldock, who has alfo the advowfon of the rectory. The parifh was inclofed by agreement previoufly to 1778, when an Act of Parliament was obtained to confirm it. An allotment of land was affigned in lieu of tithes to the rector. Nicholas Rowe, the dramatic poet, was born at this place in 1661.

BARTON, fometimes called *Barton in the Clay*, from its fituation at the commencement of the clayey foil under Barton hill, is in the hundred of Flitt and deanery of Dunftaple, about feven miles from Luton, on the road to Bedford. The manor of Barton was given to the Monks of Ramfey by their firft Abbot Eadnothus, afterwards Bifhop of Dorchefter[e]. After the reformation it paffed through various hands, having never continued long in the fame family. It is now the property of Edward Willes efq. whofe father, the Bifhop of Bath and Wells, purchafed it of Mr. Jenkins of Harpenden. The rectory is in the gift of the crown.

BATTLESDEN, in the hundred of Manfhead and deanery of Dunftaple, is a fmall village about three miles from Woburn, between the two great roads. In the 13th and 14th centuries the manor was in the family of Firmband or Fremband[f], who twice reprefented the county in parliament in the reign of Edward III. It was afterwards in the Chetwodes. About the reign of Queen Elizabeth it became the property of the Duncombes, by the marriage of William Duncombe efq. with Ellen, daughter and heir of William Saunders efq. of Potfgrave.

It was to one of this family, Sir Saunders Duncombe, a gentleman penfioner to King James and Charles I. that we are indebted for the accommodation of fedans or clofe chairs; the ufe of which was firft introduced by him in this country in the year 1634, when he procured a patent, which vefted in him and his heirs the fole right of carrying perfons " up and down in them" for a certain term. It is probable that Sir Saunders, who was a great traveller, had feen them at Sedan, where Dr. Johnfon fuppofes that they were firft made. It is remarkable, that Capt. Bayley firft introduced the ufe of hackney coaches in London the fame year[g].

In 1706[h] the manor of Battlefden was purchafed by Allen Bathurft efq. a diftinguifhed political character during the reigns of queen Anne and George I.; by

[e] Dugdale's Monafticon.   [f] Efcheats in the Tower.   [g] See the Strafford Papers, vol. i. p. 336.
[h] Sir G. P. Turner's Papers.

the

the former of whom he was in 1711 created Baron Bathurſt of Battleſden, which continued for ſome years to be the country-ſeat of that nobleman, and the occaſional reſort of the celebrated conſtellation of wits, of whom he was the patron and the friend. In 1724 Lord Bathurſt ſold Battleſden to Sir Gregory Page, great uncle of the preſent proprietor, Sir Gregory Page Turner bart. In the church are monuments of the Duncombe family from 1603 to 1688. Sir Gregory Page Turner is patron of the rectory.

BEDFORD, the county town, is ſituated on the river Ouſe, which divides it into two parts, and is fifty miles from London.

It is generally ſuppoſed that Bedford was the *Bedicanford* of the Saxon Chronicle, where the battle was fought between Cuthwulf and the Britons in 572; and it is ſaid to have been the burial-place of Offa king of the Mercians. Matthew Paris ſpeaks of the chapel in which he was interred, as having been dilapidated and carried away by the floods. Edward the Elder, as Camden informs us on the authority of Hoveden, repaired Bedford, which had been ruined in the Daniſh wars, and built a new town on the ſouth ſide of the river, called Mikeſgate; but the author of the Saxon Chronicle, and other writers, ſpeak of the building on the other ſide of the river as a fortreſs only, or citadel. Authors vary conſiderably alſo as to the date of this building. Bromton makes it 907, the Saxon Chronicle 919. The Daniſh army was repulſed by the townſmen of Bedford in 921 [i]; in 1010 they were more ſucceſsful, and burned the town [k].

The record of Doomſday ſpeaks of the town of Bedford as being taxed as half a hundred both for ſoldiers and ſhipping. Remigius, biſhop of Lincoln, is ſaid to have taken it away from the church of St. Paul, and to have retained it unjuſtly in his own hands.

King William Rufus gave the Barony of Bedford to Pain de Beauchamp [l], who built a ſtrong caſtle adjoining the town. Bedford caſtle ſuſtained a ſiege againſt King Stephen and his army in 1137; but hiſtorians differ very much in their accounts, both as to the event of the ſiege, and who were the defenders. Dugdale, quoting ancient authorities, ſays, that Milo de Beauchamp and his brothers, hearing that the king had beſtowed their ſiſter in marriage, together with the whole Barony of Bedford, which had belonged to Simon de Beauchamp their father, unto Hugh Pauper, brother to the Earl of Leiceſter, garriſoned the caſtle of Bedford, then a fort of great ſtrength environed with a mighty rampire of earth, and a high wall, within which was an impregnable tower; ſo that the king, *not being able to get it by aſſault,* brought his army before it, and, after a long and hard ſiege, obtained it by

---

[i] Sax. Chron.   [k] Ibid.   [l] Dugdale's Baronage.

ſurrender,

furrender, through the mediation of his brother Henry de Blois bifhop of Winchefter, Milo de Beauchamp and his foldiers marching out upon honourable terms [m]. Camden, without entering into particulars, merely mentions that Stephen was the firft who took this caftle with great flaughter. Holinfhed informs us, that during the wars between Stephen and David king of Scotland, Bedford, which had been given to David's fon Henry, as appertaining to the earldom of Huntingdon, was garrifoned by the Scots; and that after being befieged for thirty days together, by Stephen, who every day gave an affault or alarm, it was at length won by him *by pure force and ftrength*. The circumftance, of Bedford having been thus for a time annexed to the earldom of Huntingdon, is confirmed by a record of parliament, by which it appears that the abbefs of Elftow, in 1327, preferred a petition, claiming the third penny in the town of Bedford, under a grant of Malcolm king of Scotland and earl of Huntingdon. The burgeffes of Bedford, in reply, affirmed that Malcolm never had the lordfhip of the town [n]. It is moft probable, that before his time it had been reftored to the Beauchamps. In 1190 Simon de Beauchamp gave 100l. for the government of Bedford caftle [o].

In 1216 William de Beauchamp, being then poffeffed of the barony of Bedford, took part with the rebellious barons, and received them as friends into his caftle, which they were advancing to befiege [p]. The king having fent his favourite, Faukes de Brent, to fummon the caftle, it was furrendered within a few days, and given to him for his good fervices [q]. The king appears to have been there in perfon the fame year [r]. Matthew Paris informs us that Faukes de Brent (being thus poffeffed of the barony by the king's gift) rebuilt and fortified the caftle, for which purpofe he pulled down the collegiate church of St. Paul; and that the abbefs of the neighbouring convent of Elftow, hearing of his facrilege, took the fword out of the hand of that faint's image in her church, and would not replace it till juftice had overtaken the offender: but a charter of the firft of Henry the third entirely exonerates Faukes de Brent from this charge, for by it the king grants the church of Tindene to the Monks of Newenham, as a compenfation for his father king John having ordered the church of Saint Paul's at Bedford, to them belonging, to be pulled down, when he caufed Bedford caftle to be fortified [s]. It is certain that Faukes de Brent, when he was in poffeffion of this caftle, prefuming upon its impregnable ftrength, fet at nought all law and authority; and having been fined by the king's juftices itinerant at Dunftaple, in the year 1224, for his various outrages and depredations upon the property of his lefs powerful neighbours, he fent a party of foldiers, who feized Henry de Braybroke one of the king's juftices, and treating him with great barbarity,

---

[m] Baronage, Vol. i. p. 223, 224.   [n] Parl. Rolls.   [o] Dugdale.   [p] Ibid.   [q] M. Paris.
[r] Pat. 18. Joh.   [s] Pat. 1 Hen. III. printed in Dugdale's Monafticon, Vol. ii.

brought

brought him prifoner to the caftle at Bedford ʳ. The king hearing of thefe outrages, marched to Bedford in perfon, attended by Stephen Langton archbifhop of Canterbury, and the principal peers of the realm. On this occafion the archbifhops, bifhops, and abbots granted a voluntary aid to the king, and two labourers from every hide of their lands to work the engines employed in the fiege ᵘ.

Camden has extracted from the Chronicle of Dunftaple, the following account of the fiege written by an eye-witnefs: "On the eaft fide," fays the writer, "was one *Petraria* and two *Mangonella* which daily battered the tower, and on the weft fide two *Mangonella* ruined the old tower, and one *Mangonell* the fouth, and one on the north made two breaches in the wall oppofed to them. Befides thefe, there were two wooden towers raifed above the height of the caftle for the crofs-bow-men and fcouts, alfo many others in which the crofs-bow-men and flingers lay in ambufh. There was alfo a machine called a cat, under which miners had free paffage to fap the walls of the tower and caftle. The caftle was taken by four affaults. In the firft was taken the barbican, in the fecond the outer bail, in the third the wall near the old tower was overthrown by the miners, through the breach of which they with great danger made themfelves mafters of the inner bail: on the fourth affault the miners fet fire to the tower, and when the fmoke burft out and great cracks appeared in the tower the befieged furrendered." The men of Dunftaple made the fecond affault here mentioned, in which the outer bail was taken, for which fervice they had a confiderable fhare of the plunder ˣ. Many lives were loft by the fall of the old tower. The fiege lafted two months, uncommon efforts being ufed to get poffeffion of this nurfery of fedition, as Camden ftiles it, which was deemed by its owner to have been of fuch ftrength as almoft to defy any mode of affault then in ufe. The fuccefs of the befiegers was attributed chiefly to the ufe of a lofty wooden caftle, higher than the walls, which gave the befiegers an opportunity of obferving every thing that paffed within. Faukes de Brent was not in the caftle at the time of its capture; his brother William with four and twenty of his officers were executed; Culmo another brother received the king's pardon; Faukes himfelf haftened to Bedford to crave for mercy, under the protection of the bifhop of Coventry, and was pardoned on condition of being banifhed the realm. The king ordered the caftle to be difmantled, and the ditches to be filled up. The ftones were given to the monks of the two neighbouring priories, Newenham and Caldwell ʸ. The barony of Bedford was reftored to William de Beauchamp, who obtained the king's leave to erect a manfion on the fite of the caftle, and to inclofe it with a wall, not exceeding the height of that which belonged to the fecond ward, and to be without any battlement ᶻ.

ʳ M. Paris.　ᵘ Chron. Dunft.　ˣ Chron. Dunft.　ʸ Chron. Dunft.　ᶻ Dugdale.

The

The king's orders, with refpect to the total demolition of the caftle, appear not to have been carried into effect, for John lord Moubray, who, through a female heir, inherited a part of the eftates of the Beauchamps, is faid in the inquifition taken after his death, in 1361, to have died feifed of the *ruinous* caftle at Bedford; and Camden fpeaks of its ruins as exifting in his time, overhanging the river on the eaft fide of the town. There is not a ftone now remaining, but the veftiges of the caftle are to be feen at the back of the Swan Inn. On the keep is a bowling-green, formerly of much celebrity. After the death of John Moubray, the laft duke of Norfolk of that name, the fite of Bedford caftle appears to have defcended by a co-heir of the Moubrays to William marquis of Berkeley, who gave it to Sir Reginald Bray[a]. The fite of the caftle with the Swan inn is now the property of the duke of Bedford, and it is prefumed that it paffed from the Goftwicks by purchafe to the Marlborough family, and from them, together with feveral other eftates which had been in the Goftwicks, to the Duke of Bedford's grandfather.

The barony of Bedford, confifting of feveral manors in Bedfordfhire and Buckinghamfhire, was divided among the three daughters of William de Beauchamp, who died in the reign of Edward I. Maud, wife of Roger de Moubray, Ela, wife of Baldwin Wake, and Beatrix, wife of Thomas Fitzotes. Some of the defcendants of thefe co-heirs continued for many generations to poffefs, either entirely or in portions, manors which had been parcel of this barony. The barons of Bedford having been anciently lord almoners to the kings of England on the day of their coronation, Thomas de Moubray, as one of their co-heirs by the marriage of his anceftor with Maud de Beauchamp, and John Lord Latimer, as inheriting a part of the barony which had paffed in marriage with Maud, daughter of Beatrix de Beauchamp, to the Botetorts, claimed this office with its perquifites at the coronation of king Henry IV. The claim of Lord Latimer was allowed, and Sir Thomas Grey was appointed to reprefent Thomas de Moubray, whofe lands were then in the king's hands[b]. At the coronation of James II. the earl of Exeter, defcended from the Latimers by the marriage of his anceftor Thomas earl of Exeter with one of the co-heireffes of John Neville, the laft Lord Latimer[c]; Sir George Blundell defcended from

Ela

[a] See the Rolls of Parliament, Vol. vi.   [b] Vincent's MSS. in Coll. Arm.

[c] The immediate defcendants of the Latimers who inherited from the Botetorts, failed by the death of John Neville, the firft Lord Latimer of that family without iffue; but the manors, which were parcel of the barony of Bedford, were entailed on his brother Ralph Neville earl of Weftmorland, whofe fon George became Lord Latimer, and defcended to John Neville the laft Lord Latimer, who left four daughters co-heireffes, from one of whom the Marquis of Exeter is defcended. The other daughters married the Earl of Northumberland, Sir William Cornwallis, and Sir John Danvers. The only known defcendants in lineal fucceffion from the three daughters of William de Beauchamp, baron of

Bedford

Ela de Beauchamp through the Pigots and Gafcoignes ; and Thomas Snag efq. who, it is prefumed, poffeffed fome lands parcel of the barony by purchafe, claimed the office of almoner, which was adjudged for that time to the earl of Exeter[d]. In the reign of Henry VIII. the Goftwicks acquired a confiderable portion of this barony by purchafe, partly from the Bedingfields. It is prefumed that the intereft which the Goftwick family had in the barony paffed with the eftates, which were fold by them to the duchefs of Marlborough, and were afterwards purchafed of the Marlborough family by John duke of Bedford. The manor of Bedford, which was formerly part of the barony, has long been vefted in the corporation.

Before the conqueft, there was a collegiate church at Bedford, dedicated to St. Paul. Rohefia or Roife, wife of Pain de Beauchamp, changed the prebendaries into canons regular. Her fon Simon removed them to a new fite in the neighbour-ing parifh of Goldington, afterwards called Newenham[e], about a mile from Bedford down the river ; from which circumftance and his extenfive benefactions he was efteemed their founder, and was fo called on his tomb, which in Leland's time exifted in the prefent church of St. Paul, having been removed, it is probable, from the ancient collegiate church, which was pulled down by king John as mentioned before.

Caldwell or Cawdwell Priory, about a quarter of a mile weft of Bedford, on the banks of the Oufe, was founded in the reign of king John, by Simon Barefcot or Baf-ket, alderman of Bedford, for brethren of the order of the Holy Crofs or Holy Sepulchre, and was dedicated to the Virgin Mary ; Robert de Houton gave the fite. The founder conferred the patronage of this convent on Roger le Marefchal. It paffed afterwards to the Latimers and Uffords[f]. The order of the Holy Sepulchre falling to decay not long after the eftablifhment of this monaftery, it is probable that it was replenifhed with Auftin canons ; for at the time of its fuppreffion by Henry VIII. it was ftated to be a priory of the laft-mentioned order, and was then dedicated to St. John the Baptift and St. John the Evangelift. Its clear yearly income was ftated to be 109l. 8s. 5d. The fite was granted in 1563 to Thomas Leigh[g], whofe defcendants continued there in 1620[h]. In 1682, it was the property of Edmund Gardiner efq.[i] who had a feat there, which has been pulled down many

Bedford (as traced by Francis Townfend efq. Windfor Herald), are Lord Stourton, Lord Petre, and the Earl of Berkeley from Maud the elder daughter ; the Earl of Peterborough, the Duke of Leeds, Sir William Wake bart. Sir John Reade bart. the Earl of Guildford, and Sir Richard Bedingfield bart. all defcended from Ela the fecond daughter of William de Beauchamp (through the Patefhulls) ; and the Duke of Beaufort, the Earl of Leicefter, the Duke of Marlborough, and Thomas Clifford efq. defcended (through the Botetorts), from Beatrix third daughter of William de Beauchamp.

[d] Sandford's Hiftory of the Coronation of James II. [e] Leland's Collectan. [f] Dugdale's Monaft. [g] Tanner. [h] MS. Diary of Th. Archer, rector of Houghton Conqueft. [i] Monument of his daughter-in-law Mary Lyfons in St. Mary's Church.

years ago, and a farm-houfe built in its place. The eftate continued in the Gardiner family till about the year 1780. It now belongs to George Livius efq. Traces of the conventual buildings may be feen in a field adjoining the farm-houfe.

The houfe of Grey-Friars, or Francifcans, in Bedford, was founded by Mabel Patefhull, lady of Bletfoe, before the year 1311[k]. Leland defcribes her tomb as being on the fouth fide of the high altar of the conventual church, under an arch, with an epitaph, in which fhe was called the foundrefs. He fpeaks alfo of the tomb of queen Eleanor, with her "image of plaine plate of braffe encrounid;" that of one of the Lord Moubrays, (John Lord Moubray,) who died in 1361 ; and Sir Richard Irencefter, who was faid to have made the body of the church. The revenues of this monaftery, when fuppreffed, were eftimated only at 3l. 15s. 2d. clear yearly value. Its fite, on which is now a farm-houfe, (to the north-weft of the town in the parifh of St. Paul's,) was granted by Henry VIII. to John Goftwick, mafter of the horfe[l]; it is now the property of the earl of Afhburnham. The few remains which ftill exift of the conventual buildings, exhibit fome veftiges of the cloifters. A barn adjoining to the houfe is faid to have been the refeċtory.

St. Leonard's hofpital, on the fouth fide of the town, was founded before the year 1302, by a townfman of Bedford. A record of that date calls it "the poor houfe of St. Leonard, in which were fix freres chapleynes wearing a religious habit[m]." The patronage of this hofpital was given by the town to Sir Reginald Bray, for his good offices in getting their fee-farm rent reduced[n]. It appears that the manor of Everton, on the borders of the county, belonged to this hofpital[o], the revenues of which were valued in 1535 at 16l. 6s. 8¼d. *per annum*[p]. The fite, which is in St. John's parifh, is now a farm of the duke of Bedford.

The hofpital of St. John the Baptift was founded in the year 1280[q], by Robert de Parys, for a mafter and two or more brethren, priefts, who were to pray for the fouls of the founder, John St. John, Henry St. John, and John St. John, grandfon of John; and likewife for the reception and fupport of decayed freemen of the town of Bedford. Many years before the reformation the hofpital had ceafed to be occupied according to the direċtions of the founder; and it appears by the furveys made of chantries and hofpitals in the reign of Henry VIII. and Edward VI., that the hofpital and parifh church of St. John had long been confolidated, and that there was no minifter in that parifh with the cure of fouls but the mafter of

---

[k] Leland.   [l] Tanner.   [m] Rolls of Parliament, Vol. i. p. 154.   [n] Leland.

[o] Placit. Inquif. &c. de terris in Com. Bed. in Turr. Lond.   [p] Tanner.

[q] The foundation is by fome writers faid to have been in the year 980. The miftake has been occafioned by a memorandum in bifhop Longland's regifter at Lincoln, where the date is thus erroneoufly written, An° Dni Mill° nonocentefimo lxxx[m]°. Other ancient records mention 1280 as the date of the foundation, which correfponds with the pedigree of the St. Johns.

the

the said hospital. It appears also, by other records, that the presentation to these joint offices was vested in the corporation of Bedford. The right of the corporation has been frequently contested by persons claiming the houses and lands belonging to the hospital under grants from the crown; but the corporation, or rather the master and co-brethren, have been always successful. It was determined so early as 1552, upon a suit which took place after the first grant, that the hospital did not come under the description of superstitious establishments, intended to be abolished by the statute. Since the last decision in 1743, the master and co-brethren have continued in quiet possession, and the corporation have enjoyed, unmolested, their right of presentation. The master or rector and co-brethren have been, from very ancient time, a body corporate, and have had a common seal. The co-brethren, who are poor freemen of Bedford appointed by the master, have no apartments in the hospital, which adjoins St. John's church, and has been long appropriated as the rectory-house. The ancient hall is still remaining. The estate is held on lease under the master and co-brethren. The co-brethren receive a weekly allowance of 9d. each.

The bridge over the Ouse, which connects the north and south parts of the town of Bedford, is of great antiquity. There was formerly upon, or adjoining to it [r], a free chapel or oratory, with a hospital, dedicated to St. Thomas the Martyr. It was built by the townsmen in the early part of the 14th century, and endowed with lands for the support of a warden or chaplain, who enjoying the endowment for life, was to repair the bridge at his own expence [s]. The appointment of a warden appears to have been in dispute between the townsmen of Bedford and the crown. As no mention appears of it on the Chantry Roll, it is supposed to have been dilapidated before the reformation. Two gateways, one of which served for the town gaol, were taken down in 1765, to render the passage over the bridge more commodious.

Not far from St. Paul's church is an ancient Gothic building, now used as a brewery. This is supposed to have been part of one of the prebendal houses, which Leland speaks of as existing in his time at Bedford, notwithstanding their stalls had been removed to Lincoln. The building above-mentioned is held on lease under the dean and chapter of that church.

The Gothic building in the George-yard is nothing more than part of the original structure of that ancient inn, which is spoken of by the same name in a record of the year 1481 [t]. In the centre is a large gateway, and on one side the figure of St. George under a Gothic niche.

---

[r] Most Records (Pat. 42 Edw. III. &c.) describe it as on the bridge; but a petition to parliament in 1338, (see Rolls of Parliament, Vol. ii. p. 100.) speaks of it as close adjoining to the bridge on the land of Lord Moubray.

[s] Rolls of Parliament II. p. 100.   [t] Esch. 20 Edw. IV. See under the name of Illingworth.

Bedford is esteemed a borough and corporation by prescription, and is so called in all legal proceedings. The first charter on record is that of Henry II. who, in 1166, granted and confirmed the town of Bedford to the burgesses, subject to a payment of 40l. *per annum* as a fee-farm rent to the crown. His son Richard confirmed their mercantile guild and all their ancient privileges, and granted other new privileges and immunities similar to those enjoyed by the burgesses of Oxford. Richard II. granted more extended privileges, and, among others, a view of frank-pledge within the borough. In his charter the corporation are styled the mayor, bailiffs, and burgesses ; their present style of mayor, bailiffs, burgesses, and commonalty, first occurs in an inquisition of the reign of Henry VI. They consist of a mayor, recorder, an indefinite number of aldermen, two chamberlains, and thirteen common council-men. The number of aldermen is necessarily uncertain, the office of mayor being always filled by a burgess, who has previously served the offices of bailiff and chamberlain, and who immediately after the expiration of his mayoralty, becomes an alderman. The mayor, bailiffs, and chamberlains, are elected annually on the first of September. The common council are elected annually, from among the burgesses, on the Wednesday before St. Matthew's day. The bailiffs for the time being are sheriffs of the borough, and lords of the manor.

In the reign of Henry VI. the fee-farm rent payable by the burgesses to the crown, being then 46l. *per annum*, was remitted in part for a time, on a representation of the poverty of the town [u]. By the intercession of Sir Reginald Bray, when he was prime minister to Henry VII. it was permanently reduced to 20l. *per annum ;* and at some subsequent time to 16l. 5s. 8d. which is now payable to Lord Carteret and the Rev. John Pery, as representatives, it is presumed, of those who purchased the rent of the crown. Lord Carteret's share, about 12l. *per annum*, has been long given in augmentation of the vicarage of St. Paul's, which is in the patronage of that nobleman.

The town-hall, or sessions-house, (in which are held the assizes for the county) was built in 1753. It is situated in the area before St. Paul's church. The town gaol, which stood formerly on the bridge, was taken down in or about the year 1765, after which, a temporary gaol was fitted up under the town-hall, and afterwards a new gaol was built in St. Lloyd's, near the alms-houses ; but being found inconvenient, was taken down, and another has been lately erected to the North-west of the town, near the road to Kettering ; where a new county gaol also was completed in the year 1801, towards the building of which the late

---

[u] Among other causes which led to the decay of the town, is stated the building of Barford bridge, which diverted many travellers from passing through Bedford. See the charter of 25 Henry VI. extracts from which, and various other charters, have been obligingly communicated by Mr. Theed Pearse, with permission of the corporation.

Mr.

Mr. Whitbread left a legacy of 500*l*. The prifoners fleep in feparate rooms; and the fyftem of folitary confinement is occafionally adopted. In 1803 an act of parliament paffed, enabling the inhabitants of Bedford to pave and light the town, to build a new bridge, to pull down the butchers' fhambles, and to build a new market-place, with a feffions-houfe above it, and a butter-market on the fite of the old gaol. This act has been partly carried into effect, and a pent-houfe is now placed on the fite of the old gaol, where the new market-houfe is hereafter to be erected.

Bedford fent two members to parliament as early as the year 1295. The right of election was determined, in 1690, to be in the burgeffes, freemen, and inhabitant houfeholders not receiving alms. Browne Willis, in his laft edition of the Notitia Parliamentaria, fpeaks of their number as above 700. At the laft contefted election in 1790, 1148 voters polled; and the number is fince increafed by the addition of feveral honorary freeman. The mayor and bailiffs are the returning officers.

The principal manufacture of the town is lace: a confiderable trade is carried on in coals, which are brought by the Oufe from Lynn and Yarmouth.

The population of Bedford has increafed very much of late years. The number of inhabited houfes, in 1801, as appears by the returns then made to Parliament, was 783; of inhabitants 3948, of which 2221 are ftated to be perfons chiefly employed in trade, manufactures, or handicraft. Seventy-two houfes on the north fide of the town, being for the moft part very mean cottages, were deftroyed by fire on the 25th of May 1802. The fire was occafioned by a piece of a red-hot horfe-fhoe, from a blackfmith's forge, falling on the thatch of a houfe. The damage amounted to about 2000*l*. The fufferers being moftly of the poorer fort, a very liberal fubfcription was made for them in the town and county, amounting nearly to the whole of their lofs. Neat cottages have been built on the fite of thofe which were deftroyed by the fire.

The principal market at Bedford, which is held on Saturday, on the north fide of the river, is a confiderable mart for corn. The Monday's market, on the fouth fide of the river, is chiefly for pigs. There are fix annual fairs, viz. the firft Tuefday in Lent, April 21, Old Midfummer-day, Auguft 21, October 12, and December 19. Befides thefe, an annual fair is held at St. Leonard's farm, on the 17th of November.

There are in Bedford five parifh churches, St. Paul's, St. Peter's, and St. Cuthbert's, on the north fide; St. Mary's and St. John the Baptift's on the fouth fide of the river.

St. Paul's is a very handfome Gothic building, with a fpire. In the fouth

chancel,

chancel, which is fitted up for the archdeacon's court, is an altar-tomb with brafs figures of Sir William Harper and his lady. Sir William, who died in 1574, was fometime Lord Mayor of London, and a great benefactor to this his native town. On the eaft wall is a modern monument, with medallions of Sir William and Lady Harper, put up in 1768 by the truftees of the Harper charity, with an infcription recording their benefactions. On the fouth wall of the nave is painted a recumbent figure of king Charles the Firft under an open canopy, by the fide of which are infcribed fome very indifferent lines, alluding to his trial and execution.

The pulpit is of ftone, ornamented with gilt tracery, on a blue ground.

In the church-yard is the tomb of a couple, " Shadrach and Patience Johnfon," who had 24 children.

The benefice of this church is an endowed vicarage, in the gift of Lord Carteret. Thomas Chriftie efq. being poffeffed of the great tithes, gave them, in the year 1697, to the vicar and his fucceffors, charged with the payment of a fhilling each weekly, to eight poor perfons, in the alms-houfes built by him.

The churches of St. Peter and St. Cuthbert contain nothing remarkable. In the church-yard of the former is the tomb of Mr. Afpinal, a rector of that parifh, who affifted the learned Dr. Caftell in his laborious refearches in the Oriental languages. The churches of St. Peter (called St. Peter Martin, to diftinguifh it from another church of the fame name, formerly on the fouth fide of the river) and St. Cuthbert, are both rectories in the gift of the crown.

The parifhes of St. Paul, St. Peter, and St. Cuthbert, were inclofed by an act of parliament paffed in 1795, when allotments of land in lieu of tithes were affigned to the feveral perfons entitled to them.

The churches of St. Mary and St. John contain nothing remarkable. The latter, as before-mentioned, is annexed to the hofpital of that name, and is confidered as a rectory, of which the corporation have the patronage. St. Mary's is a rectory in the patronage of the bifhop of Lincoln. The parifh of St. Mary has been inclofed by an act of parliament paffed in 1797, when an allotment of land was made to the rector in lieu of tithes. It was computed that there were then about 400 acres belonging to this parifh lying in open fields. The rector of St. John's was entitled to the tithes of about twelve acres of land in this parifh, for which an allotment was alfo made.

In the regifter of this parifh are entries of the burial of three nuns of Elftow, " dame Ann Prefton, dame Elizabeth Fox, and dame Elizabeth Napier," who died in 1557 and 1558.

Oppofite to St. Mary's church, where is now a void fpace, ftood formerly a church called St. Peter's Dunftaple, which before the year 1400 was a feparate

parifh :

parifh: it was afterwards annexed to St. Mary's, the fervice being performed at each on alternate weeks, and the books and ornaments removed from one church to the other. In 1545 the parifhioners were permitted by Sir Edward North, chancellor of the Augmentations, to pull down St. Peter's church, on condition of their ufing fuch materials as were not wanted, for the repairs of St. Mary's (to which they had then lately added a new aifle) in mending the ftreets, and repairing the bridge.

The old Independent meeting-houfe in Mill-lane was originally eftablifhed in 1650, under the miniftry of John Gifford, who had been a major in king Charles's army [x]. The celebrated John Bunyan was ordained co-paftor of this congregation with Samuel Fenn in 1671, and continued in that fituation till his death in 1688 [y]. His memory is much revered by the congregation; and the chair in which he ufed to fit is preferved as a kind of relick in the veftry. On the wall of the cemetery is a tablet to the memory of his great-grand-daughter, with an epitaph, which ftates, that he exercifed his miniftry in and about Bedford for thirty-two years, during which time he fuffered twelve years imprifonment. The prefent meeting-houfe was built in 1707. The congregation are a mixture of baptifts and pædo-baptifts. They have a baptiftery for adults under their communion table, in the centre of the meeting, for fuch as difapprove of infant baptifm. In 1772, fome members of this congregation formed themfelves into a feparate fociety, and built a new meeting-houfe, not far from the old one, in the fame lane. The members of the new meeting are pædo-baptifts.

The Moravians, or fociety of *Unitas fratrum*, have had an eftablifhment at Bedford ever fince the year 1745. They have a neat chapel built in 1751. Adjoining it are houfes for the fingle brethren and fifters, who refpectively live in community. In the fifters' houfe are nearly forty fingle women, who are employed in working tambour. Behind the chapel is a cemetery, in which is a memorial of one of their bifhops. It is kept extremely neat, in four compartments: the tomb-ftones are all flat, fmall, and uniform, as in their burial-ground at Chelfea.

The free-fchool at Bedford was founded by Sir William Harper, alderman of London, for the inftruction of children of the town in grammar and good manners. The letters patent bear date 1552, the founder's deed 1566. The fchool-houfe, conveyed by that deed to the corporation, had been built by Sir William Harper between thofe periods. It was rebuilt by the truftees in 1767, when a ftatue of the founder was placed in the front. The warden and fellows of New College in Oxford are vifitors of the fchool, and appoint the mafter and ufher, or fecond mafter.

[x] Printed acccount of the rife and progrefs of this meeting, annexed to a Funeral Sermon.
[y] Ibid.

The

The mafter's falary, under the laft act for regulating the Bedford charities, is 260l. with coals and candles; that of the fecond mafter 160l., with the like perquifites. Under the fame act, the writing-mafter has a falary of 80l. *per annum.* The prefent head-mafter is the Rev. John Hook, B. C. L.; the fecond mafter, Charles Abbot, D.D.

Sir William Harper, when he founded the free-fchool at Bedford, conveyed to the corporation thirteen acres of land in the parifh of St. Andrew Holborn, for its fupport, and for the marriage of poor maidens of this town; the overplus, if any, to be given in alms to the poor. This land having been let on building leafes, Lamb's Conduit-ftreet, Theobald's-road, Bedford-ftreet, Bedford-row, and fome leffer ftreets were built on it; the rents were in confequence advanced to 150l. *per annum;* and when the greater part of the leafes fell in, which happened about the year 1763, they were advanced to nearly 3000l. *per annum!* The truftees then applied to parliament for an act to regulate the difpofal of this noble income, which was accordingly obtained: but fome of the regulations having been productive of inconvenience to the town, a new act was procured in 1792; at which time other leafes having nearly expired, the eftates were about to experience a further advance of almoft 1000l. *per annum.* The truftees were made a body corporate by the act of 1764. By the laft act they are to confift of the lord lieutenant and the two members for the county, the members for the town, the corporation of Bedford, and eighteen other elective inhabitants. The eftates now produce about 5800l. *per annum.* A farther increafe is very foon expected, and at a future period they will be capable of much greater improvement.

Under the laft act, three exhibitions of 40l. *per annum* each are given to fcholars from the free-fchool, either at Oxford or Cambridge, during the fpace of fix years. The fum to be appropriated for marriage-portions is fixed at 800l. *per annum,* to be given by lot in portions of 20l. each to forty poor maidens of Bedford, of good fame and reputation, not under fixteen years of age, and not exceeding fifty. They muft marry within two months after drawing the fortunate lots, otherwife they forfeit the portion. The men to whom they are to be married muft not be vagrants, or perfons of bad fame or reputation. At a future opportunity, it is probable that the truftees will procure fome farther regulations to be made refpecting the hufbands, fince the object of the donation, which is intended to fettle a poor couple comfortably in life, is fo often defeated by the maidens marrying foldiers belonging to marching regiments quartered in Bedford; the almoft inevitable confequence of which is, that the portion is no fooner received than diffipated, and it not unfrequently happens that the women return, after a time, with orphan families, and, unable to prove their hufbands' fettlements, become heavy burdens to the town.

If,

If, for want of a sufficient number of applications, there should be any overplus of the 800l. appropriated annually for marriage-portions, it is to be given to poor women of good fame and reputation, who have lived five successive years in service in the town of Bedford, and have been married within the preceding year.

The act appropriates the sum of 300l. *per annum* for the support of twenty-six boys in a hospital or school of industry, and 700l. to be laid out in apprentice-fees for fifteen poor boys and five girls, to be chosen by lot. Alms-houses have been built also, pursuant to the directions of the act, for ten poor men and the same number of women. The weekly allowance to each is 3s., and 40s. annually for clothing. If a poor man and his wife live together, they are allowed to the amount of 5s. a week. The sum of 100l. *per annum* was appropriated to be given in sums of 5l. each to twenty poor girls at their going out to service. The residue, after providing for the above-mentioned purposes as expressed in the act, is to be laid out in building and endowing more alms-houses, or building cottages, to be let at low rents to the poor.

If another opportunity should offer, upon the expected farther increase of the charity estates, of making any change in the present regulations, or any new disposition of the additional fund, the trustees would find the plan of Mr. Raine's charities, in the parish of St. George in the East, Middlesex, not unworthy their notice, particularly his hospital for girls. Mr. Raine gave two annual marriage-portions of 100l. each, to be drawn for by six of the most deserving young women of the age of twenty-two or upwards, who had been educated in his hospital. The husbands must be of the church of England, and inhabitants of the parish of St. George in the East, or either of two adjoining parishes. If such a regulation should be thought too limited, it might perhaps remedy the inconvenience complained of at Bedford, if the maidens portioned by Sir William Harper's charity were restricted to marrying inhabitants of their own town or county.

A charity-school for twenty children of the parishes of St. Paul and St. Cuthbert, was founded by the Rev. Mr. Leith and others, before the year 1737.

Thomas Christie esq. built, in his life-time, an alms-house for eight poor persons, to whom he bequeathed one shilling each weekly, payable out of the great tithes of St. Paul's.

The house of industry at Bedford, a large and handsome brick-building to the north of the town, was begun in the year 1794, and finished in 1796. It is fitted up with every useful accommodation; and great attention has been paid to the health as well as comfort and convenience of the inhabitants. In point of œconomical contrivance, perhaps, it is inferior to some buildings of a like nature. A manufacture of flannel has been established in this house on an extensive scale; it is in a

flourishing

flourifhing ftate; and the good effects of the inftitution begin to be felt in the reduction of the poors' rates.

A general infirmary for the county has been lately erected in St. Mary's parifh. The late Mr. Whitbread bequeathed 4000l. towards the ftructure, (which was aided by donations from the nobility and principal gentry of the county, particularly the duke of Bedford, the earl of Offory, and the prefent Mr. Whitbread,) and another fum of 4000l. towards its endowment, which is farther provided for by the intereft of various fmaller donations, and by annual fubfcriptions. The infirmary was opened for the reception of patients on the 13th of Auguft 1803; it is now completely finifhed, and ready for the reception of 38 in-patients, which is its full complement.

BIDDENHAM, a fmall village on the Oufe, about two miles weft of Bedford, is in the hundred of Willey. The manor, at the time of the Norman furvey, belonged to William Spec, anceftor of Walter de Efpec, founder of Warden Abbey. It was afterwards in the earls of Gloucefter and Stafford [z]; under whom, as lords of the fee, it feems to have been held for feveral generations by the St. Johns, who were in poffeffion of it till 1582 [a], and perhaps later. It is now the property of the Right Hon. Lord Hampden, in whofe family it has been for nearly a century. In the church are feveral memorials for the family of Boteler, who were fettled at Biddenham for ten generations [b]. Sir William Boteler, of this family, was Lord Mayor of London in 1515. There was a chantry in this church dedicated to St. William; and the chantry of Biddenham Bridge, which had a confiderable endowment in lands [c], charged probably with the repairs of the bridge which leads from Bedford to the north of Buckinghamfhire, and is now known by the name of Bromham Bridge. The great tithes, which were appropriated to the priory of Denny, in Cambridgefhire, are now the property of Lord Hampden. He is patron alfo of the vicarage, which is in the deanery of Bedford.

BIGGLESWADE, in the hundred of that name, and in the deanery of Shefford, is a confiderable market town, 45 miles from London, fituated on the great road to York, and on the banks of the Ivel. The market is held on Wednefdays, by what charter does not appear on record, but it is probable that it was granted to fome of the bifhops of Lincoln, to which fee the manor was annexed by Henry I. in 1132 [d]. Bifhop Holbeach furrendered it to Edward VI. in 1547. It is now

[z] Efch. Edw. III. and Rich. II.   [a] Collins's Peerage—Article Bolingbroke.
[b] Pedigrees Brit. Muf.   [c] Chantry Roll in the Augmentation Office.
[d] Dugdale's Monafticon, Vol. iii.

held

held on leafe under the crown by the Right Honourable Lord Carteret, in whofe family it has been for a confiderable time.

In 1785, this town fuftained great damage by a fire, which confumed about 120 houfes. The number of houfes in the parifh, (including Stratton and Holme,) according to the returns made to Parliament under the Population Act, in 1801, was 317; that of the inhabitants, 1794.

There are five annual fairs at Bigglefwade; February 13, Saturday in Eafter week, Trinity Monday, Auguft 2, and November 8.

The parifh church is a handfome Gothic ftructure. The chancel was rebuilt about the year 1467, by John Ruding archdeacon of Bedford, whofe arms are to be feen under the feats of fome ancient wooden ftalls in the north aifle. He died in 1481, and lies buried in the chancel. A plate of his tomb (from which his effigies in brafs has been removed) is to be feen in Gough's Sepulchral Monuments. The rectory, to which the advowfon of the vicarage is annexed, is the corps of a prebend in the church of Lincoln.

The manor of *Stratton*, a hamlet in this parifh, now the feat of Charles Barnett efq. was, at the time of the Norman furvey, the property of Ralph de Lifle. It was afterwards fucceffively in the Latimers [f], Nevils, and Enderbys. Francis Pigott became poffeffed of it by marrying Eleanor, the daughter and heir of John Enderby who died in 1509 [g]. The Pigotts had been fettled at Stratton long before, and had ferved the office of fheriff of the counties of Bedford and Bucks fo early as the year 1408. About the latter end of the fixteenth century, Stratton became the property of the Anderfons of Eyworth. Edmund, the eldeft fon of Sir Francis Anderfon, left an only daughter, Dorothy, an infant, who became the wife of Sir John Cotton bart. the munificent donor of the valuable Cottonian Library, which had been collected by his grandfather. This national treafure, we are told, was, during the civil wars in the reign of King Charles I. preferved at Stratton, whither it had been removed, for greater fecurity, from Connington, the ancient feat of the Cottons [h]. Sir John Cotton, the laft heir male of this family, died in 1752. Stratton was purchafed of his reprefentatives in 1764, by the truftees of Mr. Barnett's father, Curtis Barnett efq. who died, in 1746, at Fort St. David, on the coaft of Coromandel, being commander in chief of his Majefty's fhips on that ftation. About 300 rofe-nobles of Henry V. and VI. were found by a plowman, in 1770, upon the fite of the old manfion. There was anciently a chapel at Stratton, mentioned in records of the reign of Edward III. [i] The manor of Holme-cum-Langford, the greater part of which is in this parifh, belongs

---

[f] Efch. Edw. II.—Hen. VI. [g] Cole's Efcheats, and Bedfordfhire Pedigrees, Brit Muf.
[h] Stukeley's Itin. Curiof. [i] Mr. Stratton's papers.

to the dean and chapter of Weftminfter. Lord Spencer has moft of the landed property in the hamlet of Holme.

Sir John Cotton bart. who died in 1752, by his will bearing date 1726, founded a charity fchool at Stratton, for the inftruction of twelve poor children of the parifh of Bigglefwade; and having devifed the fum of 1800l. to be laid out in lands for charitable purpofes, directed that two-ninths of the rents fhould be appropriated as a falary for the mafter of this fchool, who is to be nominated, from time to time, by the lord of the manor of Stratton. The eftate purchafed purfuant to the donor's intention, was the lay rectory of Flitwick in this county. The proportion paid out of the prefent rent, to the mafter of this fchool, is 14l. 19s. 6d. Sir John Cotton's will gives a proportion of one-ninth of the faid rents, now 7l. 9s. 9d. to the vicar of Bigglefwade.

Edward Peake efq. of Southill, in the year 1557, founded a fchool at Holme, for teaching eight poor boys of the parifh of Bigglefwade, Englifh, writing, and accounts; and endowed it with a rent-charge of 13l. *per annum*, and a houfe at Holme, valued at 2l. 3s. *per annum*. Thefe fchools are at prefent under the fame mafter.

BLETSOE, in the hundred of Willey, and deanery of Clopham, is a fmall village about fix miles north-weft of Bedford, on the road to Higham Ferrers. The manor, at the time of the Norman furvey, was part of the large poffeffions of Hugh de Beauchamp; it was afterwards in the family of Patfhull. Mabel Patfhull, lady of this manor, founded the monaftery of Grey Friars at Bedford, in the reign of Edward the Firft. In 1327, John de Patefhull obtained the king's licence for embattling his manfion at Bletfoe [k]. In 1344 he was fummoned to parliament as a baron. Sir Roger de Beauchamp, chamberlain to King Edward the Third, having married his eldeft daughter, on a partition of the eftates after the death of a fon who died without iffue, became poffeffed of this manor, made it his chief feat, and was fummoned to parliament in 1373 as baron Beauchamp of Bletfoe. Margaret his grand-daughter, who, on failure of male iffue, became his fole heir, married Sir Oliver St. John, a defcendant of the ancient family of St. John of Bafing, who were already poffeffed of large eftates in Bedfordfhire, inherited by a female heir, from the Pavelys [l]. Her fecond hufband was John Beaufort, duke of Somerfet, by whom fhe had one daughter, Margaret, the wife of Edmund Tudor, Earl of Richmond and mother of king Henry VII. This illuftrious lady, who was foundrefs of St. John's and Chrift's Colleges in Cambridge, is faid to have been born at Bletfoe. That her mother, the duchefs of Somerfet, refided there in great ftate,

[k] Pat. 1. Edw. III.   [l] Collin's Peerage.

may

may be collected from the epitaph of Ralph Lannoy, formerly in Bletfoe church. He died in 1458, and is ftyled cofferer and keeper of the wardrobe to the moft noble Margaret duchefs of Somerfet, then married to a third hufband, Leo Lord Welles. Sir Oliver St. John's defcendant of the fame name, was, in 1559, created Lord St. John of Bletfoe. Oliver, the fourth baron, was, in 1624, advanced to the title of Earl of Bolingbroke. The earldom became extinct in 1711. The barony devolved to the pofterity of Sir Rowland St. John, a younger fon of Oliver Lord St. John, the third baron; and is now enjoyed by his immediate defcendant, Henry Beauchamp, Lord St. John, to whom the manor of Bletfoe ftill belongs. The greater part of the manfion has been long ago pulled down; what remains is converted into a farm houfe. It appears to have formed one fide of a large quadrangular building, of the ftyle of architecture which prevailed in the early part of the feventeenth century. Veftiges of the ancient caftellated manfion are plainly difcernible near the houfe.

In the north aifle of the parifh church, which is the burial-place of the noble family of St. John, there is a monument, with the effigies of a knight in armour, and his lady; intended for Sir John St. John, father of Oliver, the firft Lord St. John, whom he lived to fee created a peer. The word *matertera* in the epitaph muft be underftood to mean *great* aunt; the infcription cannot apply to the father of this Sir John, who was, properly fpeaking, the nephew of Margaret countefs of Richmond: fince we find by the *probate* of his will, that *he* died in 1525. It appears by the following infcription, that the countefs of Richmond brought him up with her grandfon King Henry VIII.; who made him guardian of his daughters, the princeffes Mary and Elizabeth; and that he died in the office of chamberlain to the latter, when queen.

" Infans, vir, fenior, femper clariffimus Heros:
Principibus puerum primis eduxit ab annis
Richmundæ Comitiffa, fui matertera alumni,
Inde vir effectus, Regis pervenit ad aulam
Henrici Octavi, geminas hoc tempore natas
Rex habuit quibus ambabus lectiffimus heros
Huic datus eft cuftos, datus eft camerarius illi.
O quoties illius opem bello Anglia fenfit;
Nunc vefana fremit Lincolnia, nunc fremit ingens
Gallia bis hujus notà virtute fubacta;
Mota fub Edwardo pendit Norfolcia fexto,
Mittitur huc inter proceres; quos inter & omnes
Vel fuit hic primus, vel nulli Marte fecundus.
Denique jam Senis faturatus honoribus annis,
Reginæ electus camerarius Elizabethæ;
Occidit & prolem fimilem virtute reliquit."

In the fame aifle is the monument of Frances, countefs of Bolingbroke (daughter of William Duke of Newcaftle). The patronage of the rectory is vefted in Lord St. John.

BLUNHAM, a fmall village in the hundred of Wixamtree, and deanery of Shefford, about eight miles nearly eaft of Bedford, had formerly a market on Wednefdays, and a fair at the feftival of St. James, granted, in 1315, to John Lord Haftings [m]. The manor was anciently in the Valences, earls of Pembroke, from whom it defcended by female heirs to the noble families of Haftings and Grey; and is now the property of their reprefentative, the Right Honourable Lady Lucas.

Charles Grey, earl of Kent, refided at the manor-houfe of Blunham, (now a farm,) and died there in 1625, as appears by his epitaph in Flitton church. In the parifh church at Blunham, is the monument of Lady Sufan Longueville, his daughter and heir, who carried the barony of Grey of Ruthin into the family of Longueville, afterwards earls of Suffex. There are fome memorials alfo of the Longuevilles, and of the family of Bromfall; one of whom ferved the office of fheriff of the county in 1650, and was inftrumental in preferving the Cottonian library, then depofited at Stratton, during the civil war. The rectory of Blunham is in the patronage of Lady Lucas.

The manor of *Mogerhanger*, a hamlet in this parifh, was anciently in the Trompetons or Trompingtons [n]. It was afterwards in the noble family of Ferrars of Groby [o]; and is now the property and feat of Godfrey Thornton efq. who has alfo the manors of Chalton and South Mills, in this parifh; all of which he inherited from his uncle the late Richard Aftell efq. of Everton. Mrs. Campbell, relict of the late Colonel Campbell, deputy-governor of Chelfea Hofpital, has a feat in this parifh, formerly belonging to the Bromfalls, who, it is fuppofed, were poffeffed of the eftates which are now the property of Mr. Thornton.

The parifh of Blunham has been inclofed by an act of parliament, paffed in 1796, when an allotment of land was affigned to the rector in lieu of tithes, excepting thofe of Mogerhanger, which were allotted to Mr. Thornton, and a corn rent affigned in lieu of them to the rector.

BOLNHURST, in the hundred of Stodden, and deanery of Eaton, is about eight miles north-eaft of Bedford. The manor belonged to the family of St. John, as early as the reign of Edward III. and continued their property fo lately as the 17th century. It was afterwards in the Fleetwoods and Churchills; of the latter of

᠊ Cart. 8. Edw. II.　　ᵖ Efch. Edw. I. Edw. III.　　ᵒ Efch. Ric. II.

whom

whom it was purchased about the year 1780 by the present proprietors, Jacob Turner, John Caldecot, and Samuel Wyatt. The manor of Maverns and Glintells (in this parish, and Great Barford), now the property of John Franklin esq. has been in his family for more than two centuries. George Franklin esq. of Maverns, was sheriff of the county in 1600. Maverns has long ceased to be the family-seat; they resided afterwards at Great Barford, and are now removed out of the county. In the parish church is the monument of Sir John Franklin, one of the masters in chancery, who died in 1707, and several other memorials of the family. The advowson of the rectory was formerly vested in Thorney abbey, to which two-thirds of the great tithes, now in lay hands, were appropriated. The rector has the remaining third of so much of the parish as was comprised in the inclosure, which took place by act of parliament in 1778 [p]. The advowson is now vested in the Rev. Mr. Dolling the present incumbent.

Bromham, in the hundred of Willey and deanery of Clopham, is a small village situated on the banks of the Ouse about three miles from Bedford, near the road to Newport Pagnell. The manor was, at the time of the Norman survey, part of the large property of Hugh de Beauchamp, and upon the extinction of the male line of his family, became divided into severalties, which passed through the families of Munchensi, Tyes, Moubray, Boteler, Wake, Latimer, and Nevil [q]. It appears to have been again united in the 16th century. Sir John Dyve, who died in 1607, inherited it by female descent from the family of Wylde. His son, Sir Lewis Dyve, was a distinguished officer on the king's side, during the civil war. It was purchased of the Dyves about the year 1707 by Sir Thomas Trevor, who, in 1711, was created a peer by the title of Baron Trevor of Bromham; and it is now the property of his descendant, the Right Hon. Thomas Hampden Trevor, Viscount Hampden.

The manor-house, although small and inconvenient, and from its situation near the Ouse liable to frequent floods, was for many years a country-seat of the noble family of Trevor. The late Viscount Hampden frequently resided there. The pointed door-way at the entrance appears to have belonged to a much more ancient mansion. In the hall are several family portraits, among which are those of Sir Richard Trevor, a distinguished naval and military officer, knighted in the field by Queen Elizabeth; Sir Richard Trevor of Placetage, a fine picture in the style of Cornelius Jansen; Sir John Trevor of Trevallyn; Sir Thomas Trevor, chief baron of the exchequer; and Thomas, the

[p] Allotments of land were assigned to the lord of the manor and the rector for such parts as were then inclosed.

[q] Dugdale's Baronage, and various Escheats.

first

firſt Lord Trevor. There is a portrait alſo of Lord Chief Juſtice Dyer, and a few others.

In the chancel of the pariſh church is a very handſome monument of the firſt Lord Trevor, an eminent lawyer, who had been Lord Chief Juſtice of the common pleas, and at the time of his death, in 1730, was Lord Privy-Seal and Preſident of the Council. There is a handſome monument alſo of John, the third Lord Trevor, who died in 1764, by Prince Hoare. On the chancel floor are the figures, in braſs, of Sir John Dyve, his mother, who was heireſs of Thomas Wylde, lord of the manor of Bromham, and his wife Iſabel, daughter and heir of Sir Ralph Haſtings. In the north aiſle is a handſome monument, with the effigies of a man in armour, lying under a canopy ſupported by Ionic columns, which, from the arms, appears to be that of John Dyve eſq. who married a Walcot. The rectory of Bromham belonged to the monaſtery of Caldwell near Bedford, and was granted by King Edward VI. to Eton college, together with the advowſon of the vicarage [r].

CADDINGTON, in the hundred of Manſhead and deanery of Dunſtaple, lies about two miles from Luton. The church, with about a fifth of the pariſh, is in Bedfordſhire ; the remainder in the adjoining county of Herts. The manor of Caddington Bury has been in the church of St. Paul ever ſince the latter end of the eleventh century. In Edward the Confeſſor's time it was held under the crown [s]. The dean and chapter of St. Paul's have alſo the impropriation of the great tithes, and are patrons of the vicarage. Two prebendal eſtates in the ſame church, known by the names of Caddington Major, and Caddington Minor, are in this pariſh. William Beckford eſq. who is leſſee of the rectory under the church of St. Paul, has an eſtate in this pariſh called the manor of Zouches, which was anciently in the families of Cantelupe and Zouch, and ſeems to have paſſed through the ſame hands as the manor of Eaton-Bray.

On the Hertfordſhire ſide of the pariſh is *Market Cell*, the ſite of a nunnery of the Benedictine order, founded by Geoffrey abbot of St. Alban's, about the year 1145 [t]. We are told, that Humphrey, a natural ſon of Lord Berners, beſtowed much coſt and art in building a houſe on this ſite, but did not live to finiſh it [u]. It was after this, in 1548, granted to George Ferrers [w], whoſe deſcendant Sir John Ferrers died ſeiſed of it in 1640 [x]. After this it was for a conſiderable time the ſeat of the family of Coppin, of whom there are ſome memorials in the pariſh church of Caddington. The ſite of this monaſtery, together with the manor of Markyate, are now the property and ſeat of Joſeph Howell eſq. The manor of

[r] Records in the Augmentation Office.   [s] Dugdale's Monaſt. Vol. iii.   [t] Tanner.
[u] Dugdale's Baronage, Vol. ii.   [w] Tanner.   [x] Cole's Eſcheats, Brit. Muſ.

Humberſhoe,

Humberſhoe, partly in Bedfordſhire and partly in Herts, lying within the pariſhes of Caddington and Studham, was alſo in the families of Ferrers [y] and Coppin, and was ſold a few years ago by J. Pitman Coppin eſq. to John Lambert eſq. of whom it was purchaſed in 1802, by Mr. William Shone.

Market-ſtreet, on the road from London to Dunſtaple, is in the pariſhes of Caddington and Studham. In the former pariſh, and in the county of Herts, is a chapel of eaſe, founded by John Coppin eſq. which by an act of parliament, paſſed in the year 1741, was made a perpetual cure and benefice. The pariſh of Caddington has been incloſed by a late act of parliament: an allotment of land was aſſigned to the impropriator in lieu of tithes, and an allotment of 20 acres to the vicar, excluſive of his glebe, together with a corn-rent equivalent to his farther intereſt. The vicar was entitled to the tithes of hay and wood. The pariſh was eſtimated to contain 2000 acres.

CAMPTON, anciently called CAMELTON, is a ſmall village in the hundred of Clifton, about a mile from Shefford. The manor of Camelton-cum-Shefford was, at a remote period, in the noble family of Liſle [z]. Sir John de Liſle, who died ſeiſed of it in 1356, was one of the original knights companions of the garter. Theſe Liſles appear to have been a diſtinct family from the Liſles of Kingſton Liſle in Berkſhire [a], whoſe heireſs married into the noble family of Berkeley. It is probable, that on ſome attainder or failure of iſſue, their eſtates fell to the crown. The manor of Camelton-cum-Shefford became annexed to the honour of Ampthill; and as parcel of that honour was for many years on leaſe to the Bruces earls of Elgin and Ayleſbury; the leaſe is now veſted in the Duke of Bedford, whoſe anceſtor purchaſed it of the earl of Ayleſbury in 1738.

The ſite of the manor of Campton was granted in 1548 to Sir Thomas Palmer [b]. The capital manſion on it became the property and ſeat of the Ventris family. Sir Charles Ventris, in the year 1645, very narrowly eſcaped aſſaſſination at this houſe. The circumſtance is recorded in the following inſcription, ſtill preſerved on a pannel, which having received the contents of a muſket-ſhot has never been repaired.

" In the year 1645, Sir Charles Ventris knight banneret, created by king Charles for his bravery in the civil wars, was (in the night time) by Oliver's party, ſhot at, as he was walking in this room, but happily miſſed him." This houſe and the eſtate belonging to it were purchaſed of Sir Charles Ventris Field knight, repreſentative of the Ventris family, by Sir George Oſborn bart. of Chickſand. The houſe is now occupied as a ſchool.

[y] Cole's Eſcheats, Brit. Muſ.   [z] Eſch. Edw. I.—Edw. III.   [a] Dugdale's Baronage.
[b] Pat. 2. Edw. VI.

In

In the parish church is a *Columbarium* for the Osborn family; and in the aisle, above, are the monuments of Sir John and Sir Peter Osborn (successively lord treasurers remembrancers) put up in 1653, by Henry Osborn, younger son of Sir Peter, afterwards Sir Henry Osborn knt. and one of the commissioners of the navy. The rectory of Campton-cum-Shefford is in the patronage of Sir George Osborn bart. The parish has been inclosed by an act of parliament, passed in 1797, when an allotment of land, not exceeding 100 acres, was given to the rector in part of compensation for his interest in the tithes, and a corn-rent charged on lands belonging to Sir George Osborn for the remainder.

Shefford, a post-town 10 miles from Bedford on the road to London, is a chapelry within this parish, and gives name to the deanery, in which it is situated. It lies between two brooks, which unite their streams not far from the town, and fall into the Ivel. Till of late years Shefford had a market on Fridays. It has still four fairs, held on the 23d of January, Easter Monday, the 19th of May, and the 10th of October; the two first are considerable marts for sheep and cows; the last, which is now a holiday-fair, was granted in the reign of Edward II. to Robert de Lisle, and originally lasted for six days. The number of houses in the town, according to the returns made to parliament in 1801, under the Population Act, was 90, of inhabitants 474. The chapel is a small mean building: it may be considered, perhaps, as some excuse for its present state, that the inhabitants are not only bound to repair their chapel, but to contribute also to the repairs of the mother church. They have distinct officers and maintain their own poor. The Roman Catholics have a chapel in the town, endowed with an annual stipend left in trust for that purpose; Sir John Throckmorton being the present trustee. Robert Lucas, in the reign of Queen Elizabeth, bequeathed some houses and lands for the purpose of keeping in repair the bridges, roads, and causeways, in the town of Shefford; the remainder to be given to the poor.

CARDINGTON, a very neat village, about 2½ miles south-east of Bedford, is in the hundred of Wixamtree. The manor belonged to the Beauchamps, and was parcel of their barony of Bedford. After the death of the last heir male of that family it became divided, and seems to have formed separate manors, which passed to the families of Munchensi, Wake, Pigott, Botetort, Latimer, and Nevil[c]. James Gascoigne, son of the celebrated Chief Justice by his second wife, settled at Cardington in the reign of Henry VI. and became possessed of a manor, which seems to have been the principal manor, by marrying the heiress of Pigott; his grand-

[c] Esch. Edw. I.—Ed. IV.

son,

fon, Sir William, who twice ferved the office of fheriff of the counties of Bedford and Buckingham, was comptroller of the houfehold to Cardinal Wolfey. On each fide of the altar in Cardington church is a monument with an open arch, in the Gothic ftyle, but of no very ancient date. That on the fouth fide is in memory of one of the Gafcoignes, perhaps Sir William Gafcoigne, grandfather of John Gaf-coigne, the laft heir male of the family : the other is the monument of Sir Gerrard Hervey, of the Thurleigh family, who died in 1638. This Sir Gerrard, who was knighted by the Earl of Effex for his bravery at the fiege of Cadiz, he being the firft man who entered the town [d], poffeffed a temporary intereft in the manor of Carding-ton, of which in his epitaph he is called Lord, by marrying one of the co-heireffes of John Gafcoigne. The manor afterwards became the property of Sir George Blun-dell, who married the other co-heirefs. George Blundell efq. of Cardington manor, ferved the office of fheriff in 1731. The manor was purchafed of his reprefenta-tives by the late Mr. Whitbread, and is now the property of his fon Samuel Whitbread efq. M. P. who has the manor alfo of Cardington-Cotton-end, which, it is probable, belonged anciently to fome of the co-heirs of the Beauchamps : in the reign of Queen Elizabeth it was in the families of Tamworth and Colby. The late Mr. Whitbread purchafed it of the Rev. Mr. Bedford, who inherited under the will of his grandfather's widow.

The manor of *Fenlake* or *Fenlake-Barns* is alfo the property of Mr. Whitbread, who occafionally refides at the manor-houfe called the Barns.

In the parifh church of Cardington, is a tablet in memory of the celebrated John Howard, who fell a victim to his exertions in the caufe of philanthropy, being feized with the plague at Cherfon in Tartary, where he died January 21, 1794. He refided for fome years at Cardington, in a houfe near the church-yard, and in 1773 ferved the office of fheriff for the county. The late Samuel Whitbread efq. whofe name ftands high in the lift of thofe who have been diftinguifhed for works of benevolence and public utility, has a very fplendid monument to his memory in Cardington church. It was put up in 1799, being the laft work of the deceafed ftatuary Bacon, and efteemed one of his beft. The principal figure reprefents Mr. Whitbread as a dying man, fupported by religion, who points to the glories of heaven : benevolence is weeping at his feet. There are fome other monuments of the Whitbread family, who firft fettled at Cardington in 1650, and memorials of the Blundells of whom the late Mr. Whitbread purchafed the manor.

The great tithes of Cardington were appropriated to the priory of Newenham, and are now vefted in the mafter and fcholars of Trinity College in Cambridge,

[d] Bedfordfhire Pedigrees, Brit. Muf.

under whom Mr. Whitbread is leffee. The college prefents to the vicarage, which is in the deanery of Bedford. The parifh has been inclofed by an act of parliament paffed in 1802: the lands were not exonerated from tithes. The parifh was then computed to contain 3000 acres.

CARLTON, a village on the borders of Buckinghamfhire, about a mile from Harold, is in the hundred of Willey and deanery of Clopham. The manor belonged at an early period to the family of Pabenham [e], who had large poffeffions in this county. In the year 1313, John de Pabenham had a licence to impark his woods in this parifh and Harold, being within the King's foreft [f]. The manor was afterwards in the family of Vaux. On the attainder of William Lord Vaux, it was granted by King Edward IV. to Ralph Haftings [g], whofe daughter and heir married Sir John Dyve. It has been for a confiderable time in the family of Alfton, and is now the property of Thomas Alfton efq.

The following epitaph in the parifh church, records a very remarkable inftance of long incumbency. "To the memory of Mr. Thomas Wills, who lived parfon of Carlton and Chellington about threefcore and ten years. He died the fecond of Auguft 1642, aged above an hundred." The rectories of Carlton and Chillington, which were confolidated by act of parliament in 1769, are in the patronage of Lord Hampden.

CHALGRAVE, in the hundred of Manfhead and deanery of Dunftaple, is a village about a mile from Toddington. A manor in Chalgrave was held under the Beauchamps, in the 12th century, by the family of Loring [h]. Sir Nigel or Neale Loring, who was knighted by King Edward III. for his bravery in a fea-fight at Sluys in 1340, who attended that monarch in his glorious campaign in France, in the year 1359, and was one of the knights companions of the garter at the original inftitution of that order [i], retired to fpend his latter days at Chalgrave, where, in 1365, he had the royal licence to inclofe a park [k]. This Sir Neale Loring was founder of a chantry in Chalgrave church. Two ancient altar tombs (one on each fide the nave), with effigies in ftone of knights in armour with mail gorgets, have been fuppofed to belong to fome of this family; but it muft be obferved, that none of the fhields, of which there are feveral on the tombs, exhibit the arms of Loring. This manor was afterwards in the Broughtons, and paffed by heirs female to the Cheneys and Wentworths. It is now vefted in the truftees of their reprefentative, the late Rt. Hon. Thomas Conolly [l].

[e] Efch. H. III.—Edw. III.   [f] Pat. 6 Edw. II.   [g] Pat. 4 Edw. II.   [h] Chron. Dunft.
[i] Afhmole's Inftitution of the Garter.   [k] Cart. 39 & 40 Ed. III.
[l] See the defcent more particularly defcribed in Toddington.

The

The mercers' company have also a manor in this parish, and Richard Gilpin esq. of Hockliffe has the manor of *Wingfield* (a hamlet of Chalgrave), which has been a considerable time in his family.

The church was appropriated, in the 12th century, to the priory of Dunstaple, by Rose Loring, with consent of Simon de Beauchamp, the lord paramount [m]. The rectory now belongs to Trinity-Hall in Cambridge. Mr. Gilpin is patron of the vicarage. The parish has been inclosed by an act of parliament passed in 1797, when allotments of land were given in lieu of the rectorial and vicarial tithes. The number of acres in the parish was then estimated to be about 1780.

Tebworth, a considerable hamlet in this parish, had formerly a chapel endowed with 36 acres of land. The inhabitants in 1277 endeavoured, but without success, to oblige the prior and convent of Dunstaple, in whom the rectory and advowson of Chalgrave were then vested, and who were in possession of the lands which formed the endowment, to provide a chaplain to celebrate divine service in Tebworth chapel [n]. There have been no remains of this chapel within the memory of man.

CHICKSAND, an extraparochial place in the hundred of Clifton, about a mile from Shefford, was the site of a priory, founded about the year 1150, by Pain de Beauchamp and Roese his wife, relict of Geffrey de Mandeville, founder of Walden Abbey, for nuns and canons of the order of St. Gilbert of Sempringham [o]. So anxious was this good lady to promote the interests of her favourite convent, that when her son Geffrey de Mandeville, Earl of Essex, whose patronage and benefactions she had in vain endeavoured to induce him to transfer from his father's monastery of Walden to Chicksand, died at Chester, she being then residing at this convent with her nuns, sent an armed troop to intercept his corpse on its way to Walden for interment, and forcibly convey it to be buried at Chicksand, to which monastery she hoped his kindred would by that means be induced to become benefactors; but her intention being made known to the knights, who were to attend the body, they provided themselves with a sufficient guard, and with their swords drawn, conveyed it safe to Walden [p]. Simon de Beauchamp, son of Pain, gave the church of Chicksand to the nuns there, and John Blondel, in 1317, the manor [q]. The priory was dissolved in 1538, when its clear yearly value was estimated at 212l. 3s. 5½d. [r]. The site was granted in 1539 to R. Snow, of whose family it was purchased, about the year 1600 [s], by Sir John Osborn

---

[m] Chron. Dunst.   [n] Ibid.   [o] Tanner.   [p] Dugdale's Baronage.   [q] Tanner.   [r] Ibid.
[s] From the information of Sir George Osborn.

knt. Lord Treafurer's Remembrancer, whofe grandfon of the fame name was created a baronet in 1660.

Chickfand priory is now the property and feat of General Sir George Ofborn bart. It retains much of the monaftic appearance, and exhibits confiderable remains of the conventual buildings. The fouth and eaft fronts were either rebuilt or altered about the middle of the laft century by Ware the architeᶜt. Two fides of the cloifters are nearly entire. Sir George Ofborn has fitted up the windows with ancient ftained glafs, and has depofited, in the cloifters, various antiquities, which have no immediate conneᶜtion with the place, excepting two ancient tombs, dug up near the priory. In one of the walls is placed the tomb of an abbot of Pipwell, brought from the fite of that monaftery in Northamptonfhire. A part of the building, now ufed as a chapel, and fome adjoining offices, have ftone roofs, vaulted and groined. The quadrangle within the cloifters is 64 feet by 51 feet 6 inches.

Chickfand-houfe contains fome valuable portraits, particularly of the Ofborn family: the moft remarkable of which are thofe of Peter Ofborn, Privy Purfe to Edward VI. and one of the commiffioners for ecclefiaftical affairs in the reign of Queen Elizabeth; Sir Peter Ofborn, governor of Jerfey; Francis Ofborn, a younger fon of Sir John Ofborn knt. an ingenious and entertaining writer, author of Advice to a Son, and Effays on King James and King Charles; Col. Henry Ofborn, killed at the battle of Nafeby; and Henry Ofborn, a diftinguifhed naval officer, who died in 1771, vice-admiral of Great Britain. Among the portraits, not conneᶜted with the family are, Sir Philip Warwick and his lady; a fine whole length of Edward VI. by Holbein; and a very valuable portrait of Oliver Cromwell, by Sir Peter Lely. It is a fine piᶜture, and exhibits the ftrong features of his countenance, with all the roughneffes and warts, which, we are told, he charged the artift by no means to omit [1]. It was taken after he was Proteᶜtor, and is faid to have been a prefent to Sir John Danvers, one of the Judges of King Charles I, whofe daughter married Sir John Ofborn the firft baronet.

Sir George Ofborn has built a bed-chamber in imitation of the chapter-houfe at Peterborough. In this room is a ftate-bed which belonged to King James I. as appears from the initials I. A. with the crown. The traditionary account of it is, that it was the bed on which the Pretender was born, and that, upon that occafion, it became a perquifite of the chamberlain, by whom it was given to the Ofborn family.

CHILLINGTON, in the hundred of Willey and deanery of Clopham, is a fmall village fcarcely a mile from Harold. The manor was anciently parcel of the barony

[1] See Walpole's Anecdotes of Painting, Vol. iii. p. 17.

of Trally; and, for a great length of time, had the fame proprietors as Carlton. On the attainder of Lord Vaux, both thefe manors were granted to Ralph Haftings. The manor of Chillington has been for a confiderable time in the noble family of Trevor, and is now the property of Lord Vifcount Hampden. The church is fituated at a diftance from the village, on a hill which commands a fine view of Odell caftle, Harold, and the river Oufe. The rectories of Carlton and Chillington were confolidated in 1769. Lord Hampden is patron.

CLAPHAM, in the hundred of Stodden, gives name to the deanery[u] in which it is fituated. It is a fmall village, two miles from Bedford, on the road to Higham-Ferrers. The manor belonged fucceffively to the families of Spigurnell, Vaux, and Fitzjeffry[v]. In 1648 the manor-houfe, being then a feat of Sir Philip Warwick, was for feveral months the prifon of the learned and pious Dr. Hammond[w]. This manor is now the property of the Earl of Afhburnham, whofe great uncle, William Lord Afhburnham, became poffeffed of it by marriage with the daughter and heir of Thomas Taylor efq.[x] The manor-houfe has been improperly defcribed as a feat of the Earl of Afhburnham; it has been for many years a farm-houfe. Lord Afhburnham is patron of the vicarage, and impropriator of the great tithes which belonged to the priory of Caldwell. Clapham was formerly a chapelry of Oakly; and it is fingular, that although it has long been a diftinct parifh, the inhabitants ftill bury their dead there.

CLIFTON, about one mile and a half eaft of Shefford, gives name to the hundred in which it ftands. The manor, on the death of Sir Michael Fifher in 1549, without furviving male iffue, came to the St. Johns, by marriage with his daughter and heir[y]. It is now, by a late purchafe, the property of Simpfon Anderfon efq. In the north aifle of the parifh church is an altar-tomb, in memory of Sir Michael Fifher: the fides are richly ornamented with tabernacle work. Near it is the tomb of his fon, who died without iffue in his father's life-time. Mrs. Olivier, mother of the prefent incumbent, is patronefs of the rectory, which is in the deanery of Shefford.

CLOPHILL, in the hundred and deanery of Flitt, is a populous village, about three miles and a half weft of Shefford. The manor belonged to the Barons de Albini; whofe caftle, the feat of their barony, was at Cainhoe in this parifh[z]. It appears to have been a place of confiderable ftrength. The keep, which is ftill called the

[u] The ancient orthography (Clopham) is retained in the name of the deanery.
[v] Efch. Edw. II. Edw. III. and Edw. IV.   [w] Ant. Wood.   [x] Collins.
[y] Cole's Efcheats, Brit. Muf.   [z] Dugdale's Baronage.

Caftlehill,

Castlehill, is lofty, and overgrown with coppice-wood. After the extinction of the family of Albini, it is probable that the manor of Clophill, or Cainhoe, was sold by the co-heirs. It passed through the families of Lacy, Nowers, and Norton[a]: after which it came to the Greys, earls of Kent; and is now the property of their representative the Right Honourable Lady Lucas.

Robert de Albini, founder of the priory of Beaulieu, in Hertfordshire, gave an estate in the parish of Clophill, or Cainhoe, to the monks there[b]. His charter mentions a monastery at Clophill[c], of which nothing farther is known. It is probable that it was a cell to St. Alban's, and was of short duration. After the reformation, Sir Michael Fisher became possessed of the estate which had belonged to the monks of Beaulieu, and had acquired the name of the manor of Clophill-Hall. His grand-daughter and heir married the first Lord St. John of Bletsoe[d]. This estate has been held for a considerable time with the principal manor of Clophill, and is now the property of Lady Lucas.

The manor of *Beadlow*, partly in this parish, was for many years in the Charnock family; and is now vested in their representatives the Herveys.

The parish church stands on a hill, at a considerable distance from any part of the village. The great tithes of this parish were appropriated to the abbey of St. Alban's[e] about the year 1097[f]. They are now annexed to the vicarage by the benefaction of one of the earls of Kent. Lady Lucas has the patronage.

COLMWORTH, a village in the hundred of Barford and deanery of Eaton, is about eight miles N. E. of Bedford. The monastery of St. Neot's had considerable estates in this parish, which were granted in 1542 to Sir Richard Williams, *alias* Cromwell. Sir Edward Montagu, Lord Chief Justice of the Common Pleas, died seised of the manor of Colmworth in 1557[g]. It had been for many years in the family of Ray previously to 1797, when it was purchased by the present proprietor the Reverend Leonard Towne.

The parish church is a handsome Gothic structure, with a lofty spire, which is a conspicuous object for several miles round. In this church is the tomb of Eleanor wife of Sir Gerard Braybroke, daughter and heir of Aylmer Lord St. Amand, who had large possessions in this county in the fourteenth century; and a very sumptuous monument, erected in 1641 by Lady Dyer, in memory of her deceased husband Sir William Dyer knt. The inscription quaintly informs us, that " they multiplied

---

[a] Esch. Edw. I. Edw. II. and Edw. III. [b] Dugdale's Monasticon. [c] The words of the charter are, " Nec non mansio quædam de dominio domini juxta monasterium de Clophelle quam monachi sibi-ipsis ædificent." [d] Cole's Escheats, Brit. Mus. [e] The *Liber Regis* erroneously says to Chicksand. [f] Lives of the Abbots of St. Alban's. [g] Cole's Escheats.

themselves

themfelves into feven children," one of whom was Sir **Ludowick Dyer**, created a baronet in 1626. The following is a fpecimen of the poetry:

" My deareft duft, could not thy hafty day
Afford thy drowfy patience leave to ftay
One hour longer, fo that we might either
Have fat up, or gone to-bed together:
But fince thy finifh'd labour hath poffefs'd
Thy weary limbs with early reft,
Enjoy it fweetly, and thy widowe bride
Shall foon repofe her by thy flumbering fide;
Whofe bufinefs now is only to prepare
My nightly drefs, and call to prayer.
Mine eyes wax heavy, and the day grows old,
The dew falls thick, my blood grows cold:
Draw, draw the clofed curtains, and make room,
My dear, my deareft duft, I come, I come."

John Hele efq. is patron of the rectory of Colmworth, having purchafed the advow-fon of the Hillerfdons of Elftow.

COPLE, in the hundred of Wixamtree, is a fmall village about four miles and a half from Bedford. The Duke of Bedford has the manor of Cople, together with the manors of Woodend, Wiggen, Rolands, and Howcots, all in this parifh. They were purchafed in 1774, of the Duke of Marlborough, by John, Duke of Bedford. Cople had been fucceffively in the Beauchamps, Mowbrays, and Goftwicks[h]; Woodend for many years in the Lukes; Rolands belonged anciently to a family of that name: it had been in the Spencer family before 1642[i].

In the parifh church are tombs with brafs figures of the families of Launcelyn, Ro-land, and Gray. The Launcelyns were benefactors towards the building of the church, as appears by their arms cut in ftone on one of the pillars. In the chancel are two altar tombs, with effigies in brafs, in memory of Sir Walter Luke, juftice of the common pleas, who died in 1544; and Nicholas Luke, baron of the exchequer, who died in 1563. Sir Walter's Lady was Anne Launcelyn, nurfe to King Henry VIII.[k] The Lukes refided at Woodend in this parifh, by moft writers miftaken for a place of the fame name near Toddington. Sir Oliver Luke of Woodend and his fon Sir Samuel were both in the fervice of the parliament during the civil wars; the latter was fcout-mafter for Bedfordfhire and fome adjoining counties[l]. His name has attained much celebrity, as the fuppofed original of Butler's Hudibras. It is certain that the poet lived fome time in his houfe, acting in the capacity of his

[h] Cole's Efcheats, Brit. Muf.   [i] Ibid.   [k] Bedfordfhire Pedigrees, Brit. Muf.
[l] Myfteries of the Good Old Caufe.

clerk;

clerk; and it is obfervable, that in his poem of Dunftaple Downs, he exprefsly calls Sir Samuel Luke, Sir Hudibras [m]. Sir Samuel was buried at Cople, in 1670. His defcendants continued at Woodend, now a farm-houfe, till the death of George Luke, the laft of the family, in 1732.

The great tithes of Cople were given to the priory of Chickfand, by Simon de Beauchamp [n]; the impropriate rectory and the advowfon of the vicarage, which is in the deanery of Bedford, are now vefted in Chrift-church college, Oxford. The Duke of Bedford is leffee of the rectory.

CRANFIELD, in the hundred of Redbornftoke and deanery of Flitt, is a village on the borders of Buckinghamfhire, about nine miles fouth-weft of Bedford. The manor was given to the monks of Ramfey by Ailwin Niger, who died in 998 [o]. It was granted in 1621 to Sir Lionel Cranfield, who was the fame year created a baron, taking his title from this place. In 1672, it became the property of the Monoux family; and in 1729, was purchafed of them by Wriothefley, Duke of Bedford, from whom it defcended to the prefent Duke. The manor of Wafhingleys in this parifh was in the Leighs of Stoneleigh, from whom it paffed, by purchafe, to the family of Field, and from them, by female heirs, to the Bakers and Colemans, of whom it was inherited by the prefent proprietor, Mr. Theed Pearfe of Bedford. There was anciently a gild or brotherhood in the church of Cranfield, and lands given for a *drinking*, and for the maintenance of a lamp. The Rev. George Davies, the prefent incumbent, is patron of the rectory.

DEAN is a fmall village in the hundred of Stodden and deanery of Eaton, fituated in the north part of the county, on the borders of Northamptonfhire and Huntingdonfhire, about four miles from Kimbolton. The manor of Over or Upper Dean, a hamlet in this parifh, was in the Cheney family for feveral generations [p]. The priory of Huntingdon had another manor, which perhaps was that of Lower or Nether Dean. They are now both the property of Lord St. John, and have been a confiderable time in his family. In the church is an altar-tomb with the effigies in brafs, in very fair prefervation, of Sir Thomas Barker, prebendary of the the collegiate church of St. Mary in Shrewfbury, and rector of Dean, who died in 1501. The church of Dean was given by Alice de Clermont, countefs of Pembroke, to the knights hofpitallers [q], who were patrons of the rectory till the reformation. King Henry VIII. gave the rectory of Dean to the church of Wor-

[m] See the fubject difcuffed in Biograph. Brit. new edit. Vol. iii. p. 86, 87. in the notes.
[n] Dugdale's Baronage.   [o] Dugdale's Monafticon.
[p] See Nom. Villarum, No. 1316. in Brit. Muf. No. 6281. and Efch; Hen. VI.
[q] Dugdale's Monafticon.

cefter

ceſter, in 1547, ſince which time the great tithes have been veſted in the dean and chapter, who appoint a curate. Sir John Smith bart. of Sidling in Dorſetſhire is leſſee under the impropriators. Over and Nether-Dean have been incloſed, by an act of parliament, paſſed in 1800, when an allotment of land was aſſigned to the impropriators in lieu of tithes.

Dean is ſaid to have been the birth-place of Francis Dillingham, one of the tranſlators of the Bible: the family of Dillingham appears to have been very numerous in this pariſh, but no record of his birth appears in the regiſter.

DUNSTAPLE, in the hundred of Manſhead and in the deanery to which it gives name, is a market town on the great road to Cheſter and Holyhead, 33 miles from London. Its origin is attributed to the provident care of king Henry I. who, finding that this neighbourhood, through which a much frequented road towards the north paſſed, was much infeſted by robbers, ordered the woods to be cut down and grubbed up, and having built a royal manſion for his own reſidence, called Kingſ-bury, encouraged ſome of his ſubjects to ſettle near him, by granting them lands at a ſmall rent, a market, and various liberties and privileges[r]. The monkiſh legends add, that the town took its name from Dun or Dunning, the chief of the rob-bers. Modern etymologiſts have ſuppoſed with greater probability, that it was called Dunſtaple from its market or ſtaple on the downs. *Duna* or *Dunum* in bar-barous Latin, is a hill or down, and frequently occurs in the chronicle of Dunſtaple, in the deſcription of lands in this neighbourhood, as either *infra* or *ſuper Dunam.*

The king kept the new town in his own hands till about the year 1131, when he beſtowed it, with all its rights and privileges, on a priory of Black Canons, which he had founded near the manſion, where he occaſionally reſided, and where, in 1123, he had kept his Chriſtmas with great ſplendour, receiving an embaſſy from the earl of Anjou[s]. This palace he reſerved in his own hands, becauſe, as yet, there were no apartments in the convent fit for his reception[t]. The king kept his Chriſtmas at Dunſtaple again in 1132[u], as did his ſucceſſor king Stephen in 1137[w]. In 1154, the war being terminated, a friendly meeting took place at Dunſtaple, between Stephen and Henry duke of Normandy, who ſucceeded him on the throne[x]. In 1204, king John gave his palace and gardens, on the ſite of which is now a farm-houſe on the road to Luton, near Mrs. Marſh's hoſpital, to the prior and convent[y], who, upon occaſion of all future royal viſits, accommo-dated the monarch and his ſuite within their own walls[z]. In 1213, the town was deſtroyed by fire. In 1214, a great ſynod was held at the priory[a]. In 1215,

---

[r] Dugdale's Monaſticon.   [s] Sax. Chron.   [t] Dugdale's Monaſticon.   [u] Holinſhed.
[w] J. Bromton inter Decem Scriptores, vol. i. 1343.   [x] Holinſhed.
[y] Dugdale's Monaſticon, vol. ii.   [z] Chron. Dunſt.   [a] Ibid.

king John lay at Dunſtaple, on his journey towards the north[a]. In 1217, Lewis the Dauphin, with the Engliſh barons, who were in arms againſt the king, halted for a night in this town [b]. In 1244, a great number of difcontented barons and knights aſſembled at Dunſtaple, and Luton, under pretence of holding a tournament, although their meeting was in reality for political purpoſes. The tournament was prohibited by the royal mandate, to which they yielded obedience, but gave a convincing proof of their formidable power, by ſending Sir Fulk Fitzwarren to the pope's nuncio, whoſe proceedings had given great umbrage to the Engliſh, with a peremptory order, in the name of the barons and knights, aſſembled at Dunſtaple and Luton, that he ſhould inſtantly quit the kingdom ; an order which the nuncio, finding the king's authority inſufficient to protect him, was obliged to obey [c]. It appears by the chronicle of Dunſtaple, that king Henry III. frequently honoured the convent with his preſence. In 1247, he was there with his queen, prince Edward and the princeſs Margaret ; on which occaſion the prior preſented their majeſties with a gilt cup, and the prince and princeſs with a gold buckle each. In 1265, the king and queen, with cardinal Ottoboni the pope's legate, and Simon Montford, earl of Leiceſter, made ſome ſtay at Dunſtaple. In 1276, ſome of the king's falconers, who were lodged in the priory, having had an affray with the chaplains and the prior's ſervants, the king came in perſon to try the matter, and ſummoned a jury of 36 men, out of two hundreds, unconnected with the convent or the town. It appeared, that the falconers had begun the affray, and killed one of the chaplains. When the corpſe of queen Eleanor was depoſited one night at the priory of Dunſtaple, in 1290, two bawdekyns or precious cloths were given to the convent, and 120 pounds weight of wax. As it paſſed through the town, the bier ſtopped in the middle of the market-place whilſt the chancellor and nobility marked out a proper ſpot for the erection of a croſs, the prior aſſiſting at the ceremony, and ſprinkling the ground with holy-water. This croſs was demoliſhed during the civil wars, probably by the ſoldiers of the earl of Eſſex, who appear to have been quartered at Dunſtaple in 1643 [d]. In 1341, king Edward III. with his queen were preſent at a grand tournament held at Dunſtaple [e]. No mention has been found of any other royal viſits to this town, excepting that king Henry VI. was there in 1457 [f], and queen Elizabeth, on her progreſs in 1572 [g].

The priors of Dunſtaple enjoyed very extenſive liberties and privileges. They had the power of life and death, and ſat with the king's juſtices itinerant, who, on their circuit, always came to Dunſtaple for the purpoſe of trying ſuch offences as had been committed within the juriſdiction of the town. They had more than one

---

[a] Holinſhed. [b] M. Paris. [c] Holinſhed. [d] Pariſh Regiſter. [e] Holinſhed. [f] Ibid.
[g] Queen Elizabeth's Progreſſes.

gaol, for it appears by the chronicle of the priory, that their *principal* gaol was rebuilt in 1295; and they had a gallows at a place without the town, called Edefcote. During the infurrections, in the reign of Richard II. in 1371, the townfmen exacted of the prior a charter of liberties, but it was cancelled afterwards, as having been extorted by force[h].

The revenues of the priory, at its diffolution, were eftimated at 344l. 13s. 3d. clear yearly value. The laft prior was Gervafe Markham, who took an active part in the proceedings relative to the divorce between king Henry VIII. and Catharine of Arragon, his queen. The commiffioners fat at Dunftaple priory, and the fentence of divorce was pronounced by archbifhop Cranmer, on the 23d of May 1533, in the chapel of our lady there[i]. Prior Markham, after the diffolution of his convent, had a penfion of 60l. *per annum.* He died in the month of September 1561, and was buried at Dunftaple, as appears by the parifh regifter. The fite of the priory, which was granted in 1554 to Dr. Leonard Chamberlayne, is now the property and refidence of Col. Maddifon. The only remains of the conventual buildings (excepting what is now the parifh church), are fome rooms with vaulted and groined ftone roofs; one of them has been converted into a parlour.

The prefent parifh church, which contains only the nave of the conventual church, exhibits various ftyles of architecture. The infide is chiefly Norman, and undoubtedly part of the original ftructure. The ftone gallery at the weft end, now hid by the organ-loft, has pointed arches; the windows are of a much later date. The weft front is very richly decorated with niches of the early Gothic architecture. The great weftern door has a fine femicircular arch, which has been very richly ornamented with foliage, grotefque heads, &c. neatly cut in Toternhoe ftone, now much mutilated. It is faid that king Henry VIII. intended to eftablifh a cathedral at Dunftaple, of which Dr. Day was to be the firft bifhop; and that when the defign was laid afide, a great part of the conventual church was pulled down[k].

In the parifh church of Dunftaple are feveral memorials of the families of Dickenfon, Aynfcombe, Marfh, and Chew, great benefactors to the town. The ftory of an epitaph on a woman who had 19 children at five births, has been fufficiently exploded; it arofe from a mifconftruction of the quaint manner in which the number 19 was expreffed in Latin verfe[l]. The brafs plate on which this epitaph was infcribed has been removed; it has been frequently printed.

Over the altar is a large painting of the Lord's fupper by Sir James Thornhill, given to the parifh by Mrs. Cart and Mrs. Afhton in 1720. In the church of Dun-

---

[h] Chron. Dunft.   [i] Strype's Memorials of archbifhop Cranmer, and Herbert's Life of Hen. VIII.

[k] Willis's Mitred Abbies.

[l] " Ter tres, bis quinos hæc natos fertur habere
    Per fponfos binos."

ftaple

ſtaple was a fraternity of St. John the Baptiſt. A very richly embroidered altar-cloth, with portraits of the family of Fayrey, and a figure of St. John the Baptiſt, ſaid to have been given to this fraternity by Henry Fayrey, who died in 1516, is in the poſſeſſion of John Miller eſq. of Bedford. It was ſome years ago occaſionally uſed as a funeral pall at Dunſtaple, by the permiſſion of Mr. Miller's family, who then reſided there. The brotherhood-houſe belonged to the Wingate family in 1642[m].

The friars preachers, or black friars, eſtabliſhed a convent of their order at Dun-ſtaple in 1259, ſorely againſt the will of the prior and canons[n]; but the friars being patronized by the court, it was in vain for them to reſiſt. In a few years they were ſo far reconciled to their new neighbours, that the prior condeſcended to become their gueſt[o]. The yearly revenue of the friars, when their convent was ſuppreſſed, amounted only to 4l. 18s. 4d. The ſite was granted to Sir William Herbert; it is ſuppoſed to have been in a field of Mrs. Foſſey's near her houſe, which is ſituated weſt of the pond, in the South-ſtreet of Dunſtaple.

There was alſo at this place a houſe or hoſpital for lepers, belonging to the prior and canons of Dunſtaple, who appointed the warden. It exiſted as early as the beginning of the thirteenth century[p].

King Henry I. is ſaid to have founded ſchools at Dunſtaple. It appears by the chronicle of the convent, that in 1224, diſputes ran ſo high between the ſcholars and the townſmen, that many were wounded on both ſides, and ſome mortally[q].

The manor of Dunſtaple, which was given by king Henry I. to the prior and convent, was, after the reformation, annexed to the honour of Ampthill, and is now held, on leaſe under the crown, as parcel of that honour, by the Duke of Bedford.

The charter of king Henry I. granted two markets to this town, and a fair, at the feſtival of St. Peter, to whom the convent was dedicated. The markets were held on Sundays[r] and Wedneſdays. King John granted another fair at the feſtival of St. Fremund. The chronicle of the priory mentions a great loſs which the market at Dunſtaple ſuſtained in 1294, by the long ſtay of prince Edward at Langley, his kitchen conſuming more than 200 meſſes a-day, and his ſervants taking up all the cheeſe, eggs, and other commodities which they could find in the market, and even from the tradeſmen's houſes, and paying for nothing. There is now only one market held on Wedneſdays, and four fairs, Aſh Wedneſday, May 22, Auguſt 12, and November 12; all fairs of buſineſs, chiefly for the ſale of horſes, cows, and ſheep. The number of houſes in the pariſh, according to the returns made under the Population Act, in 1801, was 243, that of inhabitants 1296.

[m] Cole's Eſcheats, Brit. Muſ.   [n] Chron. Dunſt.   [o] Ibid.   [p] Ibid.   [q] Ibid.
[r] It was not unuſual in ancient times to hold markets and fairs on Sundays and other great feſtivals. See the account of Thatcham and Wallingford in Berkſhire.

Dunſtaple had ſummons to ſend members to parliament in the reign of Henry II.[s] The town, which is governed by four conſtables, retains but few of the privileges which the townſmen formerly enjoyed under the charter of king Henry I. The aſſizes for the county were held at Dunſtaple in 1607[t]. The frequent communication between this town and London, occaſioned the plague to be very fatal here in 1603 and 1625; the regiſter of burials for the year 1665 is imperfect.

Edward VI. in 1552, granted the rectory and advowſon of Dunſtaple to the dean and canons of Windſor[u]. It is probable that the grant was reſumed, the rectory being now in the patronage of the crown.

Mrs. Frances Aſhton, Mrs. Jane Cart, and Mr. Thomas Aynſcombe, in purſuance of the intention of their relation, Mr. William Chew, who died in 1712, built and endowed a charity-ſchool in this town. By two indentures, bearing date 1724 and 1727, the ſchool is endowed with lands in Caddington, Luton, Houghton-Regis, Flamſted, Toternhoe, and Whipſnade. The maſter has a ſalary of 40l. *per annum* for teaching forty boys; and 37l. *per annum* is allowed for their clothing. The management of the charity is veſted in ſeven truſtees. If a ſufficient number of boys for the object of this charity ſhould not be found at Dunſtaple, they may be filled up from the pariſhes of Caddington, Kenſworth, Edleſborough, Houghton-Regis, or Luton. In conſequence of the increaſed rents of the eſtates, forty boys and fifteen girls are now clothed, educated, and apprenticed, by this charity.

Mrs. Cart and Mrs. Aſhton each founded an alms-houſe for ſix poor widows. Mrs. Aſhton, by her will bearing date 1727, left lands for the purpoſe of paying 6l. *per annum* each to the poor women in her alms-houſe, to buy them a gown, firing, and other neceſſaries. The remainder, after deducting for repairs, and paying ſome ſpecific charitable bequeſts, to be divided, in equal portions, between the ſix poor women.

Mrs. Blandina Marſh, in 1713, built neat houſes for the reſidence of ſix decayed maiden gentlewomen, which, by her benefaction, and that of another lady, are endowed with an income of about 180l. *per annum* for their ſupport.

Elkanah Settle, a well-known dramatiſt and political writer in the reign of Charles the Second, was born at Dunſtaple on the firſt of February 1647-8[w]. He was the antagoniſt of Dryden; and during the biaſs of party prejudice, there were not wanting thoſe who preferred his compoſitions to thoſe of his rival.

It may, perhaps, be thought worthy of remark, that the firſt attempt at theatrical repreſentation in this kingdom is ſuppoſed to have been at Dunſtaple, where the

---

[s] Willis's Notit. Parliament. [t] Note in the Regiſter at Houghton Conqueſt, by Mr. Archer.
[u] Tanner. [w] Pariſh Regiſter.

play

play of the miracles of St. Catherine was performed under the direction of Geoffrey, a fecular prieft, afterwards abbot of St. Alban's[x].

DUNTON, a village in the hundred of Bigglefwade and deanery of Shefford, is fituated about four miles eaft of Bigglefwade, on the borders of Hertfordfhire. The manor of Dunton, which had belonged to the Chamberleynes, and the manor of Joyes in Dunton, were granted, in 1475, to Lord Grey of Ruthin[y]. They are now, by the name of the manors of Goyes or Joyes, and Chamberleynefbury, the property of Earl Spencer, and have been a confiderable time in his family. King Edward the Confeffor gave the monks of Waltham a manor in Milnho (now called Millow or Milhow) a hamlet of this parifh[z]. Another manor, which at the time of the Norman Survey was part of the extenfive property of Walter Giffard, was, in later times, in the Enderbys, Goftwicks, and Powleys[a]. This manor has been nearly two centuries in the Spencer family, and is now the property of Earl Spencer, who has alfo the impropriate rectory of this parifh which belonged formerly to the priory of Holiwell, and is patron of the vicarage. The parifh of Dunton has been inclofed under an act of parliament paffed in 1797, when the number of acres in the parifh was eftimated at 2200.

EATON-BRAY, in the hundred of Manfhead, is a village about four miles from Dunftaple. The manor of Eaton was given by king John to Ardulfus de Braci[b]. Not long afterwards it was in the Cantilupes, barons of Bergavenny, who built a caftle there in 1221, which the chronicle of Dunftaple reprefents as very injurious to that town. It paffed in 1273, by a female heir, to the family of Zouche[c]. Katherine, relict of William Lord Zouche, died feifed of it in 1471[d]. It is fuppofed to have been forfeited by attainder, and to have been granted to Sir Reginald Bray in 1513, when he obtained a grant of the neighbouring parifh of Toternhoe, which had been alfo in the families of Cantilupe and Zouche.

The family of Bray were of confequence in the county at an early period. Thomas de Bray was knight of the fhire in 1289, and Roger de Bray in 1312. When they fettled at Eaton-Bray, to which they gave their name, does not appear; but it was long before they were poffeffed of the manor. Edmund Bray, grandfather of Sir Reginald, the faithful minifter of king Henry VII. was defcribed as of this place[e]; and it appears on record, that the parifh was called Eaton-Bray in the reign of Edward III[f]. It is probable that the Brays held the manor under the Barons Cantilupe and Zouche. Sir Edmund Bray, nephew of Sir Reginald, was fummoned to parliament in 1530

[x] See Bibliotheca Top. Brit. Bedfordfhire, p. 237, where is a reference to Warton's Hiftory of Englifh Poetry, vol. i. p. 236.

[y] Pat 14. Edw. IV.   [z] Dugdale's Monafticon.   [a] Efch. Hen. VII.—Hen. VIII.—Eliz. and Car. I.   [b] Regifter of the Priory of Dunftaple in the Britifh Mufeum.   [c] Chron. Dunft.

[d] Efch. 11 Edw. IV.   [e] Biograph. Brit.   [f] Inq. ad q. dam. See alfo Harleian MSS. 5193. fol. 75.

as baron of Eaton-Bray. The title became extinct by the death of his son John Lord Bray without issue in 1557. The manor of Eaton-Bray passed to the posterity of William Lord Sandys, who married the only child of John Bray, uncle of the first Lord Bray; and from them, by marriage, to the family of Sandys of Latimers, in Buckinghamshire. Sir Edwin Sandys of Eaton-Bray died in 1608 [g]. The manor was purchased of his representatives in 1623 by the Huxleys of Wyer-Hall in Middlesex [h]. It has since been in the family of Potter. In 1763 it was purchased of Thomas Potter esq. by William Beckford esq. alderman of London, and is now the property of his son. There are no remains of the castle, nor of the mansion of the Lords Bray. A house, which was built on the site about a century ago, has recently been pulled down.

In the chancel of the parish church is the monument of Jane, wife of Edmund Lord Bray, who died in 1558. In the south aisle is a fragment of stone-work, richly carved and ornamented with the royal arms, and the arms and device of Sir Reginald Bray. The great tithes of Eaton-Bray, which were formerly appropriated to the priory of Merton in Surrey, now belong, together with the advowson of the vicarage, to Trinity College in Cambridge. Eaton-Bray is in the deanery of Dunstaple.

EATON-SOCON, a village in the hundred of Barford, is a great thoroughfare on the north road, 55 miles from London. It gives name to a deanery. At this place was a castle, the seat of a branch of the Beauchamp family, who were barons of the realm from the reign of Henry II. to the year 1292, when Ralph de Beauchamp died seised of the manor of Eaton, held by baronial service [i]. He left issue; but as his posterity were not summoned to parliament, Dugdale discontinues the history of the family after his death. It is probable that the manor of Eaton passed by female heirs to the family of Vaux. Leland speaks of the ruins of Eaton castle as belonging, in his time, to the Lord Vaux, whose descendant, Edward Lord Vaux, sold it in 1624 to Rowland Squire: from his family, in 1689, it passed to the Ashlys; and from them, in 1708, to the ancestors of the duke of Bedford [k], who is the present proprietor. Another manor, belonging also to the duke of Bedford, was granted in 1563, to Thomas Beverley, being described as late parcel of the possessions of the dissolved monastery of St. John of Jerusalem [l]. In 1629 it passed from Sir Henry Moore to the family of Gery of Bushmead, and in 1640 from them to the Squires; since which time it has been held with the principal manor of Eaton.

[g] MS. Diary of Thomas Archer, rector of Houghton Conquest. [h] Papers communicated by William Bray esq. [i] Esch. 21 Edw. I. [k] Duke of Bedford's Papers. [l] Ibid.

The

The manor of Eaton, or Goldingtons in Eaton, was part of the eftate of Sir Michael Fifher, who died in 1549, and paffed by marriage to the St. Johns. It is probable that this is the fame eftate which (being then called the manor of Eaton or Eyton) was in the Gery family as early as the year 1635, and was fold by them, in 1649, to Robert Dobbs. It has been fince in the families of Kent, Brewer, Sibley, and Waller; and was purchafed in 1782 of Mr. Jofeph Green by the prefent proprietor John Brickwood efq.

The manor of *Wyboldfton* or *Wybofton* in this parifh, was, in the 13th century, in the family of Bathonian [n]; afterwards, for feveral generations, in that of Greyftock. This manor is now the property of Thomas Whetham efq. in whofe family it has been, together with thofe of Honeyden and Begry, for many years.

The priory of Bifmede or Bufhmead, in this parifh, was founded in the reign of Henry II. by Oliver Beauchamp and his fon Hugh. It was inhabited by Auftin canons, and dedicated to the Virgin Mary. Its revenues, at the diffolution of monafteries, were eftimated at 71l. 13s. 9½d. clear yearly value [o]. The fite was granted in 1537 to Sir William Gafcoigne, Comptroller of the Houfehold to Cardinal Wolfey. Sir John Gafcoigne in 1545 conveyed it to Anthony Cocket; from whom, in 1552, it paffed to William Gery efq. [p] anceftor of the late William Gery efq. of Kimbolton. Bufhmead is now the property and feat of his fon-in-law the Rev. Hugh Wade Gery, who has a cartulary of the priory very fairly written on vellum; and Buck's drawing of the conventual buildings, no part of which now remains, excepting the refectory, converted into a ftable and offices.

Baffmead, in this parifh, was, in the reign of Henry VIII. the feat of Sir Thomas Wauton [q]. A branch of the family of Aftrey afterwards fettled themfelves there. After the death of the late Sir John Danvers, whofe anceftors had poffeffed it for feveral generations, it was put up to fale, and is now the property of Thomas Smith efq.

The windows of the parifh church at Eaton were ornamented with ftained glafs, of which there are confiderable remains in the north aifle, reprefenting fubjects from the legends of St. Nicholas and St. Etheldreda. Among the ancient difburfements of the church, as ftated in Bacon's *Liber Regis*, was 5s. *per annum* for ftraw. The duke of Bedford is patron of the vicarage, and proprietor of the rectory which formerly belonged to the knights of St. John of Jerufalem. The parifh was inclofed by an act of parliament paffed in 1795, when an allotment of land was given to the impropriator in lieu of tithes, and a fmall allotment, with a corn-rent, to the vicar.

[n] Efch. Hen. III.   [o] Tanner.   [p] Papers in the poffeffion of Mr. Wade Gery.
[q] Bedfordfhire Pedigrees Brit. Muf.

EDWORTH,

EDWORTH, a small village on the borders of Hertfordshire, about six miles from Shefford and five from Baldock, is in the hundred of Bigglefwade. The manor was part of the estate of Walter de Langton, prime minister to king Edward I [r]. It had been before in the Seymours [s], and was afterwards successively in the families of Peverell, Lisle, Talbot, Zouche, Enderby, and Powley [t]. It is now the property of William Hale esq. of King's Walden in Hertfordshire, in whose family it has been for many years. Mr. Hale is also patron of the rectory, which is in the deanery of Shefford. The advowson formerly belonged to the priory of St. Neot's [u].

ELSTOW, a considerable village about a mile and a half from Bedford, is in the hundred of Redbornstoke. It has fairs on the 15th and 16th of May; and on the 5th and 6th of November.

Judith Countess of Huntingdon founded an abbey here, in the reign of William the Conqueror, for Benedictine nuns, which was dedicated to the Holy Trinity, St. Mary, and St. Helen. Its revenues, when dissolved, were estimated at 284l. 12s. 11¾d. clear yearly value [w]. The site was granted in 1553 to Sir Humphrey Ratcliffe, a younger brother of the Earl of Suffex, who resided in the abbey house, and died in 1566, as appears by his monument over the altar in Elstow church. In the reign of Charles the First [x], and perhaps at an earlier period, it belonged to the family of Hillersdon, who built a large mansion adjoining to the church, now in ruins, the greater part of it having been pulled down a few years ago. The site of the abbey, and the manor, which belonged also to the convent, are now the property of Samuel Whitbread esq. M.P. whose father purchased it, in 1792, of the daughters of the late Mr. Hillersdon.

There are very few remains of the conventual buildings excepting the church (now the parish church), which retains considerable traces of the original structure. The north door is of Norman architecture; some of the columns are square and very massy, and most of the arches circular. At the south-west corner of the church is a small building with a vaulted roof, supported in the centre by an octagonal fluted column, probably a vestibule. In the south aisle of the chancel is the tomb, with her effigies in brass, of Elizabeth Hervey, the last abbess of Elstow, placed there in her life-time, with blank spaces for the dates. As she survived the dissolution of the abbey, it is probable that her body never reached its intended place of sepulture. Some of the nuns, who died after the reformation, were buried in St. Mary's church at Bedford. In the church at Elstow are several memorials of the families of Crompton, Lovett, and Hillersdon.

[r] Esch. Edw. I.   [s] Ibid.   [t] Esch. and Cl. Rot. Edw. III.—Eliz.
[u] Placit. &c. de terris in Com. Bedf. in Turr. Lond.   [w] Tanner.   [x] Cole's Escheats, Brit. Muf.

The great tithes of Elſtow were appropriated to the abbey; they are now the property of Mr. Whitbread. He is alſo patron of the vicarage, which is in the deanery of Bedford. The pariſh has been incloſed by an act of parliament which paſſed in 1797, when an allotment of lands was made in lieu of the rectorial tithes. The number of acres in the pariſh was then eſtimated at 1060.

John Bunyan, author of the celebrated theological romance called the Pilgrim's Progreſs, was born at Elſtow in 1628, of mean parentage.

EVERSHOLT, a village in the hundred of Manſhead and deanery of Flitt, lies about two miles and a half eaſt of Woburn. The manor, which had belonged to the monaſtery, was, after the reformation, annexed to the honour of Ampthill. In 1601 it was granted to Henry Aſtrey, who, the ſame year, conveyed it to the Hillerſdons. In 1702, it was purchaſed of that family by Wriotheſly Duke of Bedford [y], from whom it has deſcended to the preſent duke. The manor of Wakes in this pariſh, now the Duke of Bedford's, was purchaſed with Everſholt in 1702. In 1504 it was the property of Giles Lord Daubeny. In 1531 it paſſed to the family of Hinton; and in 1604 from them to the Hillerſdons [z]. The manor of Kingſhoe or Kinſes, in this pariſh, is alſo the Duke of Bedford's. It was purchaſed by the late duke. The advowſon of the rectory, which belonged formerly to the priory of St. John of Jeruſalem [a], has been many years in the noble family of Sandys. The reverſion, with other large eſtates of the late Lord Sandys, is veſted, after the death of his Lady, in the ſecond ſon of the late Marquis of Downſhire.

EVERTON.—This pariſh is partly in Bedfordſhire, partly in Cambridgeſhire, and partly in Huntingdonſhire. As the church ſtands in Cambridgeſhire, it will be treated of under that county.

EYWORTH, in the hundred of Biggleſwade and deanery of Shefford, lies on the borders of Cambridgeſhire, about three miles from Potton and five from Biggleſwade. The manor belonged, at an early period, to the Leybourns [b]. It was afterwards in the families of Charlton and Francis [c]. In the reign of Queen Elizabeth, Eyworth was the property and ſeat of Sir Edmund Anderſon, Lord Chief Juſtice of the Common Pleas; a man of conſiderable eminence in his profeſſion, and one of the judges who ſat at the trial of Mary Queen of Scots. His great-grandſon Stephen was created a baronet in 1664; their poſterity continued at Eyworth till the death of Sir Stephen Anderſon bart. in 1773, when the title became extinct. The manor is

[y] Duke of Bedford's Records.   [z] Ibid.   [a] Placit. &c. de terris in Com. Bedford. in Turr. London.   [b] Eſch. Edw. I.—Edw. III.   [c] Eſch. Hen. V. &c.

now

now the property of the Right Hon. Lord Yarborough, whofe family name was Anderfon [d], being lineally defcended from Stephen Anderfon, a grandfon of the chief juftice.

In the church are feveral monuments of the Anderfons. That of the Chief Juftice, on the fouth fide of the chancel, has the effigies of himfelf and his lady, under a richly-ornamented arch. He is reprefented in his robes and cap, with a collar of S.S.; the face bears a ftrong refemblance to his portrait, as engraved by Faithorne. On the oppofite fide of the chancel is the monument of Sir Francis Anderfon, eldeft fon of the Chief Juftice, whofe effigies in gilt armour is reprefented between thofe of his two wives, kneeling and fronting the chancel. On the fouth fide of the chancel is the monument of Edmund Anderfon efq. of Stratton, eldeft fon of Sir Francis, who died in 1638. It has half-length figures of himfelf and his wife Alice in white marble, their hands jointly holding a heart, on which are infcribed thefe words—"To God." On the floor is the tomb of Alice, Vifcountefs Verulam and Baronefs St. Alban's, widow of the great Lord Chancellor Bacon, who died in 1656, probably at the houfe of Mr. Anderfon, to whom fhe was related.

The great tithes of this parifh were appropriated to the priory of St. Helen's in London. They are now the property of Lord Yarborough, who is patron of the vicarage. Edmund Chifhull, a learned antiquary and divine, was born in this parifh.

FARNDISH, in the hundred of Willey and deanery of Clopham, is a fmall village on the borders of Northamptonfhire, into which county a confiderable part of the parifh extends. It is about five miles from Higham-Ferrers. In the 13th and 14th centuries the manor was fucceffively the property of the Pabenhams and Tyringhams [e]. During the laft century, and perhaps for a longer period, it was in the family of Maydwell, from whom it paffed, by marriage and bequeft, to the Lockwoods ; and is now the property of William Lockwood Maydwell efq. Charles Chefter efq. is patron of the rectory. The parifh of Farndifh, computed to contain 672 acres, has been inclofed by an act of parliament paffed in 1800, when an allotment was made to the rector in lieu of tithes.

FELMERSHAM, in the hundred of Willey and deanery of Clopham, lies on the banks of the Oufe, about feven miles north-eaft of Bedford. The manor, at an early period, was in the family of St. John, in which it continued till 1640, when it was fold by the Earl of Bolingbroke and his brothers to Mr. Leach, of whofe defcendants it was purchafed in 1717 by Thomas Orlebar gent. It is now vefted in the

---

[d] Some years ago he took the name of Pelham in addition. [e] Efch. Edw. II.—Rich. III.

Rev.

Rev. Thomas Orlebar Marfh, the Rev. Edward Orlebar Smith, and other reprefent-atives of Mr. Orlebar. The Mafter and Scholars of Trinity College in Cambridge have alfo a manor here, together with the rectory and advowfon of the vicarage. The parifh was inclofed by an act of parliament paffed in 1765, when allotments of land were affigned to the impropriators and to the vicar.

The weft end of the church affords a curious fpecimen of the earlieft Gothic archi-tecture. Between the nave and chancel is an ancient wooden fcreen very richly ornamented.

From a very early period there were two manors at *Radwell*, a hamlet of this parifh, which has a bridge over the Oufe. One of thefe manors was granted, by William the Conqueror, to Euftace de St. Giles, who gave it to his brother Ofbert le Mordaunt [f], anceftor of the Peterborough family. From the reign of Henry III. to that of Henry VI. it was in the Radwells [g]; and paffed from them by an heir female to the family of Rands [h], who continued to poffefs it till the year 1753, when it was fold to the late Jeffrey Fifher efq. of Flitwick, whofe only child Anne, late the wife of James Heffe efq. and now of George Brooks efq. has given it to her two daughters by her firft hufband, Anne wife of William Horne efq. and Martha wife of the Rev. Arthur Bold. The manor-houfe is a very ancient building, and has, in the windows of an old hall, the arms of Radwell impaling S. a chevron between three lions' heads erafed Arg. crowned Or (Beauchamp). The other manor, at the time of the Norman furvey, belonged to the Albinis; in 1316 to the Patfhulls [i], from whom it paffed by female heirs to the St. Johns; and is now the property of the Right Hon. Lord St. John.

FLITTON was anciently called Flictham, Flutte, and Flitt. It gives name to the hundred and deanery in which it lies. The village is about four miles fouth-eaft of Ampthill. The manor, which, at the Norman furvey, belonged to Robert Fafiton, and was afterwards in the Fitz-Richards, before the year 1324 became the property of the ancient family of Grey of Ruthin [k], who, at an earlier period [l], had been poffeffed of the manor of Wreft in this parifh, now the feat of their reprefent-ative Lady Lucas. Edmund Lord Grey of Ruthin was created Earl of Kent in 1465. The barony paffed to an heir female on the death of Henry Earl of Kent in 1639, but the earldom continued in the family of Grey. In 1706 Henry de Grey, Earl of Kent, was created Marquis, and in 1710, Duke of Kent. He died in 1740 without furviving male iffue, when the dukedom became extinct. The marquifate was

---

[f] Collins's Peerage.   [g] Efcheats.   [h] Bedfordfhire Pedigrees, Brit. Muf.
[i] *Nomina Villarum*, Brit. Muf.   [k] Efch. 17 Edw. II.
[l] Reginald Grey died feifed of Wreft in 1308. See Efch. 1 Edw. II.

WEST VIEW OF FELMERSHAM CHURCH BEDFORDSHIRE.

Published by T. Cadell & W. Davies, Nov 1, 1804.

not long before his death entailed on his eldeſt grand-daughter, Jemima, the lady of Lord Chancellor Hardwicke, and daughter of John Lord Glenorchy, by Lady Amabel Grey, the duke's eldeſt daughter, and her iſſue male. On the death of Marchioneſs Grey, in 1797, without male iſſue, that title became extinct; but the barony of Lucas, which in 1663 was extended to the heirs male and female of Anthony Earl of Kent by Mary, ſole heireſs of John Lord Lucas, deſcended to her eldeſt daughter Amabel, relict of Lord Polworth, now baroneſs Lucas, who is the preſent proprietor of the manors of Flitton and Wreſt.

Wreſt Park was in 1524 the ſeat of Sir Henry Grey [m]; who, being then heir to the title, on the death of his half-brother, found the eſtates ſo much impoveriſhed, that he neglected to aſſume it; and it remained dormant till re-aſſumed by his grandfon Reginald. The peerages are inaccurate in ſtating that his ſon declined to aſſume the title, the fact being, that he never had the opportunity, for he died in the lifetime of his father in the year 1545, as appears by his tomb in Flitton church; ſo that Reginald ſucceeded to the eſtates on the death of his grandfather in 1562, and was the fifth only, and not the ſixth, as the peerages ſtate, to whom the dignity of an earl, which he did not aſſume till 1571, belonged. Wreſt Park has been ever ſince the principal ſeat of the family.

The houſe, in its preſent ſtate, retains little appearance of antiquity, having been, at various times, altered and modernized. It contains a great number of portraits, forming nearly a ſeries of the noble family of Grey from Henry Earl of Kent, one of the peers who ſat on the trial of Mary Queen of Scots, down to the preſent time. Among theſe are Elizabeth Counteſs of Kent, who, reſiding at Wreſt in her widowhood, there patronized Butler the poet, and frequently entertained the learned Selden as her gueſt; Anthony Grey, rector of Burbach, who ſucceeded, in 1639, to the title on the death of Henry Earl of Kent, huſband to the above-mentioned lady; Lady Suſanna Grey, daughter of Charles Earl of Kent, who carried the barony of Grey of Ruthin to the Longuevilles; Henry Earl of Kent, who died in 1651, and Amabel his ſecond counteſs, commonly called the good Counteſs of Kent; Anthony Earl of Kent and his lady, the ſole heireſs of John Lord Lucas, in their robes, by Sir Peter Lely, &c. &c. &c. There are ſeveral portraits alſo of the Crew family, and others; among which are Sir Randolph Crew, Lord Chief Juſtice of the King's Bench, a fine picture of Thomas Lord Crew by Sir Peter Lely, Nathaniel Lord Crew Biſhop of Durham, and Sir Charles Lucas, brother of the firſt Lord Lucas, the eminent loyaliſt, who was ſhot at the ſiege of Colcheſter; and of that celebrated lawyer and ſtateſman, the late Lord Chancellor Hardwicke.

The gardens at Wreſt Park exhibit a ſpecimen of the old ſtyle improved by Brown,

[m] Collins's Peerage.

who

who made the ferpentine river, a very fine piece of water, about three quarters of a mile in length, furrounding the garden, and fupplied by a fpring which rifes not far from the houfe. At the fpring-head is a cold-bath, over which is a building in imitation of a Roman temple, defigned by Sir William Chambers. The duke of Kent, who was very partial to his country-feat, adorned the gardens with obelifks and various other buildings, particularly a magnificent banqueting-houfe, which terminates a fpacious avenue in front of the manfion, and a large room where he fpent many convivial hours with fome of the great ftatefmen who were his contemporaries, after partaking of his favourite amufement in the adjoining bowling-green.

It is probable that the parifh church of Flitton was built by Reginald Lord Grey, Lord Admiral of England, fubfequent to the year 1410, when the court of chivalry adjudged him the right of bearing the arms of Haftings [n], which are quartered with his own on the porch of Flitton church. It is principally remarkable for the monuments of the noble family of Grey, whofe burial-place it has been fince the reign of Henry VIII. The aifle adjoining the nave was built by Henry Earl of Kent in 1605. In this aifle are the monuments of Henry Earl of Kent, the founder, who died in 1614, with the effigies, in their robes, of himfelf and his countefs, Mary daughter of Sir John Cotton, who died in 1580, and was buried at Great Gaddefden;—Elizabeth Countefs of Kent, daughter of Gilbert Earl of Shrewfbury, who died in 1651, with her effigies in white marble;—Henry Earl of Kent, who died in 1651, and his fecond wife Amabel, called from her works of charity the *good* Countefs of Kent, who died in 1698, at the age of 92. Their effigies in white marble are very heavy and ungraceful;—and Lady Jane, relict of Sir Euftace Hart, who died in 1671, with her effigies in white marble. Charles Earl of Kent, who died in 1623, and Henry Earl of Kent, who died in 1639, have only memorials on the floor; where is alfo a figure in brafs, removed, probably, from the nave or chancel, of Henry, eldeft fon of Sir Henry Grey, who died in 1545, during the life-time of his father. The duke of Kent built three additional rooms, in which are the monuments of the duke himfelf, who died in 1740, and his only fon Anthony, Earl of Harold, who died in 1723, with their effigies in white marble in Roman habits; his two duchefses, Jemima Crew, who died in 1738, and Lady Sophia Bentinck, who died in 1748; his three daughters, Amabel Lady Glenorchy, who died in 1727; Lady Henrietta De Grey, 1717; and Lady Anne Cavendifh, 1733, with their effigies in white marble; an urn to the memory of Lady Mary Gregory, a fourth daughter, who died in 1761; and another in memory of the late Earl of Hardwicke, who died in 1790. In the chancel is the effigies in brafs of Thomas Hill, receiver-general to three earls of Kent, who died in 1628, aged 101 [o].

---

[n] Collins's Peerage.   [o] Mr. Hill's age, and the date of his death, were incorrectly printed in Pennant's Journey to London, and have been from thence copied into other works.

The

The great tithes of Flitton, which were appropriated to the priory of Elftow, are now vefted, together with the advowfon of the vicarage, in Chrift-Church College, Oxford, and are held on leafe under the college by Lady Lucas.

Silfoe, a hamlet in this parifh, on the road from Luton to Bedford, had formerly a market on Tuefdays, granted in 1319 to Ralph Fitz-Richard, then lord of the manor, together with a fair on the feftival of St. Philip and St. James [p]. This fair is ftill held; and another on the 21ft of September. The market has been long difufed. The manor, at the time of the Norman furvey, belonged to a concubine of Nigel de Albini. It has long been in the family of Grey. An ancient record fpeaks of the manor of Blundell in Silfoe [q], as part of their property, but the name is not now known. At this hamlet is a chapel of eafe. The altar-piece, reprefenting the Adoration of the Shepherds, was painted by Mrs. Mary Lloyd, and given by her to the chapel.

FLITWICK, in the hundred of Redbornftoke and deanery of Flitt, lies about three miles fouth of Ampthill. The manor of Flitwick was anciently in the Earls of Albemarle [r]. A moiety of it paffed afterwards through the families of Flitwick, St. Amand, Cornwall Lord Fanhope, and Grey [s] Earl of Kent: by the latter it was conveyed to the crown. King Charles I. having fold it to the city of London, it was conveyed in 1639 by the city truftees to Edward Blofield and his heirs. From the Blofields this manor paffed by marriage to Benjamin Rhodes efq. who in 1736 devifed it to Humphrey Dell, M. D. Under Dr. Dell's will it was enjoyed by the late Jeffrey Fifher efq. in right of his wife, and now by George Brooks efq. as hufband of Anne daughter of Mr. Fifher, and relict of James Heffe efq. The manor-houfe is occupied by the Right Hon. John Trevor. The other moiety of the manor belonged to the priory of Dunftaple [t]; and, fince the reformation, to the families of Mofsley, Honeywood, and Mildmay [u]. It is fuppofed to be now confolidated with the other. The great tithes were appropriated to the priory of Dunftaple. They are now held, together with the glebe-land, which confifts of 95 acres, 3 roods, and 2 perches, by Mr. Brooks, on a leafe of 99 years from the feoffees, in truft for the fchoolmafter of Holme, the mafter of the free-fchool at Bigglefwade, the vicar of Bigglefwade, the rector of Connington, and the vicar of St. Neot's. The Earl of Offory is patron of the vicarage of Flitwick.

At Rokefac, or Ruxox, in this parifh, was a fmall monaftery, which appears to have been a cell to Dunftaple. The chapel of St. Nicholas de Rokefac was built

---

[p] Cart. 12 Edw. II. [q] Cole's Efcheats in the Britifh Mufeum. [r] Chron. Dunft. 1269.
[s] Efcheats, Edw. I.—Rich. II. Cl. Hen. VI. &c. [t] Chron. Dunft. [u] Cole's Efcheats.

by Philip de Sannerville about the year 1170, and dedicated by Robert de Chefney, Bifhop of Lincoln [w]. The fite of Rokefac was granted by William Earl of Albemarle, and Hawife his wife, to the canons of Dunftaple and the canons of Rokefac [x]. Alexander, canon of Rokefac, is mentioned in an old deed in the cartulary of Dunftaple in the Britifh Mufeum, which contains feveral grants to St. Nicholas of Rokefac. Mention is made in the chronicle of Dunftaple, under the year 1205, of fettling about the prior at Rokefac. Friar Michael de Peck, friar John de Hallings, and others of the houfehold at Rokefac, are mentioned in the fame chronicle under the year 1283. It is probable that the monks were removed long before the reformation, for records of that date make no other mention of Rokefac, or Ruxox, than as a manor belonging to the priory of Dunftaple, which was granted in 1558 to the family of Weft, in whom it continued for a confiderable time. In 1704 it was purchafed of the heirs female of their fucceffors, the Blofields, by Lord Bruce, and of his family, in 1738, by John duke of Bedford; from whom it has defcended to the prefent duke. The fite is moated, but there are no remains of the ancient buildings.

The manor of Preftley, in this parifh, was purchafed of the Jourdans in the year 1495, by the family of Grey. In 1541 Sir James Grey conveyed it to the crown. Queen Elizabeth, in 1560, granted it to Richard Champion and John Thompfon. It was purchafed of the Thompfon family by the Cuthberts, from whom it paffed, by a female heir, to the Sheldons. It is now part of the Duke of Bedford's eftate, having been purchafed of the truftees of Colonel Durham, who married the daughter of Cuthbert Sheldon efq. who died in 1764. The late duke kept this eftate in his own hands for the purpofe of his agricultural experiments.

GOLDINGTON, in the hundred of Barford, is fituated nearly two miles north-eaft of Bedford. The Hazeldens had a manor in this parifh as early as the year 1432 [y], which continued in their family at leaft three centuries. It is now the property of J. Polhill efq. The Goftwickes had another manor [z], which, it is probable, had been in the Beauchamps and Mowbrays. It is now the property of the duke of Bedford, whofe grandfather purchafed it of the duke of Marlborough in 1774. The great tithes of this parifh were appropriated to the priory of Newenham. After the reformation, they were many years in the Hazelden family, and are now the property of Mr. Jofeph Addington. The Duke of Bedford is patron of the vicarage, which is in the deanery of Bedford. In the church are fome memorials of the ancient family of the Hazeldens: that of lateft date is the tomb of James Hazelden gent. who died in 1732.

[w] Cartulary of Dunftaple Priory in the Britifh Mufeum.   [x] Ibid.   [y] Cl. 11 Hen. VI.
[z] Cole's Efcheats.

The

The priory of Newenham, above mentioned, was fituated in this parifh, on the banks of the Oufe, and was founded by Simon de Beauchamp, who removed hither fome canons regular from the collegiate church of St. Paul at Bedford [a]. The revenues of this priory were valued, in the reign of Henry VIII. at 293l. 5s. 11d. clear yearly income. After the diffolution, the manor of Newenham, which had belonged to the priory, was made parcel of the honour of Ampthill, as it ftill continues, being on leafe to the duke of Bedford. The fite of the priory was the refidence of Sir Robert Catlin, Chief Juftice of the King's Bench [b], who died in 1574; and was afterwards the property of William Lord Cobham [c]. The prefent proprietor is Mrs. Mary Beft. There are no remains either of the priory or manfion. A wall of brick, with a turret, marks the fituation of a court, which, it is probable, adjoined the houfe.

The caftle-mill, and fite of Rifinghoe caftle, are alfo in Goldington parifh. Rifinghoe caftle is fuppofed, by Leland, to have belonged to the Efpecs; but it feems more probable that it was the property of the Beauchamps, who appear, by the Norman furvey, to have had the chief property in this parifh. The Efpecs had no lands either in the parifh or hundred. Rifinghoe mill is mentioned in a charter of Thomas Lord Mowbray, bearing date 1391 [d]. It is now the duke of Bedford's. The keep of the caftle is of confiderable height, and adjoining it are large earth-works. The duke of Bedford has alfo the manor of Putnoe, or Puttenhoe, in this parifh, which belonged to the Beauchamps, and was afterwards in the Mowbrays and Goftwicks. The abbot and convent of Warden had alfo an eftate at Puttenhoe. King Henry III. granted them an annual penfion of 20 marks, to be paid out of the exchequer, as a compenfation for the damage he had done to their woods at Puttenhoe during the fiege of Bedford.

UPPER-GRAVENHURST, in the hundred of Flitt, lies about three miles fouthweft of Shefford. The manor belonged to the abbey of Ramfey, and was granted in 1542 to Sir Henry Grey, from whom it defcended to the prefent proprietor Lady Lucas. The great tithes belong to Trinity College, Cambridge. The benefice, which is in the deanery of Shefford, is a curacy in the gift of the parifhioners.

Ion houfe, in this parifh, was fold in 1639 by William Whitbread gent. anceftor of the prefent member for Bedford, to William Allayne, whofe daughter and heir brought it in marriage to John Sabine efq. created a baronet in 1672, being defcribed of Ion-houfe, which he fold the fame year to Morgan Hinde efq. of whofe

[a] Leland's Collect.   [b] Bedfordfhire Pedigrees, Britifh Mufeum.   [c] Efch. 39 Eliz.
[d] Dugdale's Monaft. II. 240.

family it was purchafed, in 1724, by the duke of Kent.   It is now a farm houfe, the property of Lady Lucas.

LOWER GRAVENHURST, an adjoining village, is in the fame hundred, but in the deanery of Flitt.   The manor was anciently in the families of Bocles[e], Zouche[f], and Bilhemore[g].   It was many years in the noble family of Grey, and is now the property of their reprefentative Lady Lucas.   The church was built by Sir Robert de Bilhemore, as appears by a French infcription on his tomb, without date.   In the porch is a coat of arms fuppofed to be his, a bend within a border engrailed.   In the church are monuments of the Pigots.   That of Benjamin Pigot efq. who died in 1606, has a genealogical account of the family.   His mother (the daughter of Oliver St. John of Bletfoe) was relict of Henry Grey efq. who died in 1545, during his father's life-time, and, by him, mother of three fucceffive earls of Kent,—Reginald, Henry, and Charles.   Lower Gravenhurft is a rectory in the gift of the crown.

HARLINGTON, in the hundred of Manfhead and deanery of Flitt, lies about two miles north-eaft of Toddington.   The manor was parcel of the barony of Cainhoe belonging to the Albinis, under whom it was held by the Pyrots[h]; it is probable, that it paffed afterwards to the families of Peyvre or Broughton; for it is certain, that in 1561, it was vefted in their reprefentatives the Cheneys[i], from whom it paffed, by marriage, to the Wentworths, and under the will of Thomas Wentworth, earl of Strafford, who died in 1732, to the prefent proprietor Henry Vernon efq. fon of Lady Harriot Vernon, one of the earl's daughters.

Wood-end, in Harlington, was the feat of a branch of the Aftrey family; the firft who fettled there was a grandfon of Sir Ralph Aftrey, lord mayor of London, who died in 1494[k].   Sir James Aftrey of Wood-end was a learned lawyer, and publifhed an edition of Spelman's Gloffary with his life[l].   After the death of the late Dr. Aftrey, Wood-end (which fome writers, having miftaken it for Wood-end in Cople, have erroneoufly defcribed as a feat of the Lukes) was inherited by the prefent proprietor, Francis Penyfton efq. of Cornwell in the county of Oxford.   The manor of Wadloes, belonging alfo to Mr. Penyfton, is partly in this parifh.

The Wingates had a feat in Harlington, now belonging to their reprefentative, John Wingate Jennings efq.   Edmund Wingate the arithmetician, who was fent to France to teach the princefs Henrietta Maria (afterwards the queen of Charles I.) Englifh, was of this family.   He refided at Harlington during the protectorate of

---

[e] Efch. Edw. II.   [f] Ibid.   [g] Epitaph in the church.
[h] Nomina Villarum, Brit. Muf.   [i] Cole's Efcheats.   [k] Bedfordfhire Pedigrees in the Brit. Muf.
[l] Ant. Wood.

Cromwell.

Cromwell. In the year 1654, his name occurs in the Ampthill regifter, attefting marriages as a juftice of peace.

Ralph Pyrot gave the church of Harlington to the prior and convent of Dunftaple[m], to whom the great tithes were appropriated. They are now the property of Mr. Vernon, who is patron of the vicarage. In the church are fome memorials of the Aftreys.

HAROLD, a fmall market town on the Oufe, bordering on Northamptonfhire, lies in the hundred of Willey, and deanery of Clopham, about nine miles from Bedford. The market is held on Thurfday, but is fo inconfiderable that it fcarcely deferves the name; and indeed, Harold has been overlooked by moft writers who have enumerated the market towns of this county. The number of houfes in the parifh, according to the returns made to Parliament under the Population Act in 1801, was 155, of inhabitants 763. The knights templars[n], and the family of Pabenham[o], appear to have been the principal land owners in this parifh, in the thirteenth, and at the beginning of the fourteenth century. As early as the year 1324, the manor was in the noble family of Grey[p]. When Henry de Grey, earl of Kent, was created a marquis in 1706, he took his fecond title from this place; his fon Anthony, earl of Harold, who died in his father's life-time, was the only perfon by whom it was enjoyed. The manor is the property of Lady Lucas as reprefentative of the Greys.

Sampfon le Fort, in the year 1150, founded a priory at Harold, in honour of St. Peter, for canons and nuns of the order of St. Nicholas of Arrouafia, but it was afterwards occupied by a priorefs and a few nuns of the order of St. Auftin. Its revenues, when fuppreffed, were eftimated at 40l. 18s. 2d. clear yearly value. The fite was granted, in 1544, to William Lord Parr, and again, in 1555, to John Cheney and William Duncombe[q]. It is now a farm houfe, the property of Lady Lucas. The only part of the conventual building which remains, is the refectory, now a barn, and known by the name of the Hall-barn.

In the parifh church, which has a handfome Gothic fpire, are memorials of the families of Boteler and Alfton; a monument (with her buft) of Mrs. Jolliffe, daughter of Lord Crew; and the tomb of Mrs. Mead, daughter of Sir Rowland Alfton of Odell, and widow of Dr. Mead the celebrated phyfician, who refided at the large houfe near the church, which devolved to him in right of his wife, and was inherited by his fon. It is now the feat of Robert Garftin efq. The great tithes of Harold were appropriated to the priory: the prefent proprietor of the rectorial

[m] Chron. Dunft. [n] Cart. 53 Hen. III. [o] Cart. 5 Edw. II. [p] Efch. 17 Edw. II.
[q] Tanner.

               eftate

estate is Grove Spurgeon Farrer esq. The parish has been exonerated from tithes, in consequence of the inclosure, for which an act of Parliament passed in 1797. The vicar has a small allotment of glebe under this act, and a corn-rent in lieu of his farther interest in the tithes. The parish was then computed to contain 3300 acres. Lady Lucas is patroness of the vicarage.

There is a bridge over the Ouse at Harold, with a long causeway.

HATLEY-PORT, or COCKAYNE-HATLEY, in the hundred of Bigglefwade and deanery of Shefford, is a small village two miles from Potton, on the borders of Cambridgeshire. It was anciently the estate of the Argentiens and Bryans [r]. Sir John Cockayne, lord Chief Baron of the Exchequer, who died in 1427, became possessed of this manor, and made it his country-seat [s]. From his family the village obtained the appellation, which distinguishes it from some neighbouring parishes likewise named Hatley in Cambridgeshire. The manor has lately passed by marriage to the family of Cust, and is now the property of Mrs. Lucy Cockayne Cust. In the nave of the parish church is an altar-tomb, stripped of its brass plates, said to be the monument of Chief Baron Cockayne. There are several memorials of this family, from the year 1527 to 1739. In the north aisle is a monument of Sir Patrick Home, who married one of the Cockaynes, and died in 1627.— Mrs. Cust is patroness of the rectory.

HAWNES or HAYNES, anciently HAGNES, in the hundred and deanery of Flitt, lies about five miles from Shefford, and about six and a half from Bedford. The manor was part of the large possessions of the Beauchamps, and passed from them, by inheritance, to the Mowbrays [t]. It is probable that the marquis of Berkeley, who inherited large property from the Mowbrays, gave it, as he did several other estates, to Sir Reginald Bray; for it appears, that Sir Reginald's great-nephew, Sir Edward Bray, sold it in 1563 to Robert Newdigate esq. [u]. Queen Anne, consort of James I. was entertained by Sir Robert Newdigate at Hawnes, on the 27th and 28th of July 1605, the king being then at Sir Edmund Conquest's at Houghton; on the 30th, the king and queen, with the whole court, attended divine service at Hawnes church [w]. After the death of Sir Robert Newdigate in 1613, Hawnes is supposed to have passed by purchase to the Lukes of Cople, who appear

[r] Cart. 1 Edw. II. and the Nomina Villarum in the British Museum, No. 6281. Harl. MSS.
[s] Bedfordshire Pedigrees in the British Museum.
[t] Dugdale's Baronage and Esch. Ed. III.—Hen. VI.
[u] Papers in the possession of William Bray esq.
[w] MSS. of Thomas Archer, rector of Houghton-Conquest, in the possession of the present rector.

to have refided here occafionally, from 1626 to 1654 [x]. After this it was pur-chafed by Sir Humphrey Wynch, who, in 1667, fold it to Sir George Carteret. Sir George was, in 1681, created Baron Carteret of Hawnes; and his lady (being heirefs of John Granville, earl of Bath), was in 1714, created Countefs Granville. Thefe titles became extinct in 1776, on the death of Richard, the fecond Earl Granville; when Henry Frederick, fecond fon of Thomas Vifcount Weymouth, inheriting this and other his eftates, took the name of Carteret, and, in 1784, was created Baron Carteret of Hawnes.

Hawnes houfe, which confifts of two quadrangles, has been modernized, and in great part rebuilt by the prefent Lord Carteret. Among the pictures are por-traits of Margaret, countefs of Lenox; Rembrandt's mother [y]; Sir George and lady Carteret; John earl Granville, &c. At the foot of the great ftair-cafe is an ancient view of Longleat, the feat of the Marquis of Bath. In the church is a monument of Anthony Newdigate, one of the commiffioners for the fale of abbey lands, who died in 1568; and memorials for Sir John Ofborn, bart. of Chickfand, who died in 1699, and others of that family. Hawnes is alfo the burial-place of the Carterets, but there are no memorials for them in the church.

The church of Hawnes was given by Simon de Beauchamp to the priory of Chickfand, and the advowfon having paffed, with other eftates of that monaftery, to the Ofborns, is now the property of Sir George Ofborn of Chickfand. The vicarage is endowed. Thomas Brightman, author of a Treatife on the Revelations, which attracted much notice in the reign of queen Elizabeth, was vicar of Hawnes. He died in 1607.

HENLOW, in the hundred of Clifton, lies about two miles and a half to the eaft of Shefford. There are three manors in this parifh, one of which was for many gene-rations in the noble family of Grey [z], and is now the property of their reprefenta-tive Lady Lucas. It was held under the barony of Odell. Another, called Henlow Lanthony, was as early as the year 1293 part of the poffeffions of the priory of Lanthony near Gloucefter [a]. Sir John Clarke died feifed of this manor in 1614, leaving two daughters co-heirs, from one of whom it is probable it paffed to the family of Edwards, who have poffeffed it for feveral generations. It is now the property of Mrs. Elizabeth Edwards, widow. A third manor, called Henlow-War-den, belonged to the abbey of that name. It has long been in the Edwards family, and is now the property of George Edwards efq. fon of Mrs. Edwards above-mentioned. In the parifh church are feveral monuments of this family. The

[x] Parifh Regifter.
[y] The fame perfon whofe portrait was engraved for Pennant's tour to Scotland, under the erroneous appellation of the Countefs of Defmond. [z] Efch. Rich. II., &c. [a] Cart. 21 Edw. I.

great

great tithes of this parish were appropriated to the hospital of St. Julian, near St. Alban's. When the parish was inclosed by an act of Parliament passed in 1795, the vicar, who was entitled to a portion of the great tithes, had a corn-rent assigned him, and a small allotment of land, the remainder of the land allotted in lieu of tithes was assigned to the Edwards family. The vicarage, which is in the gift of the crown, is in the deanery of Shefford.

HIGHAM-GOBION, in the hundred and deanery of Flitt, a small village about nine miles from Luton, a little to the east of the road to Bedford, derived its additional name from the family of Gobion, to whom the manor belonged from an early period till the year 1301 [c], when it passed by marriage to the Botelers, in whose possession it continued for many generations. Their arms are still to be seen over the parlour fire-place in the manor-house, now a farm. Sir Henry Boteler of Higham-Gobion died in 1608, leaving a son, Sir John [d]. William Langley esq. became possessed of this estate in 1639. In 1641 he was created a baronet, being described of Higham-Gobion. His son, Sir Roger, in 1657, sold the manor to Arabella, countess of Kent, from whom it descended to the present proprietor, the Right Hon. Lady Lucas.

This place was the residence of the learned Dr. Castell, author of the Polyglott Bible, who lived here in obscure retirement, till he fell a victim to his intense application to study, which a short time before his death deprived him of his eye-sight. Dr. Castell was buried in Higham-Gobion church, where is a monument to his memory, with the following inscription : " Edmundus Castell, S.T.D. Regiæ Majestati Carolo II. a sacris, Ecclesiæ Christi Cantuarensis Canonicus, Linguæ Arabicæ apud Cantabrigienses Professor, Regalis Societatis Socius, author Lexicon Heptaglotti, necnon hujus ecclesiæ Rector. Mortalitatis quod reliquum est tam ipsi quam lectissimæ ejus conjugi Dominæ Elizabethæ Bettesworth, Petri Bettesworth militis aurati primó relictæ, deinde Joannis Harris Arm. (cujus filius Willielmus una cum filiâ ejus Elizabethâ hic jacent) Anno Ætat. Edmundi 68, Dæ. Elizabethæ 64—Anno Christi 1674.—Vivus hic legat humandum." The advowson of the rectory is vested in Richard Lee esq. as trustee for the children of the Rev. Mr. Mead of Dunstaple, who is the present incumbent.

HOCKLIFFE, in the hundred of Manshead and deanery of Dunstaple, is a great thoroughfare on the ancient Watling-street, now the high road from London to Chester. At this village, which is about five miles beyond Dunstaple, the great road through Woburn to Manchester and Liverpool branches off. Its situation is low,

[c] Esch. 29 Edw. I.   [d] MS. Diary of Thomas Archer, rector of Houghton-Conquest.

which

which was the occasion of its having acquired the appellation of Hockliffe, or Hockley in the Hole; it was noted for its miry road, which of late years has been much improved. The manor belonged to the monaftery of Woburn [e]. In 1615, it was granted to Thomas Hillerfden efq. and in 1712, was purchafed of his defcendants by Allen Lord Bathurft, who, in 1718, fold it to John Reynal efq. It is now the property of Francis Moore efq. of Egginton, in right of his wife, who was relict of the late J. S. W. Reynal efq. In the parifh church, which ftands on a hill at fome diftance from the high road, are tombs of the family of Gilpin, one of whom, Robert Gilpin, died rector of the parifh, in 1640: his wife furvived him 50 years, and died at the age of 97. Richard Gilpin efq. is now patron of the rectory. There was an ancient hofpital at Hockliffe, dedicated to St. John the Baptift, of which there are no remains. It exifted as early as the reign of king John [f].

HOLWELL, in the hundred of Clifton and deanery of Shefford, is a fmall village on the borders of Hertfordfhire, about three miles from Hitchin, a little to the weft of the road from that town to Shefford. Henry Spigurnell had a charter of free-warren in Holwell, in the reign of Edward II. The manor was foon afterwards in the family of Malore [g]. On the attainder of Sir Robert Belknap, one of the juftices of the common pleas in 1392, being then parcel of his eftate, it was granted to John de Burton and others [h], and was afterwards in the family of Kynbell [i]. Not many years ago it was in the Forefters, from whom, either by purchafe or inheritance, it paffed to Baldwin Leighton efq. who, in 1765, fold it to the late John Radcliffe efq. It is now the property of the Right Hon. Lady Frances Radcliffe his widow. The manor is ftyled Holwell the Great, otherwife Holwell and Codicot. The advowfon of the rectory, which belonged alfo to the late John Radcliffe efq. was purchafed in 1673, by his anceftor Sir Ralph Radcliffe of the Nodes, who were for a fhort time proprietors of the manor. It is now the property of Mr. Delmé Radcliffe, who married Mifs Clarke, the niece and heirefs of the late John Radcliffe efq. The parifh of Holwell has been inclofed by an act of Parliament paffed in 1802, when an allotment of land was given to the rector in lieu of tithes. Mark Hilderfley, bifhop of Sodor and Man, was rector of this parifh 35 years.

HOUGHTON-CONQUEST, which lies in the hundred of Redborn-ftoke, and deanery of Bedford, about two miles and a half north-eaft of Ampthill, takes its

---

[e] Cooper's Hiftory of Odell in Bibl. Top. Brit.   [f] Tanner.
[g] Nomina Villarum in the Britifh Mufeum, No. 6281. Harl. MSS.   [h] Pat. 15 Rich. II.
[i] Cl. 3 Hen. V.

additional

additional name from the ancient family of Conquest, who were possessed of the manor before the year 1298[1]. The male line of this family became extinct in Benedict Conquest esq. (father of the present Lady Arundel), of whom this manor was purchased by the late Earl of Upper Ossory in 1741. It is now the property of the present earl. The seat of the Conquests was called Houghton-Bury, or Conquest-Bury. In 1605, king James paid a visit to Sir Edmund Conquest, and slept at Houghton on the 27th and 28th of July, the queen being at the same time at Sir Richard Newdigate's, at Hawnes. On the 28th, it being the feast day at Houghton, the king with his court, consisting of the Duke of Lenox, the Earls of Northampton, Suffolk, Salisbury, Devonshire, and Pembroke, the Lords Knollys, Wotton, and Stanhope, and Bishop Watson, his almoner, attended divine service at the parish church[m]. The little that remains of the old mansion at Houghton-Bury is now a farm house; the building is of brick and timber; the eaves are ornamented with grotesque figures carved in wood.

Another manor in this parish belonged to the barons St. Amand, and was held in dower by Eleanor Lady St. Amand[n], who, in 1415, petitioned parliament against Lord Grey of Ruthin, for redress on account of several outrages committed in her park at Ampthill and elsewhere[o]. From this lady the manor acquired the name of Dame-Ellensbury Manor.—It passed, with other estates that had been in the St. Amands, to Lord Fanhope, and was afterwards the property of Sir William Gascoigne, who surrendered it to the king in 1538. From this time the history of Dame-Ellensbury manor and Dame-Ellensbury park, or Houghton park, are somewhat different till they were again united in the Bruce family. The Manor was retained in the hands of the crown, till granted by king Charles I. to Ditchfield and others, who in 1630, conveyed it to Sir Francis Clerke: Sir Francis died in 1632, and his representatives not long afterwards sold it to the Pigots, from whom it passed again by purchase, in 1665, to the Earl of Aylesbury[p].

Houghton park, otherwise Dame-Ellensbury park, was occupied in the early part of king James's reign by Sir Edmund Conquest, as keeper. In 1615, he made over his interest in it to Matthew Lister and Leonard Welstead, trustees for the celebrated Mary countess of Pembroke[q], " Sidney's sister, Pembroke's mother," who holding the park under the crown in her widowhood, built a splendid mansion of which the shell now remains. In 1630, Houghton park was granted in fee to Lord Bruce[r], and was for a considerable time the country-seat of his descendants, who were Earls of Elgin and Aylesbury. Here the celebrated Christian Countess of Devonshire, spent three years in retirement at the house of her

[1] Esch. 26 Edw. I.   [m] Mr. Archer's Notes in the parish register.   [n] See Cl. 19 H. VI
[o] Rot. Parl. IV. 92.   [p] Duke of Bedford's Records.   [q] Ibid.   [r] Ibid.

brother

brother the Earl of Elgin, after the battle of Worcester in 1651, " lightening," as the author of her life obferves, " her griefs and her expences." But even in this retirement, her ardent loyalty expofed her to fome rifks ; a troop of horfe being ordered to fetch her from hence up to London, at the time that the countefs of Carlifle was imprifoned in the tower; but fhe efcaped the danger by a bribe beftowed on one of the council of ftate. In 1738, John Duke of Bedford purchafed Houghton park, with the manor of Dame-Ellenfbury, of the Earl of Aylefbury; and in 1801, in confequence of an exchange with the late Duke, they both became the property of the Earl of Offory. Houghton-park houfe was fitted up for the Marquis of Taviftock, father of the prefent Duke of Bedford, who refided there till his untimely death; after which, it was for a fhort time occupied by Lord Offory, as tenant : it has never fince been inhabited. In 1794, it was unroofed and reduced to a fhell by the late Duke of Bedford, and moft of the materials were ufed in building the Swan inn at Bedford.

Fuller and fome other writers have called this manfion Ampthill Houfe. It muft be obferved, that in his time there was no capital manfion in Ampthill park, and that part of Houghton-park houfe ftands within the parifh of Ampthill. On the north front of this houfe was a lozenge fhield with the arms and quarterings of Sydney, and an earl's coronet; on the fouth front there ftill remain, on the frieze, various monagrams and devices of the families of Sydney and Dudley. The ruins of the houfe ftand on an elevated fpot at the end of an avenue, which reaches into the vale of Bedford.

In Houghton park they fhew a tree under which Sir Philip Sydney is faid to have written fome of his works ; but it is evident that the tradition is totally void of foundation, fince Sir Philip died, many years before his fifter, the Countefs of Pembroke, had any property or intereft in Houghton park.

Lord Offory has another eftate in this parifh, called the Manor of Houghton-How-end, which belonged to the abbot and convent of Reading, and after the reformation to the Conquefts.

An eftate in this parifh called the Manor of Houghton-Conqueft, or Bryttons, alias Groves in Houghton-Conqueft, was the property of Lord Wenlock, after whofe death it paffed to the Rotherams, and at a later period was, together with another eftate in this parifh, called the Manor of Flamwells, in the family of Wylde. Sir Edmund Wylde died feifed of them in 1620[s]. They are now the property of Dr. Macqueen in right of his wife, who was daughter and heir of the late Thomas Potter efq. one of his majefty's juftices for Wales.

[s] Cole's Efcheats. Brit. Muf.

The manor of Beadlow, partly in this parifh and partly in Clophill, belonged for many years to the Charnocks of Hulcote; from them it paffed by marriage to the Herveys of Chilton in Buckinghamfhire, in the reprefentatives of which family it is now vefted.

In the parifh church are fome memorials of the Conqueft family. In the chancel is the monument of Thomas Archer, rector of Houghton-Conqueft, inftituted in the reign of queen Elizabeth, who inferted various hiftorical notes in the parifh regifter and in a large note book, now in the poffeffion of the prefent rector, the Rev. Dr. Pearce, Mafter of Jefus College in Cambridge. It appears, from thefe notes, that he preached before the king at Hawnes, July 30, 1605, on the following fingular text from the Song of Solomon. " Take us the foxes, the little foxes which deftroy the grapes, for our vines have fmall grapes." The fermon, it is to be fuppofed, pleafed his majefty, for the preacher was immediately afterwards fworn one of his chaplains in ordinary. He preached before the king and queen at Toddington, July 24, 1608, and before the king at Bletfoe, July 26, 1612. " Anno 1623," fays Mr. Archer in the parifh regifter, " I caufed my grave to be made with brick, and I made my coffin whereon are fet thefe figures 1623." The following epitaph is of his own writing :

> " Inftruxi vivens multos
> Nunc inftruo cunctos
> Quod ftruit una dies
> Deftruit una dies.
> Sic fpeciofa ruit
> Spatiofi fabrica mundi
> Sic oritur, moritur,
> Vermis, inermis, homo.
> O me felicem
> Qui carnis fafce folutus
> Mutavi veris vitrea
> Vana bonis.
> Fui Thomas Archer
> Capellanus Regis Jacobi
> Rector hujus ecclefiae
> per annos XLI.
> In vita hoc pofui
> Anno Domini MDCXXIX.
> Anno Ætatis LXXVI
> Veniet qui me in lucem
> reponet dies.

The effigies of the deceafed, who died in 1631, is reprefented in canonicals, in his pulpit, with a cufhion and book before him. In the chancel is the monument alfo

of

of Dr. Zachary Grey, rector of Houghton, editor of Hudibras, and a commentator on Shakfpere, with the following infcription :

> " Sacred to the memory of Zachary Grey, L.L.D. late rector of this parifh, who with zeal undiffembled ferved his God, with love and affection endeared himfelf to his family, with fincerity unaffected promoted the intereft of his friends, and with real charity and extenfive humanity behaved towards all mankind. He died, Nov. 25, 1766, aged 78."

The church of Houghton was formerly divided into two portionable parfonages, called Houghton-Franchife, and Houghton-Gildable. There were two parfonage houfes, one of which was moated ; the parfonages were united by the King's fpecial command in 1637 into one rectory called Houghton-Conqueft, to which Edward Martin was then inducted as the firft rector [t]. The advowfon was fold by the Conquefts to St. John's College in Cambridge.

A free-fchool and alms-houfe were founded at Houghton-Conqueft by Sir Francis Clerke, the great benefactor to Sidney Suffex College in Cambridge, who had a feat in this parifh, and died there in 1632. The mafter's falary is 16l. per annum, and the poor people, who are fix in number, have 8l. divided between them, under Sir Francis Clerke's will. Edmund Wylde efq. in 1691, left the fum of 140l. for the purchafe of lands, the profits of which are to be appropriated to the repairs of the fchool and alms-houfe, the overplus to be divided among the fix poor people.

HOUGHTON-REGIS, in the hundred of Manfhead, lies about a mile and a half from Dunftaple, on the road to Toddington. The manor was anciently, as the name of the place imports, part of the royal demefne. At a very early period it became the property of the Cantilupes, barons of Bergavenny [u]. From them it paffed by a female heir to the Zouches of Harringworth, who became poffeffed of it in 1273 [w]. It was afterwards in the Brays ; Sir Edward Bray conveyed it in 1567 [x] to Lewis Montgomery, and Jane his wife [y]. In the early part of the 17th century, this manor belonged to the Egertons, Earls of Bridgwater [z]. In 1653, it became the property of the Brandreths ; and now belongs to the Duke of Bedford, whofe grandfather purchafed it of the Brandreths in 1750. The Duke has alfo the manor of Sewell in this parifh, which was included in the fame purchafe. It was formerly the feat of an ancient family of that name, and afterwards belonged to the Dyves. It is now a farm-houfe. The Brandreths bought it, with the advowfon of Houghton-Regis, of Sir Lewis Dyve, of Bromham, an officer in the army of King Charles I. There is an

---

[t] Parifh Regifter. [u] Chron. Dunft. and Dugdale's Baronage. [w] Ibid.
[x] 20th November, 9 Elizabeth. [y] Papers communicated by William Bray efq. F.A.S.
[z] Duke of Bedford's Papers.

ancient

ancient monument in Houghton church, with the effigies of a man in armour, under a rich Gothic arch, which has the arms of Sewell; a chevron between three butter-flies. There are several memorials also for the Brandreths. Henry Brandreth esq. the representative of that family, has a seat at Houghton, and possesses the impropriate rectory which formerly belonged to the priory of Dunstaple, to which monastery they were confirmed by King Henry II. The Duke of Bedford is patron of the vicarage, which is in the deanery of Dunstaple. This parish has been inclosed by an act of parliament passed in 1796, when allotments of land were assigned to the impropriator and vicar in lieu of tithes. The commons and wastes in the parish were then computed at 4000 acres.

HULCOTE, in the hundred of Manshead, and deanery of Flitt, is a very small village on the borders of Buckinghamshire, about 11 miles South West of Bedford. The manor belonged anciently to the Firmbands and Wydvilles[a], and at a later period to a branch of the Charnocks of Lancashire, who settled at Hulcote in the reign of Henry VII. or Henry VIII.[b] John Charnock esq. of Hulcote, was created a Baronet in 1661. The title became extinct by the death of Sir Villiers Charnock in 1779. In consequence of the marriage of two of his sisters with the Herveys of Chilton in Buckinghamshire, the manor of Hulcote is now the joint property of five ladies of that family. The old manor house, built by Richard Charnock, in the reign of Queen Elizabeth, has lately been pulled down. This Richard Charnock was three times sheriff for the county; he rebuilt the parish church of Hulcote at his own expence, as appears by the inscription on his monument. There are several other memorials for the family in the church. Mrs. Barbara Hervey, who is one of the joint proprietors of the manor, is sole patroness of the rectory, which is united with that of the neighbouring parish of Salford.

HUSBORN-CRAWLEY, in the hundred of Manshead, and deanery of Flitt, lies on the borders of Buckinghamshire, about eleven miles north-west of Bedford. In the chronicle of Dunstaple, Husborn, or Husseborn, and Crawley, seem to be spoken of as two places[c], although one parish, the church being at Husborn. The manor belonged anciently to the Earls of Albemarle, and afterwards to the families of Flitwick[d] and Finaunce[e]. In the seventeenth century it was in the Thompsons. In 1691, it was purchased of Sir John Thompson, by John Lowe; and in 1721, of Francis Lowe esq. by Wriothesly, Duke of Bedford[f], from whom it has de-

---

[a] Cart. 21 Edward I. and Cart. 39 Edward III.   [b] Baronetage.   [c] See particularly Anno 1251.
[d] Chron. Dunst.   [e] Esch. 37 Henry VI.   [f] Duke of Bedford's Records.

scended

fcended to the prefent Duke. In the church is a handfome monument, with the effigies of a knight in armour, and his lady, under a canopy fupported by Doric columns : it has no infcription, but by the arms appears to be that of one of the Thompfon family. The impropriate rectory and advowfon of the vicarage, which formerly belonged to the priory of Dunftaple, were purchafed of the Thompfons, by the anceftors of the Rev. E. Williamfon, who conveyed them to the late Duke of Bedford in 1795. The fame year an act of parliament paffed for inclofing the parifh, when an allotment was affigned to the impropriator in lieu of tithes. In 1796, this vicarage (which was endowed in 1220, as appears by the chronicle of Dunftaple) was confolidated with Afpley-Guife.

KEMPSTON, in the hundred of Redbornftoke, lies about three miles north-weft of Bedford. The manor of Kempfton-Daubeny, which has been commonly deemed the paramount manor, was granted in 1309 to John de Britannia, Earl of Richmond [g], and in 1337, to William Daubeny [h]. This manor, which appears to have been afterwards in the Brays [i], together with another manor, which paffed by an heir female from the family of Fifher to the St. Johns, and has been known by the name of Kempfton-Fifhers, and Kempfton-St. Johns [k], were both in the feventeenth century in the family of Snagg, of whom they were purchafed, early in the laft century, by the anceftor of Robert Dennis efq. of Kempfton, the prefent proprietor.

Another manor called Kempfton-Greys, otherwife Haftingfbury, was parcel of the dower of Maud, Countefs of Huntingdon, and afterwards of her daughter-in-law, Helen, Countefs of Chefter, having been fucceffively in the families of Brus, Baliol, and Haftings, who married the co-heireffes of John Earl of Chefter [l], it paffed from the latter by a female heir to the Greys. In the reign of James I. it was the property of Sir Edward Cater, of whofe reprefentatives it has been lately purchafed by the prefent proprietor, William Long efq.

William de Bohun had free warren in Hardwyck, a hamlet of this parifh, in 1328 [m]. After the attainder of his defcendant the Duke of Buckingham, in 1460,

[g] Cart. 2 Edward III.   [h] Pat. 11 Edward III.

[i] Sir Edward Bray was poffeffed of it 9 Eliz. It had probably been then fome time in the family of Bray. Papers communicated by William Bray efq. F.A.S.

[k] A record of the year 1419, (7 Henry V.) See Placit. &c. in Com. Bedford in Turr. Lond. fpeaks of a manor of Draytons in Kempfton, concerning which there was then a lawfuit between the guardians of Sir John Drayton's daughter and others. It is probable that this was the eftate, which was afterwards called Kempfton-Fifhers, and Kempfton-St. Johns.

[l] Dugdale's Baronage, and Efch.   [m] Cart. 2 Edward III.

the

the manor of Kempſton-Hardwyck was in the family of Bowton. Edward Bowton conveyed it to Henry VIII. in 1542 : it was afterwards in the families of Long [n] and Fitzwilliam [o]. This manor having been for a conſiderable time in the Cater family, was purchaſed of their repreſentatives by Mr. Long. The great tithes of Kempſton were appropriated to the priory of Caldwell and to Elſtow Abbey. The preſent impropriators are George Livius eſq.; Thomas Gurney eſq.; and F. G. Spurgeon Farrer eſq. : Mr. Aſpinall, the preſent incumbent, is patron of the vicarage, which is in the deanery of Bedford. The pariſh of Kempſton has been incloſed by an act of parliament paſſed in 1802, when allotments of land were aſſigned to the impropriators, and to the vicar, who was entitled to all the ſmall tithes, as well as to the great tithes of the Holmes.

KEYSOE, in the hundred of Stodden, and deanery of Eaton, lies in the north part of the county, about eleven miles from Bedford. There were formerly two manors in this pariſh, called Keyſoe-Berryſted, and Keyſoe-Grange, both of which became united in the St. John family. One of theſe manors was granted by Edward I. in 1297 to Walter Lord Teyes [p], from whom it paſſed by heirs female to the Patſhulls [q], Beauchamps, and St. Johns. The other appears to have belonged to the Peyvres [r], and Dayrells [s], before it came into the poſſeſſion of the St. Johns, a branch of which family had a ſeat at Keyſoe. The manor was purchaſed of the laſt Earl of Bolingbroke, about the year 1700, by the anceſtors of John Crawley eſq. of Stockwood, near Luton, who is the preſent proprietor.

The pariſh church which is a handſome Gothic building, has no monumental inſcriptions of any note. On the outſide is a tablet, commemorating the providential eſcape of a man who fell from the top of the ſpire. The church of Keyſoe was given by Simon de Beauchamp to the priory of Chickſand. The impropriation is now veſted in the maſter and ſcholars of Trinity College, Cambridge, who are patrons of the vicarage. Mr. Crawley is leſſee under the college. An act for incloſing this pariſh paſſed in 1803, when allotments, in lieu of tithes, were aſſigned to the impropriators and to the vicar.

KNOTTING, in the hundred of Stodden and deanery of Clopham, is a ſmall village on the borders of Northamptonſhire, about eleven miles from Bedford. It lies a little to the north of the Higham-Ferrers road. It was for ſeveral years a manor and ſeat of the Pyes of Berkſhire, of whom it was purchaſed in 1774, for the late Duke of Bedford during his minority. The manor houſe is now occupied

[n] Eſch. Eliz.   [o] Eſch. Jac.   [p] Cart. 2 Edw. I.   [q] Eſch. Edw. III.   [r] Cl. Hen. III.
[s] Cl. Hen. VI.

as a farm. The Duke of Bedford is patron of the rectory, which has been united to Souldrop.

LANGFORD, in the hundred of Bigglefwade, lies about four miles north-eaft of Shefford. The manor was parcel of the barony of Odell, and the fee continued in the family of the Wahuls or Wodhulls[t], Lords of that Barony, till the reign of Edward IV. Of late years it has been for a confiderable time in the family of Browne, of which the late Mrs. Schutz was the heirefs. The church of Weftminfter has alfo a manor in this parifh. The rectory was appropriated to the knights hofpitallers, and afterwards, by a grant bearing date 1547, to Fotheringay College in Northamptonfhire. The prefent proprietor of the great tithes and rectorial manor is Sir John Fagg bart. in right of his wife, who was daughter of Mr. Newman of Canterbury. The vicarage, which is in the deanery of Shefford, is in the gift of the crown.

LEIGHTON-BUSARD, in the hundred of Manfhead and deanery of Dunftaple, is a market-town on the borders of Buckinghamfhire, forty-one miles from London. It is fuppofed to have been the Lygeanburgh of the Saxon Chronicle, which was taken from the Britons by Cuthwulph in 571. It has been conjectured that the addition of Buffard or Buzzard is a corruption of Beaudefert, which name, indeed, occurs in fome old papers ; but in the moft ancient records the name of the town is written Leighton-Bofard, and fometimes Bufard or Buzzard. The family of Bofard or Boffard, from whom it feems to have derived its additional name, were of confequence in the county, and knights of the fhire, in the reigns of Edward II. and Edward III[u].

The market which is on Tuefdays, is one of the moft ancient in the county ; the tolls were valued at 7l. per annum at the time of the Norman furvey. There are fix fairs, viz. February 5, the fecond Tuefday in April, Whitfun Tuefday, July 26, October 24, and the fecond Tuefday in December. Two of thefe were granted to Eton College in 1447, the fecond and laft are of modern date; fome of thefe fairs are noted for a large fale of horfes. In the market-place is a beautiful Gothic crofs of a pentagonal form, with figures of Kings, &c. The affizes for the county were held at Leighton in July 1657. The number of houfes in Leighton parifh, (exclufive of the hamlets,) according to the returns made to parliament in 1801 purfuant to the Population Act, was 376, that of inhabitants 1963.

The manor of Leighton, which was part of the ancient demefne of the crown, is now held on leafe under the church of Windfor, by the Hon. Mary Leigh, fifter of

[t] Efch. Edw. IV. Thomas Reynes who held the manor of Langford under the Wahuls, paid a fine for alienation, anno 50 Edward III.   [u] Willis's Notit. Parl.

the late Lord Leigh of Stonely in Warwickſhire, whoſe anceſtor Sir John Leigh acquired it about the year 1600, by marrying the daughter and heir of Sir Chriſtopher Hoddeſdon [u].

King Henry II. granted a manor in Leighton to the abbeſs and Ciſtercian nuns, of Font-Everard, in Normandy, who eſtabliſhed a cell of foreign monks in this pariſh, at a place called Grovebury [x], the prior of which was procurator-general for the concerns of the abbey of Font-Everard, in England. In 1316, this manor was held under the abbeſs, by Mary the king's ſiſter, who was a nun at Ambreſbury [y]. In 1411, the abbeſs of Font-Everard had the king's licence to alienate the manor of Grovebury to John Worſhip [z]. In 1413, it was purchaſed by Sir John Phelip, who ſettled it upon his wife Alice, a grand-daughter of the poet Chaucer, and their joint heirs [a]. It ſeems to have been ſeized by the crown, on the death of her third huſband, William Duke of Suffolk; for, in 1472, it was granted for life to the ducheſs, as a compenſation in part for a debt due to her from the crown [b]. It was enjoyed alſo by her ſon John Duke of Suffolk, who jointly with Elizabeth his wife, the king's ſiſter, granted the manor of Grovebury, alias Leighton-Boſard, to Windſor College [c]. The Hoddeſdons and Leighs held this manor on leaſe under the College. In 1668, Thomas Lord Leigh aſſigned the leaſe to Dr. George Bate, phyſician to King Charles II.; from his family it paſſed to the Powneys; and about 1776, from them to William Villiers Lewis eſq. father of William Villiers Villiers eſq. the preſent leſſee.

Beſides the alien priory before-mentioned, biſhop Tanner ſays, there ſeems to have been a houſe of Ciſtercian monks in Leighton, which was a cell to Woburn abbey.

In the pariſh church, which is a handſome Gothic building, are monuments for the family of Leigh, among which are thoſe of the Hon. Charles Leigh, who died in 1704, and his daughter Alice, Baroneſs Altham, who died in 1684. There are monuments alſo for the families of Wingate, Welles, and Wilkes. In the nave is a tablet to the memory of John Pulford, M. A. who died in 1710. " He made an augmentation," ſays his epitaph, " to the poor vicarage of Leighton, with a liberality not unworthy the greateſt prelate." This augmentation produces now, in lands and money, about 60l. *per annum*. The ſurvey of Doomſday ſtates the rectory of Leighton, then the property of Remigius, biſhop of Lincoln, to conſiſt of four hides of land. The rectorial manor is now a prebendal corps in that church, to which the biſhop collates. The leaſe has been held, with that of the principal manor, by the Hoddeſdons and Leighs, and is now veſted in the Hon.

[u] Collins' Peerage. [x] Dugdale's Monaſt. vol. ii. [y] Nomina Villarum in the Britiſh Muſeum.
[z] Pat. 12 Hen. IV. [a] Pat. 1 Hen. V. [b] Pat. 12 Edw. IV. [c] Pat. 20 Edw. IV.

Mrs.

Mrs. Mary Leigh. The prebendary is patron of the vicarage. William Sclater, a divine of some note, in the 17th century, was son of Anthony Sclater, who enjoyed the vicarage of Leighton-Busard fifty years, and lived to be nearly a hundred years of age[d]. There was a fraternity or brotherhood in the church of Leighton: a part of their hall is still standing in Broad-street not far from the cross.

At the entrance of the town, is an alms-house for eight poor widows, founded by Matthew Wilkes in 1630. Their allowance is 3s. a week each, besides firing and clothes. The Hon. Mrs. Leigh, about the year 1790, built a house for the Sunday-schools, to which she subscribes 20l. *per annum*.

Heath, commonly called Heath-and-Reach, Billington, Egginton, Stanbridge, and Clipson, are hamlets in this parish: the four first have chapels of ease. Heath-and-Reach lies about two miles from Leighton; Billington and Egginton about the same distance. In the returns made to Parliament in 1801, pursuant to the Population Act, all these hamlets, excepting Clipson, were numbered separately from Leighton; Stanbridge is stated to have 57 houses, and 262 inhabitants; Billington 39 houses, and 200 inhabitants; Egginton 44 houses, and 206 inhabitants; Heath-and-Reach 111 houses, and 541 inhabitants. The manor of Egginton, which, during the last century, passed through several hands, was lately the property of John Bond esq. and now of George Goodwin esq.

There are now three manors in Stanbridge, two of which it is probable belonged to the ancient family of Chamberleyne; since one of them is to be traced to the Fowlers, and the other to the Morteynes, both of which families inherited estates by female heirs from the Chamberleynes, who possessed the manor in the year 1323[e]. The manor of Stanbridge, as it is now called, was in the Fowlers about the latter end of the 16th century, afterwards in the families of Iremonger and Baldwin. From the latter it descended to the Rev. Mr. Pitman, of whom it was purchased by the husband of the present proprietor, Mrs. Gurney. The manor of Morteynes, *alias* Reynes descended by a female heir from the Morteynes to the Dicons. In 1547, it was purchased by the family of Reynes of Clifton-Reynes. After several intermediate conveyances, it came into possession of the Brandreths about the year 1700, and having passed by marriage to the Duncombes, was purchased of Brandreth Duncombe esq. in 1786, by John Franklin esq. the present proprietor. Another manor called Morrells, from a family who possessed it in the reign of Henry VI. was at that time called the manor of Stanbridge, and is supposed to have been the principal manor, since that, which is now called the manor of Stanbridge, then paid a quit-rent to it. From the Morrells, this manor passed to the family of Brocas, and from them to the Ellinghams, who were in possession at least 150 years. In 1746,

---

[d] Fuller's Worthies.   [e] Placit. &c. de terris in Com. Bed. in Turr. Lond.

Thomas Ellingham conveyed it to John Capon and John Franklin. It is now the fole property of John Franklin efq. of Rufhmore.

In the chapel at Stanbridge is a monument in memory of Henry Honner and Jane his wife, who lived together in wedlock about 60 years : he died in 1627, at the age of 95 ; fhe in 1629, at the age of 86. There have been no burials in the other chapels, nor have they any cemeteries.

LIDLINGTON, or LITLINGTON, in the hundred of Redbornftoke and deanery of Flitt, lies three miles and a half weft of Ampthill, and about 8 miles fouth-weft of Bedford. The manor, which had been parcel of the poffeffions of the abbefs and convent of Barking, was conveyed to King Henry VIII. by Dorothy Barleigh the laft abbefs, two years before the furrender of that monaftery. Having for many years belonged to the family of Chefter, who had a feat at Litlington, it was fold by the reprefentatives of the laft baronet, in 1769, to Mr. Ifaac Hawkins ; who, in 1774, conveyed it to the late earl of Upper Offory. It is now the property of the Duke of Bedford, in confequence of an exchange which took place in 1801, between the late duke, and the prefent earl of Offory.

The manor of Goldingtons, in this parifh, belonged to a family of that name, one of whom lies buried in the parifh church. On the tomb is his effigies on a brafs plate, in armour, with an imperfect date (148..) This eftate belonged afterwards to the family of Reynes, from whom it paffed by marriage to the Dicons[g]. Soon after the year 1600 it was in the Snaggs [h], of Marfton-Morteyne, who poffeffed it for more than a century. It is now the property of Earl Spencer. The tithes of this parifh were formerly appropriated to the abbey of Barking, in Effex. Under the Inclofure Act which paffed in 1775, an allotment of land was affigned in lieu of tithes to the earl of Upper Offory, then impropriator. The rectorial allotment was included in the exchange before-mentioned.

LUTON, in the hundred of Flitt and deanery of Dunftaple, is a confiderable market town on the borders of Hertfordfhire. It lies on the road from London to Ampthill and Bedford, near the 31ft mileftone. The market, which is on Monday, is noted for its abundant fupply of corn. It is of great antiquity, being mentioned in the furvey of Doomfday, where the tolls are valued at 100s. *per annum*. There are two annual fairs, April 18th and October 18th. The number of houfes in the parifh, according to the returns made to Parliament in 1801, purfuant to the Population Act, was 612, of inhabitants 3095.

The manor of Luton, having been part of the royal demefne, was given by

---

[g] Efch. Edw. VI.　　[h] Efch. Car. I.

William

William the Conqueror to Geoffrey, earl of Perch [i]. By a subsequent grant it became the property of Robert, earl of Gloucester [k], and having again reverted to the crown, was granted by King Stephen, to Richard Waudari [l], and afterwards by King Richard I. to Baldwin de Betun, earl of Albemarle [m]. William Marefhall, earl of Pembroke, who married the earl of Albemarle's daughter and heir, gave it to the famous Fulk de Brent, who, in 1216, obtained a confirmation from king John of the honour of Luton [n]. It is probable that the caftle built at Luton in 1221, which is reprefented in the chronicle of Dunftaple as having been very prejudicial to the neighbouring town, was one of the fortreffes of this haughty and oppreffive baron.

Upon the banifhment of De Brent, Luton was re-granted to the earl of Pembroke, who, thus, as the above-mentioned Chronicle obferves, recovered what with foolifh prodigality had been given away [o]. Eleanor, widow of William Marefhall, earl of Pembroke, fifter of king Henry III., who married to her fecond hufband, Simon de Montford, Earl of Leicefter, held the manor of Luton in dower till her death, which happened in 1274 [p]: it then devolved to the reprefentatives of Sibil, Countefs of Derby, who was one of the co-heireffes of William Marefhall the elder, earl of Pembroke, and died many years before, leaving feven daughters, two of whom brought parts of this manor into the families of Mohun and Kyme [q]. From one of thefe it is probable a part paffed to the family of Bonham, who had fome fhare of the manor in the reign of Edward II. [r]; but the greater part, and it is probable the whole eventually, became vefted by purchafe of the other feveralties in the family of Hugh de Mortimer, who married Agatha, one of the co-heireffes of the above-mentioned Countefs of Derby. This branch of the Mortimers became extinct in the male line in the fourth generation after this match [s]. John Creffey, as their coufin and heir, was lord of the manor of Luton in 1403 [t]. Soon after this it appears to have been vefted in the crown, for in 1406, king Henry V. granted the manor of Luton-Mortimer to John, Duke of Bedford, regent of France [u].

The next poffeffor on record is John Lord Wenlock, whofe family appears to have owned eftates in Luton at an earlier period [w]. Leland fays, that this Lord Wenlock, who was killed at the battle of Tewkefbury in 1472, left an heir-general,

---

[i] Dugdale's Baronage.   [k] Lives of the abbots of St. Alban's, annexed to Mat. Paris.   [l] Ibid.
[m] Cart. Antiq. infra Tur. Lond.   [n] Pat. 18 Joh.   [o] Hearne's Chron. Dunft.   [p] Ibid.   [q] Efch.
Edw. 1. and Dugdale's Baronage.   [r] Records of Luton manor communicated by Mr. Brown.
[s] Dugdale.   [t] Records of Luton Manor.   [u] Pat. 4 Henry V.

[w] Lord Wenlock's grandfather was a Wyvell; he married into the family of Wenlock and affumed the name. William Wenlock, prebendary of Brownfwood, who died in 1392, had eftates in Luton. He was brother to Joan Wenlock, who married Lord Wenlock's grandfather. Sir Thomas Wenlock, who was knight of the fhire in the three firft years of King Henry VI. was, it is probable, of this family.

who

who married a kinfman of archbifhop Rotheram, one of the founders of Lincoln-College in Oxford. Others have fuppofed that the Luton eftates were granted by King Edward IV. to the archbifhop, as attainted property[x]. The family alliance, mentioned by Leland, is not to be found in any of the pedigrees in the heralds college. It appears on record, that certain houfes in London which had devolved to the crown, not by the attainder, but by the death of Lord Wenlock without iffue, were granted in 1475 to Thomas Rotheram, then bifhop of Lincoln[y]. The grant of Luton does not appear on record. It is certain that John Rotheram, brother of the bifhop, was lord of the manor of Luton and the hundred of Flitt in 1476[z], and that Thomas Lawley efq. who by pedigrees of the family, appears to have been heir-general of Lord Wenlock, conveyed Luton and feveral manors or farms in that parifh to bifhop Rotheram, in 1477[a]. This conveyance, it is probable, might have been obtained for the greater fecurity of the title, even if there had been a grant from the crown. The manor of Luton continued in the Rotheram family till the year 1614, when it was purchafed by Sir Robert Napier bart. of Mercheflon, in Scotland[b]. Sir John Napier, the laft heir-male of that family, who died in 1747, bequeathed it to his aunt, Mrs. Frances Napier, by whofe bequeft it became the property of Francis Herne efq. Mr. Herne, in 1763, fold it to John, earl of Bute, whofe fon (created Marquis of Bute in 1796) is the prefent proprietor, and has his chief country feat at Luton-Hoo in this parifh.

The manor of Hoo, or Luton-Hoo, was the ancient inheritance of the family of Hoo, or De Hoo, who are faid by Sir Henry Chauncy to have been fettled there before the Norman conqueft[c]. Sir Robert de Hoo was knight of the fhire in the reign of Edward I. Sir Thomas Hoo, K. G. who was made Lord Hoo, of Hoo, in Bedfordfhire, and Lord Haftings in 1447, died in 1454 without male iffue. Anne, his only daughter by his fecond wife, brought this manor in marriage to Sir Geffrey Boleyn, who was lord mayor of London in 1460. The tradition of the place is, that his great-grand-daughter, Anne Boleyn, queen to King Henry VIII. was born at this place. Her father fold the manor of Luton-Hoo in 1523 to Richard Farmer, merchant, whofe heir conveyed it in 1575 to John Brocket efq. In 1601 it was purchafed of Mr. Brocket's reprefentatives by Robert Napier efquire[d], and paffed with the manor of Luton to the Marquis of Bute.

Luton-Hoo, the marquis's feat, ftands in the midft of a well-wooded park about three miles from the town. The old park, which confifted of about 300 acres, inclofed by Sir Robert Napier, was enlarged to 1200 by the late Lord Bute,

[x] Hiftory of Luton in Bib. Top. Brit. p. 14, 26, and 31. [y] Pat. 15 Edw. IV. [z] Records of Luton Manor. [a] Cl. 17 Edw. IV. [b] Records of Luton manor. [c] Hiftory of Hertford-fhire. [d] Records of the manor.

who

who employed Brown to lay it out. It now contains about 1500 acres. The river Lea, which rifes in the neighbouring parifh of Houghton-Regis, a little beyond Leagrave, a hamlet of this parifh, runs through the park, where it fupplies two pieces of water, the one containing 14, the other 50 acres. A part of the houfe at Luton-Hoo was rebuilt by the Napiers, but fome parts of it appear to be of a more ancient date. The late Earl of Bute began building a very ftately manfion on the fite, from a defign by Mr. Adam; the eaft front and the fouth wing only were completed. The principal rooms, particularly the library, which is 146 feet in length, the drawing-room and the faloon, are on a magnificent fcale. The collection of pictures is very large and valuable, chiefly of the Italian and Flemifh fchools. Among the portraits are, Margaret queen of Scots, with her fecond hufband Archibald Douglas; the firft Earl of Pembroke, the Earl of Strafford, General Ireton, Mr. Pym, Mrs. Lane, who affifted King Charles II. in his efcape after the battle of Worcefter; Lord Chancellor Jeffreys, Ben Jonfon, Dr. Samuel Johnfon, Dr. Armftrong, and the late Earl of Bute, by Sir Jofhua Reynolds. The chapel is fitted up with very rich Gothic carving in wood, faid to have been originally executed for Sir Thomas Pope at Tittenhanger in 1548, and brought to Luton by Sir Robert Napier. The late Earl of Bute formed a botanic garden at Luton, but he afterwards removed his valuable collection of plants to his feat at Chrift-Church in Hampfhire.

Ancient records defcribe feveral eftates in this parifh by the name of Manors, befides thofe already mentioned; as Fennel's Grove, Langley's, Bennett's, North-wood, Stapleforth, Eaft-Hide, Weft-Hide, Stoppefley, Great Hampfted-Someries, Hayes, Bailiffs, Dallowe, Leagrave, Lightgrave, or Lucy's, Bifcot, &c. It is probable, that fome of thefe originated from the divifions and fub-divifions of the manor among the heirs of Sibella countefs of Derby. None of them poffefs at prefent any manerial rights. The eight firft are enumerated in the conveyance from Mr. Lawley to bifhop Rotherham. All traces of Bennett's and Northwood appear to be loft. A wood, called Fennel's Grove, belongs to the Marquis of Bute. Langley's and Stapleforth are two farms, which paffed to the Napiers, and now belong to the Marquis of Bute; the latter now forms part of Luton park. Eaft-Hide, a reputed manor, which pays a quit-rent to the lord of the manor of Luton, was purchafed in the early part of the laft century by Philadelphia, relict of Sir Thomas Cotton bart. who, not long afterwards, fold it to Mr. Floyer, Governor of Fort St. David. It was purchafed of him by Dr. Bettefworth, chancellor of the diocefe of London, who died in 1779, and is now the property and refidence of his widow. The houfe was built by Lady Cotton. The manor of Weft-Hide, *alias* Aynell's, belongs to the Marquis of Bute: Stoppefley was anciently

in

in the Hoos; in queen Elizabeth's reign, this manor and Hayes belonged to the family of Catesby [b], and were afterwards in the Cheynes [c] : Stoppesley now belongs to the Marquis of Bute. Hayes, which is a small estate within Stoppesley, is the property of Mr. Morris. Dallowe and Bailiffs or Bailies both belong to the Marquis of Bute. Bailiffs was formerly in the family of Field [d], Dallowe in the Crawleys, of whom it was purchased by the Napiers.

The manor of Lightgrave, or Leagrave, was from 1305 to 1455 in the family of Lucy [e], and is presumed to be the same, which, in the seventeenth century, being then called Lucy's, or Lewsy's, was in the family of Wingate [f]. This estate lying principally in the parish of Toddington, is now the Duke of Bedford's, having been purchased in 1782, of John Miller esq. by the trustees under his grand-father's will. The manor of Biscot, or Limbury-*cum*-Biscot, which was also in the Wingates [g], is now the property of John Crawley esq.

The manor of Great Hampsted was, as early as the year 1309, in the baronial family of Somery [h]. In 1464, it was conveyed to Lord Wenlock by the name of Great Hampsted-Someries [i]. This estate passed from the Rotherhams to the Crawleys. A field called Grathamsted, being the site of the reputed manor or manor-farm of Great Hampsted or Grathamsted, is still the property of John Crawley esq. whose ancestors were possessed also of another farm, now the Marquis of Bute's, called Someries, where are the remains of an ancient mansion, supposed to have been begun and left unfinished by Lord Wenlock; but they appear to be of a more recent date, and are probably the ruins of a mansion belonging to Sir John Rotherham, who certainly resided at Someries, which came to the Crawleys by the marriage of his daughter with Sir Francis Crawley, one of the Justices of the Common Pleas [k], who died in 1649. John Crawley, grandfather of Sir Francis, was of Nether-Crawley in the parish of Luton. His descendant, John Crawley esq., has a seat called Stockwood in this parish.

Besides those already mentioned, the Marquis of Bute has two other inferior manors in this parish, called Brach and Farley. Brach belonged to the Rotherams and Napiers, and was purchased by the late Earl of Bute, with the Luton estate, of Mr. Herne. Farley was part of the possessions of the abbot and convent of St. Alban's; it was afterwards the seat of a branch of the Rotherams. King James, on his progress in 1605, spent a night at Sir John Rotherham's near Luton [l].

At Farley or Farleigh, which is about two miles from Luton, was an ancient hospital given by King Henry II. to the great foreign hospital of Santingfield in Picardy,

[b] Esch. Eliz.   [c] Esch. Car. 1.   [d] Esch. Eliz.   [e] Esch. Edw. I—Edw. IV.
[f] Esch. Car. 1.   [g] Ibid.   [h] Esch. 2 Edw. II.   [i] Cl. 3 Edw. IV.
[k] Bedfordshire Pedigrees in the British Museum.   [l] Leland's Collectanea, vol. i, p. 626.

Lee sculp.

PART OF THE WENLOCK CHAPEL, AND CHANCEL OF LUTON CHURCH.

Published by T.Cadell & W.Davies Strand 30th Nov.1805.

to which the mafter and brethren of Farleigh were made fubordinate [m]. William Wenlock, prebendary of Brownfwood, was made mafter of this hofpital in 1379 [n]. Having been feized by King Henry VI. as belonging to an alien houfe, it was given by him to the Provoft and Scholars of King's College in Cambridge [o]. The mafter of Farley hofpital appears to have had a manor in Farley [p]. It is probable, that it was the fame which belongs to the Marquis of Bute, and that the Provoft and Scholars of King's College, who have not at prefent any eftate in Luton, conveyed it to the abbot and convent of St. Alban's, in exchange for other lands.

The parifh church of Luton is a handfome Gothic ftructure: the tower is compofed of flint and other ftones in chequer-work. The chancel was built by John Whethamfted, abbot of St. Alban's, in the 15th century. On the fouth fide are four ftone feats richly ornamented; in the fpandrils are the arms of Edward the Confeffor, the kingdom of Mercia, the abbey of St. Alban's, king Offa, abbot Whethamfted, &c. Above is the abbot's motto *Valles abundabunt*. There is a chapel on the north fide of the chancel, feparated from it by two lofty and elegant Gothic arches. The following infcription, preferved in an heraldic manufcript in the Britifh Mufeum [q], fhews that it was built by Sir John Wenlock, before the year 1461; for, in that year, he was created baron Wenlock.

" Jefu Chrift moft of myght,
  Have mercy on John Le Wenlock Knight,
  And on his wife Elizabeth,
  Who out of this world is paft by death,
  Which founded this chapel here,
  Help them with your hearty prayer,
  That they may come to that place,
  Where ever is joy and folace."

This infcription, and the portrait of Lord Wenlock, which was formerly in the eaft window [r], have been deftroyed or removed. The arms of Wenlock ftill remain quartered with Hoo, and furrounded by the garter. The fame arms are over the fcreen which divides the chapel from the chancel, impaling thofe of Lady Wenlock, who was daughter and co-heir of Sir John Drayton. Under one of the arches is an altar-tomb, on which is the effigies of an ecclefiaftic in his robes, fuppofed to be that of William Wenlock, prebendary of Brownfwood in the cathedral church of St. Paul, and mafter of the hofpital of Farleigh, who died in 1392, and directed his body to be buried at Luton. The infcriptions on the tomb appear to confirm

[m] Tanner.   [n] Hiftory of Luton, p. 36.   [o] Pat. 26 Hen. VI. Pt. 1.
[p] Pope Nicholas's Taxation.   [q] Harl. MSS. No. 1531.
[r] Hiftory of Luton, p. 17.

the

the conjecture; but the arms, which are several times repeated, (Arg. a chevron between three crofs croflets G.) are not thofe of Wenlock. It is poffible that they might have been borne by the hofpital of Farleigh, or that of Santingfield, to which it was fubordinate. The tomb, if it be that of William De Wenlock above mentioned, muft have exifted before the arch was built, and was probably removed to its prefent fituation by Lord Wenlock (who appears to have been great-nephew of the prebendary), when he founded the chapel. The following infcriptions have been frequently, but very erroneoufly, printed; they are imperfect, but what remains is very legible.

On the north fide :—

> " In Wenlok brad I
> In this toun Lordfchipes had I
> Her am I now fady
> Chriftes moder help me Lady
> Under thes ftones
> For a tym fchal I refte my bones
> Dey mot I ned ones
> Myghtful God grant me thy wones."

On the fouth fide :—

> " —illelmus fic tumulatus
> De Wenlok natus,
> In ordine prefbiteratus,
> Alter hujus ville
> Dominus meus fuit ille
> Hic licet indignus
> Anime Deus efto benignus."

It is probable that Elizabeth Lady Wenlock was buried in this chapel, and that Lord Wenlock intended it for his own place of fepulture; but lofing his life in the battle of Tewkefbury, he was buried in the conventual church at that place, where an altar-tomb in the north wall of the nave has been afcribed to him; though, as the arms on the furcoat of the recumbent figure are not thofe of Wenlock, it is more probable that it was intended for fome other perfon. Le Neve has doubted the fact of Lord Wenlock's being flain at Tewkefbury, from the circumftance of his having found the will of John Wenlock, bearing date 1477, fubfequent to that battle'. It certainly, however, was not the will of Lord Wenlock, for King Edward IV. in 1475 granted certain houfes in London, which had efcheated to the crown by the death of John Lord Wenlock without iffue, to the bifhop of Lincoln'. There is no reafon, therefore, for doubting the accuracy of our hiftorians on this point.

' See Hiftory of Luton, p. 46.　　　' Pat. 15 Edw. IV.

In

In the Wenlock chapel are several altar-tombs, stripped of their brasses. It appears by some ancient heraldic notes in the British Museum [u], that they are the tombs of the Rotherams of Someries. One of them was that of Sir Thomas Rotheram, nephew of the archbishop of York, who married Katharine, only child of Anthony Lord Grey of Ruthin, son of Edmund Earl of Kent. This Anthony Lord Grey, who is erroneously supposed to have died without issue, lies buried in the same chapel, where also were deposited the remains of Sir Francis Crawley, one of the Justices of the Common Pleas, who, having incurred the displeasure of Parliament for favouring the claims of King Charles I. in the business of the ship-money, was removed from his situation. He died in 1649. His son Francis Crawley, one of the Barons of the Exchequer, who died in 1682, is buried also in this chapel.

In the north aisle were the monuments of the Rotherams of Farleigh [w]. John Rotheram of this family was Baron of the Exchequer in 1652 [x]. In the north aisle was also the tomb of John Hay, steward to the archbishop of Canterbury, who repaired the church of Luton at his own charge, and died in 1454 [y].

At the west end of the south aisle is the mutilated figure of an ecclesiastic, holding a cross. In the same aisle is the tomb of John Bettesworth, LL. D. chancellor of the diocese of London, who died in 1779. In the north transept is the tomb of John Ackworth esq. who died in 1513. The following motley inscription, excepting the three first words, which have been removed, remains on a brass plate round the verge:

["*O man, whoe'er*] thou be! timor mortis showlde trowble thee; for when thou leest wenyst, veniet te mors superare, and so . . . . . . grave grevys, ergo mortis memoreris. Jesu Mercy, Lady help."

At the west end of the nave is an elegant Gothic baptistery, of an octagonal form. (See p. 31.)

William, the king's chamberlain, had the church of Luton at the time of the Norman survey. It was afterwards annexed to the manor, when in the possession of Robert Earl of Gloucester. Robert, abbot of St. Alban's, procured it for his convent of Robert Waudari, to whom King Stephen had given Luton upon the Earl of Gloucester's rebellion. King Henry II. afterwards seized on this church as part of the royal demesne, but, by the intercession of the abbot, restored it to the convent; and the tithes were then appropriated to defray the expence of entertaining strangers [z]. The Marquis of Bute has now two thirds of the impropriation. The great tithes of Stoppesley, which were granted by Queen Mary to Sir Thomas

---

[u] Harl. MSS. 1531. [w] Hist. of Luton. [x] Ant. Wood. Hist. of Luton.
[z] Lives of the Abbots of St. Alban's, annexed to Mat. Paris, p. 1017.

Pope, and by him given to Trinity College in Oxford, are held by his Lordſhip as leſſee under that college : the remainder belongs to Mr. Crawley. The Marquis is patron of the vicarage.

Thomas Pomfret, father of the poet, was firſt curate, and then vicar, of Luton. Dr. Johnſon ſays that John Pomfret, the poet, died in 1703, in the 36th year of his age. Thomas, ſon of Mr. Thomas Pomfret and Mrs. Catharine his wife, was baptized at Luton, March 12, 1667, as appears by the pariſh regiſter. It is remarkable, that this entry agrees with the poet's age ; and that, among a numerous family, all of whom were baptized at Luton, the name of John does not occur.

There was a fraternity in the church of Luton, dedicated to the Holy Trinity ; a regiſter-book of which, containing the accounts of the brotherhood from the year 1528 to 1547, with many curious particulars relating to their anniverſaries, feaſts, &c. is in the poſſeſſion of the Marquis of Bute.

MARSTON-MORTEYNE, in the hundred of Redbornſtoke, and deanery of Flitt, lies about ſeven miles ſouth-weſt of Bedford, and about four from Ampthill. It had formerly a market on Tueſdays, and a fair at Lady-Day, granted to John De Morteyne[b], who was ſeveral times knight of the ſhire. The Morteynes held this manor many years under the barony of Cainhoe. It was afterwards ſucceſſively in the families of Reynes, Dicons[c], and Snagg[d]. The laſt heir male of the Snaggs ſerved the office of ſheriff in 1705. It is preſumed, that the manor was purchaſed of his repreſentatives by the Ducheſs of Marlborough, and by her bequeathed, with the reſt of her Bedfordſhire eſtates, to her grandſon, the Hon. John Spencer. It is now the property of Earl Spencer.

The manor of Nether Shelton in this pariſh, which had belonged to the priory of Caldwell, was formerly in the Cheyne family[e]. It is now the property of John Foſter eſq.

The pariſh church is a handſome Gothic building : the tower, which is ſquare, and maſſive, ſtands detached from it. In the chancel is an altar-tomb, with the effigies, on a braſs plate, of Thomas Reynes eſq. lord of the manor, who died in 1451, and his wife Alice. There are ſeveral monuments of the family of Snagg. The advowſon of the rectory is veſted in the maſter and ſcholars of St. John's College in Cambridge. The pariſh has been incloſed by an act of Parliament paſſed in 1796, but the lands were not exonerated from tithes.

Wroxill, a hamlet in this pariſh, had formerly a chapel of eaſe, dedicated to St. Leonard the Martyr : it was endowed with glebe, and the tithes of the hamlet[f].

---

[b] Cart. 17 Edw. II.   [c] Thomas Dicons, who inherited by marriage with the heireſs of Reynes, died in 1549. Eſch.   [d] Eſch. Car. I.   [e] Eſch. Eliz.   [f] Chantry Roll in the Augmentation Office.

There

There are now no traces of the building. The manor of Wroxill, in the fifteenth century, was in the family of Saunderson [g], afterwards in the Catesbys [h]; it is now the property of Mr. James Bayly.

The manor of Hoe, which was parcel of the barony of Trally, described in ancient records as in this parish, is now considered to be in the adjoining parish of Wotton.

MAULDEN, in the hundred of Redbornstoke, and deanery of Flitt, lies about a mile and a half from Ampthill. The manor belonged to the priory of Elstow, and afterwards to the Carys. King James, in 1617, granted it, on failure of male issue from Henry Cary, Lord Hunsdon, to Sir John Boteler [i]. After several conveyances, it became the property of Sir Thomas Dacres, who in 1635 sold it to the Earl of Elgin, of Houghton Park, in the adjoining parish. It is now the property of the Duke of Bedford, whose grandfather purchased it of the Earl of Aylesbury, in 1738.

In the church are some memorials of the ancient family of Faldo, who were settled here before the reign of Edward III [k]. They are now extinct. Adjoining the church is a mausoleum, of an octagonal form, erected in 1656 by Thomas Earl of Elgin, in memory of his second wife Diana, daughter of Lord Burleigh, and relict of John Earl of Oxford. In the centre is a figure, in white marble, of the Countess in her shroud rising out of an oval sarcophagus. Mr. Pennant, in his Journey from Chester, says the common people called it the Lady in the punchbowl. The mausoleum is surrounded by niches, supposed to have been intended for the statues of her descendants. One only is occupied, containing that of her husband, who died in 1663. On the floor is a bust of her grandson Edward Bruce esq. eldest son of Robert Lord Bruce. Underneath the mausoleum is a columbarium, the burial-place of the Earl of Aylesbury's family. The earl is patron of the rectory. An act for inclosing the parish passed in 1796, when an allotment of land was given to the rector in lieu of tithes, and an allotment assigned to the poor in lieu of their right to peat from Maulden Moor. John Pomfret, the poet, was rector of Maulden.

MELCHBORN, in the hundred of Stodden, and deanery of Eaton, lies near the borders of Northamptonshire, about 12 miles north of Bedford. It had formerly a market on Fridays, and a fair at the festival of St. Mary Magdalen, granted in 1264 to the knights-hospitallers [l], to whom Adeliza de Clermont, wife of Gil-

---

[g] Cl. 38 Hen. VI.   [h] Esch. Eliz.   [i] Duke of Bedford's Records.   [k] Bedfordshire Pedigrees in the British Museum.   [l] Cart. 49 Hen. III.

bert

bert de Tonbridge, Earl of Clare, gave the preceptory of Melchborn; her grandfon, Roger, Earl of Clare, gave them the manor and church [m].

Leland, who was at Melchborn in 1538, fpeaks of the preceptory as " a right
" fair place of fquare ftone ftanding much upon pillerd vaultes of ftone, with good-
" ly gardeins, orchards, and ponds, and a parke thereby [n]." The preceptory he
calls an ancient ftruꞔure, but fays that the hall was built by Sir William Wefton,
the laft prior of the knights-hofpitallers. The preceptory, which was valued at
241l. 9s. 10½d. *per annum*, was granted to the hofpitallers on the re-eftablifhment of
their order by Queen Mary, in 1558, and upon their fecond fuppreffion, was given
by Queen Elizabeth, to the firft Earl of Bedford [o]. It has been many years in
the noble family of St. John, and fince they have forfaken Bletfoe, has been their
chief refidence. The houfe appears to have been built about the reign of
King James or Charles I.: the front has been modernifed. In the drawing room
are portraits of Margaret, countefs of Richmond, and the firft Lord St. John, of
Bletfoe. The prefent Lord St. John has improved the gardens, and has built feveral hot-houfes and confervatories for the culture of exotics.

The parifh church was modernized and neatly fitted up by the late Mr. Whitbread, Lady St. John's father. A brafs plate is preferved in memory of Robert
Pavely efq. who died in 1377. The St. Johns inherited confiderable property in
Bedfordfhire by a marriage with the heirefs of this family. An organ was put up
at Melchborn in 1800, by Lord St. John, who maintains an organift at his own
expence. The great tithes, which were appropriated to the knights-hofpitallers, are
now vefted in Lord St. John, who is patron of the vicarage.

MEPPERSHALL, or MEPSHALL, in the hundred of Clifton, lies about two miles
fouth of Shefford. The manor was, at an early period, in the family of Mepperfhall, who held it by the fervice of attending the king in his wars with a horfe of no
fixed price, a coat of mail, a fword, lance, iron head-piece, and a little knife [p].
They continued in poffeffion as late as the year 1453 [q]; foon after which, their
eftates paffed by marriage to the Botelers [r]. The manor of Mepperfhall now
belongs to the daughters of the late Thomas Poynter efq. to whofe family it paffed
by purchafe, from the Fleetwoods, about the year 1768. A moated fite near the
church-yard was, it is probable, the feat of the Mepperfhalls.

The manor of Polehanger, in this parifh, which belonged to the priory of
Chickfand, is now the property of Sir George Ofborn bart.

---

[m] Dugdale.   [n] Leland's Itin.   [o] Tanner.   [p] Blount's Tenures.   [q] Efch. Edw. II.—Henry VI.
[r] See Efch. 31 and 39 Henry VI.

The

The monaftery of Warden had an eftate in this parifh called Woodhull Grange. Soon after the Reformation it was in the noble family of Grey, and is now, by inheritance, the property of Lady Lucas.

In the parifh church are tombs of the Mepperfhalls and Botelers, with their effigies in brafs. The advowfon of the rectory, which is in the deanery of Shefford, is vefted in the mafter and fcholars of St. John's College, Cambridge. The circumftance of this parifh being fituated in two counties, is noticed in the furvey of Domefday; a part of it is in an infulated portion of Hertfordfhire. The dining parlour of the old parfonage houfe, which ftood within a moated fite, and has lately been removed, was on the boundary of the two counties. The beam had the following infcription, alluding to this circumftance:

> " If you wifh to go into Hertfordfhire,
> Hitch a little nearer the fire."

The prefent parfonage-houfe ftands alfo in the two counties. The church is in Bedfordfhire.

Near this place, in Hertfordfhire, is an ancient chapel dedicated to St. Thomas, of which a farther account will be given in the defcription of that county.

MILBROOK, in the hundred of Redbornftoke and deanery of Flitt, is a fmall village, fcarcely a mile from Ampthill. At this place was a cell of Benedictine monks, belonging to the abbey of St. Alban's, which was removed about the year 1119, by Geffrey, the 16th abbot of that monaftery, to Moddry, otherwife Beaulieu, in Hertfordfhire[s], the prior of which place had a grant of free warren in Milbrook, in 1294[t]. The manor having belonged fucceffively to the St. Amands and Beauchamps, was purchafed of the latter by Sir John Cornwall, who, in 1442, was created Baron of Milbrook. Not long after the death of this brave officer, who was better known by his other title of Lord Fanhope, Milbrook became vefted in the crown, and was annexed to the honour of Ampthill. The leafe of the manor is now vefted in the Earl of Upper-Offory, in confequence of an exchange with the late Duke of Bedford, who was leffee of the honor of Ampthill.

The parifh church ftands on a hill which overhangs the village. From the church-yard is an extenfive profpect over the vale of Bedford. In the church windows are the arms of Lord Fanhope, with the garter. In the chancel is a tablet to the memory of Dr. George Lawfon, rector, who died in 1684. He was employed by his patron, Robert, earl of Aylefbury, in feveral confidential meffages relating

[s] Lives of the Abbots of St. Alban's annexed to Mat. Paris 1008. [t] Cart. 22 Edw. I.

to the Reftoration. The parifh has been inclofed by an Act of Parliament paffed in 1795, when a fmall allotment of land was given to the rector, who was farther compenfated by a corn rent, charged on lands allotted to the Earl of Offory, who is patron of the rectory. The rector had an allotment alfo in lieu of fern, on Milbrook warren, and there was an allotment to the poor for fuel.

MILTON-BRYANT, more properly MILTON-BRYEN, in the hundred of Man-fhead, and deanery of Dunftaple, lies about two miles from Woburn, a little to the north of the London road. The family of Bryen, and the abbot of Woburn had anciently manors in this parifh[u]. Since the Reformation the manor of Milton-Bryant has been fuccefſively in the families of Stanton[w] and Johnfon. It is now the property and feat of Sir Hugh Inglis, whofe firft wife was the daughter and fole heirefs of the late Henry Johnfon efq. Sir Hugh was created a baronet in 1801. Robert Fitz-Bryen, gave the advowfon of the rectory to Merton abbey, in the reign of Henry II[x]. It is now in the crown. The parifh has been inclofed by an Act of Parliament paffed in 1793, when an allotment of land was affigned to the rector in lieu of his glebe, and a corn rent, in lieu of tithes.

MILTON-ERNEST, in the hundred of Stodden and deanery of Clopham, lies about five miles from Bedford, on the road to Higham-Ferrers. It took its name from the family of Erneys, Harneys, or Erneft, (for they are thus varioufly de-fcribed in records,) who poffeffed the manor from the year 1316[y], or earlier, till 1542, when it paffed to the family of Turnor, of Haverill in Suffolk, by mar-riage with the heirefs of Sir Walter Erneft[z]. Sir Chriftopher Turnor, baron of the Exchequer, was of this family, poffeffed the eftate, refided at Milton, and lies buried in the parifh church. His fons fold the manor to Sir Thomas Rolt of Sa-comb, of whofe widow it was re-purchafed, about the year 1700, by Sir Edmund Turnor, younger brother of the judge, and his grandfon John. In 1719, Edmund Turnor efq. of Stoke-Rochford, fold it to Sir George Byng, afterwards Vifcount Torrington, who had married Margaret Mafter, a grand-daughter of Sir Chrifto-pher Turnor. It was afterwards the property of Mrs. Stukely, fifter of Margaret, Lady Torrington, who bequeathed it to Withers Bramfton efq. of Hall-Place, near Bafingftoke. In 1799, Mr. Bramfton fold it to Mr. Robert Gibbins, the prefent proprietor.

The manor of Baffets, in this parifh, was for a confiderable time in the family of

[u] Nomina Villarum, in the Britifh Mufeum. N° 6281, Harl. MSS. [w] Efch. Car. I.
[x] Manning's Hiftory of Surrey, I. 251. [y] Nomina Villarum. [z] From the information of Edmund Turnor efq. F.R.S. and F.A.S.

Rolt,

Rolt, of Milton, a branch of the Rolts of Sacomb. It is now the property of Mrs. Boyden. There is a third manor called Babbs, which is now in feveralties, between T. Fifher efq. Mr. Ellis Shipley, and Mr. Samuel Wyatt.

In the parifh church are monuments of the families of Turnor and Rolt. The great tithes of this parifh were appropriated to the abbey of St. Alban's. In the reign of Charles I. the rectory belonged to the family of Franklyn. Sir Edmund Turnor, who, it is probable, purchafed of the Franklyns, in the year 1693 muficently endowed the vicarage with the great tithes, then let at 100l. *per annum*, and a parfonage houfe. His defcendant, Edmund Turnor efq. of Panton, in Lincolnfhire, is the prefent patron. Among many other acts of charity for which Sir Edmund Turnor ftands recorded as a public benefactor, is the foundation of an almshoufe at this place in the year 1695, for fix poor perfons, which he endowed with lands in Milton, Clapham, and Oakley, now let at 34l. *per annum*. An act of Parliament paffed for inclofing the parifh in 1803, when an allotment of land was affigned to the vicar in lieu of the great and fmall tithes.

NORTHILL, in the hundred of Wixamtree, and deanery of Shefford, about eight miles nearly eaft of Bedford, was called in ancient records North-Yevel. It was parcel of the barony of Trally, or Traylly. Sir John Traylly, the laft heirmale of that family (who were not fummoned to Parliament as barons later than the reign of King John [z]), died feifed of it in 1350 [a]. It is now the property of John Harvey efq. of Ickwell-bury who purchafed it, in 1802, of John Robinfon efq. of Denfton-Hall, in the county of Suffolk. An anceftor of Mr. Robinfon's, nearly a century ago, married an heirefs of the Bromfall family, who were for a confiderable time proprietors of this manor. Owen Thomas Bromfall efq. who is fuppofed to have been the laft heir-male of the family, was buried at Northill in 1731.

The manors of Thorncote, Hatch, Brookend, and Budna, which belonged for many years to the Bromfalls, were purchafed of Mr. Thomas Smith, of Gray's-Inn, by the prefent proprietor, Godfrey Thornton efq. of Moggerhanger.

The manors of Upper and Lower Caldecot, and the manor of Ickwell, have been, for more than a century, in the family of the prefent proprietor, John Harvey efq. who has a feat in this parifh called Ickwell-bury. Mr. Harvey has two other eftates, called the manors of Hartfholm and Blundells, in the two Caldecots. Mr. Fyfhe Palmer has a feat at Ickwell, which he inherits from the Fyfhes. Humphrey Fyfhe efq. of Ickwell, was fheriff of the county in 1684. Another manor of Caldecot, in Northill, having been previoufly in the families of Fyfhe, Moore, Ratchford, and Vaughan, was conveyed in 1714, to Mrs. Stukely,

---

[z] Dugdale. [a] Efch. 34 Edw. III.

whofe

whofe nephew, the Hon. John Byng, fold it to Mr. Thomas Smith of Gray's Inn.

The parifh church, a large and handfome Gothic ftructure, is fuppofed to have been built in the beginning of Henry IV.'s reign; at which time it was made collegiate by Sir Gerard Braybroke, one of Sir John Traylly's executors. In the roof of the porch, which is of ftone, are the arms of Traylly, a crofs flory between four martlets. Northill college was founded in the year 1405, for a warden or mafter, and a difcretionary number of fellows, chaplains, or minifters, who were to pray for the fouls of Sir John Traylly and Reginald his fon, both then deceafed[b]. The lands belonging to this college, valued at 61l. 5s. 3d. *per annum*, were granted, in 1548, to William Fitzwilliam[c].

In the chancel of Northill church are monuments of the Harveys of Ickwell-bury; and the following epitaph for Capel Berrow, a theological writer of fome note, author of a treatife " On the Lapfe of human Souls," who was forty years curate of the parifh: " Quicquid fuit mortale Rev^i. Capel Berrow, A. M. Hon^{imi}. Gul. Comitis Cowper à facris, fub hoc marmore conditur; immortale vero ut pium eft credere, cœlum confcendit beatorum ordinibus afcribendum. Quippe fi quem virtus egregia, fingularis humanitas, cultufque numinis fervidus ac frequens, meritò commendant, hunc integerrima plane vita, facile ingenium ac liberale ut animus uni fceleri infenfus, laudibus abunde cumularunt. Hujus paroch. 40 circiter annos paftor miro quodam impetu verborum et delectu munus divinum illuftravit; et quid verum atque decens non dixiffe folum vifus eft orator fed infpirantem fui cordis tabulam, etiam et tranfcripfiffe. Patri quidem optime promerito, 5 Cal. Nov. 1751, vita defuncto æt. anno 70, hoc pietatis et affectus monumentum filii lugentes pofuere." The eaft window of the chancel is fitted up with ftained glafs, by J. Oliver, confifting of the royal arms, thofe of the grocers' company, and of feveral of their mafters and wardens; and the arms of Margaret Lady Slayny, with whofe money, given in truft to the grocers' company for charitable purpofes, the impropriate rectory and advowfon of Northill, formerly belonging to the collegiate church, were purchafed in 1664. The grocers' company prefent to the benefice, now called a rectory, having fince that time been endowed with fuch of the great and fmall tithes as were included in the purchafe, viz. the great tithes of Beefton, Thorncot, Hatch, Budna, and Brookend, with fome few exceptions, and the whole of the fmall tithes, excepting thofe of the college farm, and a few other lands. Mr. Harvey of Ickwell-bury has the great tithes of Northill, Ickwell, and the two Caldecots, with fome few exceptions. Allotments of land were made to the feveral proprietors of tithes under an inclofure act, which paffed in the year

---

[b] Pat. 6 Hen. IV.   [c] Tanner.

1780. Some further allotments for tithes appear to have been made to the incumbent of Northill, under an act which paffed in 1796 for the inclofing of this parifh and Blunham.

OAKLEY, in the hundred of Stodden and deanery of Clopham, lies on the banks of the Oufe, about four miles north-weft of Bedford. The manor was, at an early period, in the baronial family of Argentine[a]; it was afterwards held by the family of Reynes under the Lords Roos[b], and acquired the name of Oakley Reynes. It became vefted in the crown, on the attainder of Lord Vaux in 1464[c]. A younger fon of the firft Lord Mordaunt fettled at Oakley in the fixteenth century: it is probable that he acquired the manor either by grant or purchafe. His defcendants were certainly poffeffed of it in 1679; in which year it was alienated to Sir Creffwell Levinz, one of the Juftices of the Common Pleas[d]. It is now the property of the Duke of Bedford, whofe grandfather purchafed it of the Levinz family in 1737. The Duke has a villa at Oakley, pleafantly fituated on the banks of the Oufe, which was his country-feat before he fucceeded to the title.

The parifh church appears to have been built by one of the family of Reynes, who lies buried under an Ogie arch in the fouth wall, where is his effigies in robes, on an altar-tomb, with his arms, and two other coats. The great tithes, which were appropriated to the priory of Caldwell, are now vefted in the provoft and fellows of Eton College, who are patrons of the vicarage. The Duke of Bedford is leffee under the College. An Act of Parliament paffed for inclofing this parifh in 1803, when allotments of land in lieu of tithes were affigned to the impropriators, and to the vicar.

ODELL, in the hundred of Willey and deanery of Clopham, lies upon the banks of the Oufe, one mile from Harold, and about ten miles north-weft of Bedford, on the borders of Northamptonfhire. In 1222 William Fitzwarren had a grant of a market at this place on Thurfdays[e]. The next year a prohibition was iffued, commanding that the market fhould not be held, if it proved detrimental to the neighbouring market of Olney in Buckinghamfhire[f]. It is moft probable there was then no market at Harold. The market at Odell was confirmed in 1242[g], but has long been difufed. A fair is held annually on the Thurfday and Friday in Whitfun-week.

Odell, anciently called Wahul or Wodhull, was the feat of an ancient barony, belonging, at the time of the Norman furvey, to Walter Flandrenfis, whofe pofte-

[a] Cart. Edw. II.   [b] Efch. 17 Edw. III.   [c] Efch. 4 Edw. IV.   [d] Duke of Bedford's Records.   [e] Cart. 6 Hen. III.   [f] Cart. 7 Hen. III.   [g] Cart. 26 Hen. III.

rity were called De Wahul[h]. Several manors in Bedfordfhire, Northamptonfhire, and Buckinghamfhire, were parcels of the barony. The family of Wahul were not fummoned to parliament after the reign of Edward I. but they continued in the male line, and called themfelves the Lords Wahul till the reign of Henry VIII. when the heir female of Anthony, titular Lord Wahul, married Richard Chetwode, a younger fon of Roger Chetwode efq. of Oakley in Staffordfhire[i]. Sir Richard Chetwode, in the reign of James the Firft, being poffeffed of the manor of Odell, made an unfuccefsful attempt to obtain the title of Lord Wahul, by petition to the Houfe of Lords. His defcendant, Knightly Chetwode, renewed the claim about the middle of the laft century, but with no better fuccefs[k]. The manor of Great Wodhull or Odell had been long before fold by the Chetwodes to the Alftons[l]. Sir Thomas Alfton of Odell was created a baronet in 1642. The prefent baronet, Sir John Alfton, refides in Cambridgefhire. Odell is the feat and property of Thomas Alfton efq.

Leland, who vifited Bedfordfhire in the reign of Henry VIII. defcribes Odell Caftle as " ftrange ruins belonging to the Lord Bray." It feems difficult to reconcile this with its defcent from the Lords Wahul to the Chetwodes, which is proved by various records. Odell Caftle ftands on an eminence, and commands a beautiful view of the river Oufe, and the adjacent country : very little remains of the old building ; the prefent houfe is chiefly modern. The fouth front was built by Lady Wolftenholme, relict of Sir Rowland Alfton, who died in 1698.

The manor of Little Odell was, at the time of the Norman furvey, part of the eftate of Euftace Earl of Boloigne ; and continued, for a confiderable time, to be part of the honor of Boloigne, but was afterwards annexed to the barony of Wahul[m].

The parifh church is a handfome Gothic building, and has feveral monuments of the family of Alfton. The chantry-roll for Bedfordfhire[n] mentions, that there was an endowment, before the Reformation, for the maintenance of a lamp in this church, and for a *drinking*, that is, a church ale. Mr. Alfton is patron of the rectory. In 1556 Sir Ofwald Butler, rector of Odell, did penance in the parifh church, by order of Cardinal Pole, for living with his wife[o]. The parifh of Odell has been inclofed under an Act of Parliament which paffed in 1776, when an allotment of land was affigned to the rector in lieu of tithes.

PAVENHAM, or PAVINGHAM, in the hundred of Willey and deanery of Clopham, lies about fix miles north-weft of Bedford. The manor was anciently in the

---

[h] See Cooper's Hiftory of Odell, in Bibl. Top. Brit.   [i] Ibid.   [k] Ibid.   [l] Ibid.   [m] Ibid.
[n] In the Augmentation Office.   [o] Hiftory of Odell.

Pabenhams [p], from whom it paffed, by an heir female, to the Tyringhams [q]. It has fince been, for a confiderable time, in the Alfton family, and is now the property of Thomas Alfton efq. The Mafter and Scholars of Trinity College in Cambridge have a manor, and the impropriate rectory of this parifh, and are patrons of the vicarage, which is united to Felmerfham. In the church are tombs of the families of Alfton and Franklyn. The parifh has been inclofed by an Act of Parliament, in 1769, when allotments of land in lieu of tithes were affigned to the impropriators, and to the vicar. Stafford bridge over the Oufe, with a caufey of thirty-five arches, paffable for carriages, but without a fence, is in this parifh.

PERTENHALL, in the hundred of Stodden and deanery of Eaton, lies on the borders of Huntingdonfhire, about three miles from Kimbolton. The manor was anciently in the Peyvres [r] and Dayrells; from the latter it paffed by purchafe to the Mowbrays [s]. Sir William Compton, being feifed of it in 1518, fold it to Bifhop Fox, the founder of Corpus Chrifti College in Oxford, by whom it was given to that Society.

The knights templars had the advowfon of the church, and an eftate ftill called Knights Templars, where is the fite of a moated manfion. Sir Edward Montague, Chief Juftice of the King's Bench, had an eftate in Pertenhall, parcel of the manor of Hoo, and held under that of Kimbolton [t]. The manors of Pertenhall-How, and Bell's alias Conington's-fee, were fold by Simon Taylor efq. in 1790, to the Rev. Mr. Pagett, and are now the property of William Pagett efq. John Sifmey efq. has another manor in Pertenhall, which he inherited from the family of Deane.

In the parifh church is the monument of a crufader, with his effigies in ftone; and in the chancel that of Dr. John King, rector of Chelfea, author of feveral tracts and fermons, who died in 1732. His defcendant, the Rev. John King, is now patron of the rectory of Pertenhall. The parifh has been inclofed by an Act of Parliament, paffed in 1796, when an allotment of land was given to the rector in lieu of tithes.

POTESGRAVE, in the hundred of Manfhead and deanery of Dunftaple, lies about two miles and a half from Woburn, between the two great roads. The manor belonged to the monaftery of Woburn; and having been granted by king Edward VI. to Lord Clinton and Say, was foon afterwards conveyed to the family of Saunders; and, having fince paffed by the fame title as Battlefden, was, together

[p] Efch. Hen. III. &c.   [q] Efch. Rich. II.   [r] Cart. Hen. III.   [s] Cl. 12 Edw. IV.
[t] Cole's Efcheats in the Britifh Mufeum.

with

with the advowfon of the rectory, the property of the late Sir Gregory Page Turner bart. who died fince the account of that parifh was printed, and is fucceeded in title and eftate by his fon Gregory Ofborne, a minor. The manor of Lovelfbury in Potefgrave belonged to the family of Morton in the fourteenth century [u]. It has fince been united to the manor of Potefgrave. A third manor, which was in the family of Lucy from the reign of Edward I. to that of Edward IV. [w] and afterwards in the family of Fitzjeffrey, is fuppofed alfo to have been united to Potefgrave. In the church are fome tombs of the Saunders family.

POTTON, in the hundred of Bigglefwade and deanery of Shefford, is a confiderable market-town on the borders of Cambridgefhire, forty-eight miles from London. The market, which, though not fo great as formerly, is ftill well fupplied with all forts of grain, particularly wheat and barley, is held on Saturday. The date of the charter has not been found on record. A fair on the feftival of St. James was granted, in 1227, to Henry de Braybroke, one of the Juftices of the King's Bench [x], who is fuppofed to have been then poffeffed of the manor. There are now four fairs, Feb. 2, Old Lady-day, Old Midfummer-day, and Oct. 26. A great fire happened at Potton in the year 1783, when more than fifty dwellinghoufes were deftroyed, befides out-houfes, &c. The damage was computed at upwards of 25,000l. Above 6000l. were collected for the pooreft of the fufferers. Since this accident the market is faid to have declined. The number of houfes, according to the returns made to Parliament in 1801, purfuant to the Population Act, was 239; that of inhabitants 1103.

The manor of Potton was in the Nevills from the reign of Edward II. to the year 1431 [y], and afterwards, for many generations, in the Burgoynes of Sutton. It has fince been in the Torrington family, and is now the property of Samuel Whitbread efq. M. P. whofe father purchafed it in 1795. The De la Poles had a manor in Potton in the fourteenth century [z], which, in the reign of Henry VIII. was in the family of Tanfield [a], being then called the manor of Potton-Mynchmaured. It has long been united to the other manor [b].

The great tithes of Potton were appropriated to the priory of the Minories in London, in the year 1394. They now belong to the parifh of Thackfted in Effex, having been purchafed, under a decree in Chancery, with a fum of money bequeathed to that parifh by William Lord Maynard in 1698, for charitable ufes [c]. The vicarage of Potton is in the gift of the crown. When the parifh was inclofed, under an

---

[u] Tomb in Woburn church.   [w] Efcheats.   [x] Cart. 11 Hen. III.   [y] Efch.
[z] Cl. 36 Edw. III.   [a] Efcheats.   [b] The act for inclofing the parifh of Potton, in 1774, fpeaks alfo of the manors of Potton-Rectoria and Potton-Burdett, as being then the property of Lord Torrington.   [c] Morant's Effex.

Act

Act of Parliament, which paffed in 1774, an allotment of land was affigned in lieu of the vicarial tithes.

PUDINGTON, or PODINGTON, in the hundred of Willey and deanery of Clopham, lies on the borders of Northamptonfhire, thirteen miles north-weft of Bedford, and about five miles from Higham Ferrers. King Henry III. in 1227, granted the manor of Pudington to Ifolda de Dover, till fuch time as he fhould think fit to reftore it to the heirs of Reginald Damartin, Earl of Boloigne, whofe property it had formerly been; in which cafe he promifed to grant her an equivalent[d]. The manor was afterwards fucceffively in the Greys of Ruthin, and in the Bromfletes[e]. In the reign of Henry VIII. being vefted in the crown, it was annexed to the honor of Ampthill. In 1557 it was granted to George Bredyman[f]. In King James's reign it was in the family of Payne, from whom it paffed by an heir female to that of Child. Margaret, daughter and heir of Richard Child, who died in 1647, married George Orlebar, anceftor of Richard Orlebar efq. the prefent proprietor[g], who has a feat in the parifh, called Hinwick-Houfe, built about the year 1710. The fite of the ancient manor-houfe, which appears to have been a caftellated manfion[h], is occupied by a farm.

Hinwick-Hall, a fhort diftance from Mr. Orlebar's, anciently the property of the Pabenhams and Tyringhams[i], was the feat of General Livefay, who died in 1717, and lies buried in Pudington church, where there is a monument to his memory. He was a defcendant of Sir Michael Livefay, the regicide, of whom there was a few years ago a portrait at Hinwick-Hall. This manfion is now in the occupation of Mr. Wagftaff, defcended in the female line from General Livefay's brother. The eftate is divided among feveral co-heirs, of whom the prefent occupier is one.

In Pudington church are monuments of the families of Payne, Child, and Orlebar. The great tithes, which were appropriated to the prior and convent of Canons-Afhby in Northamptonfhire, and the advowfon of the vicarage, have of late years paffed with the manor. In the library at Hinwick-Houfe is a *Cartulary* of the priory of Canons-Afhby. The parifh has been inclofed by an Act of Parliament paffed in 1765, when allotments of land were affigned to the impropriator and vicar in lieu of tithes.

PULLOXHILL, in the hundred and deanery of Flitt, is fituated on a hill about fix miles fouth-eaft of Ampthill. It was parcel of the ancient barony of Cainhoe,

---

[d] Cart. 11 Hen. III.   [e] Efch. Edw. II.—IV.   [f] Mr. Orlebar's Papers.
[g] Cooper's account of Pudington, in Bib. Top. Brit.   [h] Ibid.   [i] See Efch. Hen. III. &c.
where it is called the manor of Hinwick.

under

under which it was for some time held by the family of Pyrot [k]. At the time of the dissolution of monasteries, the manor belonged to the priory of Dunstaple. The demesne lands and the manor-house were granted by king Edward VI. in 1548, to Sir Thomas Palmer. The manor is now the property of Lady Lucas, as representative of the Greys, earls of Kent, who possessed it for several generations. The abbot of Woburn had a manor in this parish, perhaps that of Beeches and Upbury, of which George Fitz esq. died seised in 1601, as appears by his epitaph in the parish church. The manor of Ragons, with lands in Pulloxhill and Flitton, was, in the year 1521, in the family of Hill [l], who in 1691 sold it to the Earl of Aylesbury. It is now the property of the Duke of Bedford, whose grandfather purchased it of the Aylesbury family, in 1738. In the church is the monument of Sir William Bryers, who died in 1653. The rectory and advowson of the vicarage were given by John Pyrot to the priory of Dunstaple. They are now vested in Lady Lucas.

RAVENSDEN, in the hundred of Barford and deanery of Eaton, lies four miles north-east of Bedford. The Pigots, Latimers, and Mowbrays, had manors in this parish, as parcels of the barony of Bedford. The Gostwicks purchased of the Mowbrays. Their estate, which seems to have been considered as the principal manor, was sold to the Marlborough family in the early part of the last century. In 1774 it was purchased by John Duke of Bedford, who, not long afterwards, conveyed it to the father of Miss Butcher, the present proprietor.

Mrs. Sarah Southouse, widow, gives a deputation to a game-keeper for Ravensden Grange in this parish; and E. W. Scrimshire Green esq. for Ravensden Grange in this parish, and Thurleigh. One of these, it is probable, belonged to the abbot and convent of Warden, who had a manor in this parish [m]. The great tithes of Ravensden were appropriated to the priory of Newenham: they are now the property of the Duke of Bedford, who is patron of the vicarage.

RENHOLD (anciently RONHALE), in the hundred of Barford and deanery of Eaton, lies about three miles and a half north-east of Bedford. It was parcel of the estate of the Beauchamps, barons of Bedford, from whom it seems to have passed to the Latimers and Nevills. It was afterwards in the Gostwicks [n] by purchase, and is now the property of John Polhill esq. The monastery of Warden had a manor in Renhold, which became their property in 1324 [o]. Probably this was Howberry, the seat of the Bechers from the reign of Henry VIII. till about the year 1780, when it

[k] Chron. Dunst.   [l] Duke of Bedford's Records.   [m] Augmentation Office.   [n] Esch. Edw. III.—Hen. VIII.   [o] Tanner.

was

was purchafed by the family of Polhill. It is now the property of J. Polhill efq. who has alfo the manors of Salphobury and Flavills in this parifh. The great tithes were appropriated to the priory of Newenham. Mrs. Stevens, being the impropriator in 1749, gave them, after the deceafe of one or two perfons, of whom the late Richard Orlebar efq. of Hinwick was the laft furvivor, to the vicar and his fucceffors for ever. Mr. Polhill is patron of the vicarage.

RIDGMONT, in the hundred of Redbornftoke and deanery of Flitt, which lies about three miles north-eaft of Woburn, is called in old records Rugemont, *i. e.* the red hill; a name very appropriate to its fituation and the colour of the foil. The principal manor in this parifh belonged to the abbot and convent of Woburn, and is now the property of his Grace the Duke of Bedford. Another manor, called the manor of Segenhoe-cum-Ridgmont, was, at the time of the Norman furvey, parcel of the barony of Wahul, under which it was a long while held by the Greys, Lords of Ruthin, and Earls of Kent. A branch of this family fettled at Ridgmont, which from them was called formerly Ridgmont-Grey. Thomas, grandfon of Reginald Lord Grey, was created, in 1450, Lord Grey of Rugemont. He was attainted, at the acceffion of king Edward IV. for his adherence to the houfe of Lancafter, and died without iffue. The manor of Segenhoe-cum-Ridgmont was the property of the late Thomas Potter efq. one of his Majefty's Juftices for Wales, who had a feat at Ridgmont, now, together with the manor, belonging to Dr. Macqueen, who married his daughter. Dr. Macqueen has alfo the manor of Bevans in this parifh, fo called from an ancient family which were fettled there as early as the thirteenth century[p]. The laft of the name, a refpectable yeoman, has lately quitted Ridgmont, to refide at Leighton-Bufard. There was anciently a caftle at Segenhoe, which exifted as late as the year 1276[q]: it is probable that it was then a feat of the barons of Wahull.

The manor of Brogborough in this parifh was, at the time of the Norman furvey, and long afterwards, parcel of the barony of Wahull or Odell. From 1308 till 1573[r], if not later, it was held by the noble family of Grey, under that barony. It afterwards came to the crown, and was granted, in 1628, to Ditchfield and others, conveyed in 1632 to the family of Stone, and by them, in 1702, to the anceftors of his Grace the Duke of Bedford, who is the prefent proprietor. Brogborough Park, having continued in the crown, was, after the death of king Charles I. fold to John Okey, one of the regicides. After the Reftoration it was granted to Mr. John Afhburnham, and was fold by his defcendant, Lord Afhburnham, about 1725, to the Radcliffes of Hitchin in Hertfordfhire, who for fome

[p] Chron. Dunft.   [q] Ibid.   [r] Efch. Edw. II.—Eliz.

time

time refided at Brogborough Park. The houfe has been long deferted. The eftate is now the property of the Right Hon. Lady Frances Radcliffe, relict of the late John Radcliffe efq.

Bickerings Park in this parifh, was, it is probable, the feat of John Bekeryng, who was knight of the fhire in the reign of Edward III. It was in the crown, in the 17th century, and after the Reftoration was granted to John Afhburnham efq. In 1725, Lord Afhburnham fold it to the Radcliffes; and it is now the property of Mr. Delmé Radcliffe, who has lately affumed the name, on his marriage with Mifs Clarke, niece and heir of the late John Radcliffe efq.

Mr. Cooper, in his Hiftory of Odell, fays that there was formerly a church at Segenhoe, which has been demolifhed. It is certain that Walter de Wahul gave the rectory of this parifh, by the name of the church of Segenhoe, to the priory of Dunftaple, about the year 1100[a]. The impropriation is now vefted in the Duke of Bedford, who is patron of the vicarage. The parifh has been inclofed by an Act of Parliament paffed in 1796, when an allotment of land was given to the impropriator in lieu of tithes.

RISELY, in the hundred of Stodden and deanery of Eaton, about 11 miles north of Bedford, appears to have been anciently parcel of the barony of Traylly, under which it was held by the families of Burnell[b] and Croyfer[c]. It is now the property of the Right Honourable Lord St. John, whofe anceftors poffeffed it as early as the year 1399[d]. Another manor was, at an early period, in the Dayrells[e], and Pertefhills or Percells[f]; from 1629 to 1674, it was in the family of Elmes, of whom it was purchafed by Sir Crefwell Levinz, one of the juftices of the Common Pleas[g]. It is now the property of the Duke of Bedford, whofe grandfather purchafed it of the Levinz family, in 1737. The church was given by Alice de Tonbridge to the knights templars[h], and was afterwards granted, with moft of the property of that order, to the hofpitallers. The impropriation is now vefted in Lord St. John, who is patron of the vicarage. This parifh has been inclofed by an Act of Parliament paffed in 1793. An allotment of land was affigned to the impropriator for the great tithes, and a corn rent to the vicar. The vicarage had been endowed with the tithes of hay.

ROXTON, in the hundred of Barford and deanery of Eaton, lies eight miles

---

[a] Chron. Dunft.   [b] Efch. Edw. I.   [c] Cart. Edw. III.   [d] Collins's Peerage.   [e] Cl. Hen. VI.
[f] Efch.   [g] Duke of Bedford's Records.   [h] Dugdale.

north-eaſt of Bedford, on the road to St. Neot's. The manor was, in 1316, the property of Walter de Baa[h], afterwards ſucceſſively in the St. Johns[i] and Mordaunts[k]. It now belongs to a minor of the name of Metcalfe, in whoſe family it has been for a conſiderable time. Sir George Throckmorton, in the year 1541, gave an eſtate in this pariſh to King Henry VIII. who, in 1547, granted it to William Box. This eſtate, then called the manor of Throckmortons, or Boxes, in Roxton, was, in the 17th century, in the family of Delawne[l], who poſſeſſed alſo another eſtate called the manor of Colleſdon, or Fitzjeffreys, being probably the ſame which one of that family died ſeiſed of in 1480, and which had been before for a conſiderable time in the family of Boſom[m]. Theſe eſtates have been for many years annexed to the principal manor. In the pariſh church is an altartomb in memory of Roger Hunt, of *Chalveſtone*, a hamlet of this pariſh, who was appointed baron of the Exchequer in 1439. The great tithes of Roxton, formerly appropriated to the priory of Caldwell, are veſted in the maſter and ſcholars of Trinity-College, in Cambridge, who are patrons of the vicarage.

SALFORD, in the hundred of Manſhead and deanery of Flitt, lies on the borders of Buckinghamſhire, about 12 miles ſouth-weſt of Bedford. It was formerly the property of a family who took their name from the place, afterwards of the Drakelows[n], and, at a later period, of the Charnocks, of Hulcot, from whom it paſſed by marriage to the Herveys, of Chilton in Buckinghamſhire: it is now the joint property of the four daughters of the late Rev. Edward Hervey. In the pariſh church are ſome ancient monuments of a family who bore, for their arms, a plain chevron. One of them has the effigies of a cruſader, with an angel at his head, and two lions at his feet, under an ogie arch, richly ornamented. The great tithes of Salford, which were appropriated to the priory of Newenham, are now the property of Mrs. Barbara Hervey, ſole patroneſs of the vicarage, which is united to Hulcot.

SANDY, in the hundred of Biggleſwade and deanery of Shefford, ſo called from the nature of its ſoil, lies about nine miles eaſt of Bedford, three from Potton, and about the ſame diſtance from Bigglefwade. The manor in 1346, after the death of Roger de Beauchamp, of Eaton, who appears to have had only a life-intereſt in it, paſſed, in conſequence of ſome family ſettlement, to the Engaynes[o]. Thomas

[h] Nomina Villarum in the Britiſh Muſeum.   [i] Collins's Peerage.   [k] Mr. Cooper's Papers.
[l] Eſch. Car. I.   [m] Nomina Villarum, and Eſch. Hen. VI.   [n] Cart. Edw. III. and Cl. Rot. Hen. VI.   [o] Eſch. 20 Edw. III.

Lord Engayne, who died feifed of it in 1367, left only female heirs. William Lord Spencer died feifed of this manor in 1636 [p]. Lewis, fecond fon of Sir Humphrey Monoux, of Wootton, in this county, who was created a baronet in 1660, was of Sandy, which has ever fince been in the family, and is now the property and feat of Sir Philip Monoux bart.

The Hafells in this parifh is the feat of Francis Pym efq. whofe father, William Pym efq. of Radwell, became poffeffed of it, together with the manor of Halelefs, alias Hafells, by a marriage with the heirefs of Heylock Kingfley efq. who died in 1749. This manor was in the Burgoynes as early as the reign of Queen Elizabeth, and was fold by John Burgoyne efq. in 1633, to Ephraim Huit, who the next year fold it to Robert Brittain, great-grandfather of Baron Brittain, of whom it was purchafed by Mr. Kingfley, in 1721.

Mr. Pym has alfo the manor of *Girtford* in this parifh, a confiderable hamlet on the great north road, with a bridge over the Ivel. This manor belonged to the priory of Caldwell, and was granted in 1540 to the Burgoynes. In 1613 it was fold by William, Earl of Salifbury, to Francis Lord Ruffel. Having paffed by fucceffive alienations to the families of Taylor, Bromhall, Edwards, and Pulleyne, it was purchafed of the latter by Mr. Kingfley, in 1741.

Beefton, another hamlet in this parifh, lies on the oppofite fide of the river, in the hundred of Wixamtree. The manor belonged formerly to the abbot of Warden, who became poffeffed of it about the year 1386, in exchange for two manors in Cambridgefhire [q]. It is now the property of Godfrey Thornton efq.

In the parifh church are monuments of the Kingfleys and Pyms. The burial place of the Monoux family is at Wootton. Sir Philip Monoux is patron of the rectory, to which a manor is annexed.

Certain fields in this parifh were inclofed by an Act of Parliament paffed in 1780, and the remainder by an Act which paffed in 1798, when an allotment having been made in lieu of tithes, one third was affigned to the rector, and the remainder to Sir Philip Monoux, charged with a corn-rent to the rector : an allotment of land was given to the poor for fuel, and a fmall allotment to the parifh clerk in addition to his falary.

An account of the ancient encampment in this parifh, and of the antiquities difcovered in its neighbourhood, will be found in the introduction, under the head of Roman remains, p. 24.

SHARNBROOK, in the hundred of Willey and deanery of Clopham, lies about

[p] Efch. Car. I.   [q] See Pat. 10 Ric. II.

nine

nine miles north-weſt of Bedford. The principal manor, which appears to have been, at an earlier period, in the St. Johns[r], was for ſeveral generations in the Botelers, who had for ſome time a ſeat at Sharnbrook. It was purchaſed of Sir Philip Boteler bart. of Teſton, in Kent, by Admiral Samuel Corniſh, who was created a baronet in 1765, being deſcribed of Sharnbrook, in Bedfordſhire, and died in 1770. This manor, with Tofte and Temple-Hills, was given by Sir Samuel to his nephew Samuel Pitchford, who took the name of Corniſh, and is now admiral of the white. The manor of Tofte belonged to the Botelers, by a grant from the crown: the manor of Temple-Hills is ſuppoſed to be the ſame eſtate, which, having belonged to the knights templars, was granted, in 1316, to John Lord Grey, and by him conveyed to truſtees for the ſervice of the Holy Land[s]. Theſe manors were all purchaſed of Sir Philip Boteler, by Sir Samuel Corniſh, in or about the year 1765.

The priory of Newenham had a manor in this pariſh; the family of Cobb, who were ſettled at Sharnbrook for ſeveral generations, had two manors here, called Parentynes and Langtons, one held under the hundred of Willey, the other of the manor of Harold[t]. Theſe, together with the manor of Ouſe, are now the property of John Gibbard eſq. whoſe uncle purchaſed them of the family of Bullock. Mr. Gibbard has alſo a ſmall eſtate called Cobb-Hall, and the impropriate tithes, which formerly belonged to the Cobbs, and afterwards to the Orlebars. Before the Reformation they were appropriated to the abbey of St. Mary at Leiceſter. The vicarage is in the gift of the crown. In the pariſh church, which is a handſome Gothic building, with a ſpire, are memorials of the families of Boteler and Antonie.

Colworth Houſe in this pariſh, the ſeat of William Lee Antonie eſq. M.P. became the property of the Antonie family about the year 1700. It devolved to the preſent poſſeſſor, who was ſon of William Lee eſq. of Totteridge, and grandſon of Sir William Lee, Lord Chief Juſtice of the King's Bench, by the bequeſt of Richard Antonie eſq. The principal part of the houſe was built by John Antonie eſq. chief clerk of the Court of King's Bench; the wings were added by Mr. Lee, during his ſon's minority. It is now one of the moſt elegant manſions in the county.

SHELTON, in the hundred of Stodden and deanery of Eaton, lies on the borders of Northamptonſhire, 14 miles from Bedford. The manor was formerly in the St. Johns[u], afterwards in the families of Bendiſh[w] and Dillingham, and now belongs to Mr. Harris, yeoman. Lord St. John has two turns in the patronage of the rec-

[r] Collins's Peerage.   [s] Ibid.   [t] Eſch. Eliz.   [u] Collins's Peerage.   [w] Eſch. Car. I.

tory;

tory; and Mr. Freeman, of Long-Buckby, in Northamptonshire, one. The parish has been inclosed by an Act of Parliament, passed in 1794, when a corn-rent was given to the rector in lieu of tithes.

SHITLINGTON, anciently *Sethlingdone*, in the hundred of Clifton and deanery of Shefford, lies about four miles from that town. The manor was in the Napier family as early as the year 1651 [x]; and it is not improbable that it had been before in the Rotherams, who preceded the Napiers in the possession of the manor of Luton. After the death of Sir John Napier, the last baronet of that family, in 1747, the manor of Shitlington was sold. It is now the property of Joseph Musgrave esq. who purchased it, in 1760, of Robert, Earl of Holderness.

Shitlington-Bury, which seems to have been formerly the manor house, was left, in 1764, by John Briscoe esq. to Henry, Earl of Suffex, for life, which has occasioned Shitlington-bury to be described, in some books and maps, as a feat of the earls of Suffex. After the earl's death, Mr. Briscoe gave the estate in fee to the heirs at law of the two daughters of Grey Longueville esq. of Shitlington. On the earl's death, in 1800, one moiety descended to Grey Arnold, whose father, Thomas Arnold, although in the humble station of a toll-gatherer at a turnpike near Dunstaple, and supporting a numerous family with a small pittance, honourably refused to deprive his son of his patrimony, by selling his reversionary interest in this estate, though the money arising from the sale would have rescued himself and family from poverty. This Thomas Arnold was grandson of Margaret, the elder daughter of Grey Longueville esq. above-mentioned. The other moiety descended to the wife of Mr. George Antt, as representative of the younger daughter of Mr. Longueville.

The manor of Afpley-bury, in this parish, was many years in the family of Franklin. It is now the property of Joseph Musgrave esq. whose uncle, of the same name, inherited it by bequeft, from his relation, Sir Thomas Franklin bart. who died in 1728. This manor extends into Ion and Gravenhurst.

The parish church is a large and handsome Gothic structure. The tower, which fell down in 1701, was re-built in 1750, through the exertions of Mr. George Story, then curate, by a brief, a subscription, and a parish rate. In the church are monuments of the families of Longueville and Briscoe; and the tomb, with his effigies on a brass plate, of Mathew de Affchton, rector of Shitlington, and canon of Lincoln, who died in 1400. The rectory and rectorial manor, given in ancient

[x] Court Rolls of the Manor.

times

times to the abbey of Ramfey, by Ætheric bifhop of that fee, who purchafed them of fome Danes, to whom they had been given by King Canute[y], are now vefted in the Mafter and Scholars of Trinity College, Cambridge. The vicarage, which is endowed, is in the gift of that College. The parifh of Shitlington has been inclofed by an Act of Parliament paffed in 1802, when an allotment of land was affigned to the impropriator in lieu of tithes.

SOULDROP, fometimes written SOUTHDROP, in the hundred of Willey and deanery of Clopham, lies in the north part of the county, about eleven miles from Bedford. The manor belongs in part to Admiral Cornifh, and in part to the Duke of Bedford. That which belongs to the Admiral was formerly in the Cobbs, and was purchafed, with Sharnbrook, of Sir Philip Boteler, in or about 1765, by Sir Samuel Cornifh. The other has paffed with the manor of Knotting. The parifh church has been lately re-built, excepting the fpire, which, being fituated on high ground, is, though not lofty, a confpicuous object for feveral miles round. The Duke of Bedford is patron of the rectory, which is confolidated with Knotting. The parifh of Souldrop has been inclofed, under an Act of Parliament which paffed in 1770. An allotment of land was affigned to the rector in lieu of the tithes of open fields, and a tithe-rent of two fhillings in the pound for the old inclofures.

SOUTHILL, in the hundred of Wixamtree, lies about two miles north of Shefford, about four miles fouth-weft of Bigglefwade, and about nine miles from Bedford. In ancient records it is called South Yevel. The manor belongs to Lord Ongley, by defcent in the female line from Samuel Ongley efq. who was fheriff of the county in 1703, and was afterwards knighted. His Lordfhip has alfo the manor of Stanford or Stamfordbury in this parifh. The monks of Warden Abbey had a manor in this parifh in 1369, called Gatelins-Bury.

Sir George Byng, a celebrated naval officer in the reign of Queen Anne and George I. purchafed an eftate, and fettled in this parifh. In 1721 he was created a peer, by the title of Baron Byng of Southill, and Vifcount Torrington. He died in 1733, and lies buried in the parifh church. His unfortunate fon, Admiral John Byng, who feems to have fallen a victim to the violence of party, was born and interred at Southill. There is an infcription to his memory in the family *columbarium*, which may be thought to betray too much refentment for fo facred a place, though fome allowance is undoubtedly to be made for the feelings of his family. The prefent Lord Torrington fold his eftate at

[y] Hift. Ang. Scrip. III. 445.

Southill to the late Mr. Whitbread in 1795. It is now the property of his son, Samuel Whitbread efq. M. P. whofe feat ranks among the firft in the county.

Southill-Houfe was built about the year 1795, by Holland. The internal decorations are very elegant. Over the doors of fome of the principal rooms are animals in baffo-relievo by Garrard, and paintings of live game by Gilpin. In the billiard-room is a collection of Garrard's models of fheep and cattle. Over the book-cafes in the library are portraits of the principal clerks in the late Mr. Whitbread's brewery ; and over the chimney-piece, that of Mr. Whitbread himfelf, placed there by his fon, with the following appropriate and modeft motto, " Nobis hæc otia fecit."

In the parifh church is a monument for Dilly the bookfeller, who died in 1779, and feveral memorials of the family of Nodes. In the *columbarium* belonging to the Byngs are feveral infcriptions in memory of that family ; George Vifcount Torrington, 1732-3 ; Pattee Vifcount Torrington, 1746-7 ; George Vifcount Torrington, 1750, &c. &c. It is fhut up from public view. The great tithes of Southill were appropriated to the priory of Newenham. The vicarage, which is now confolidated with Old Warden, is in the deanery of Shefford. Mr. Whitbread is the patron. The parifh has been inclofed by an Act of Parliament paffed in 1797, when allotments of land were made to Mr. Whitbread and Mr. Barber, as impropriators of the great tithes, and to the vicar. The number of acres in the parifh was then computed at 2600.

STAGSDEN, in the hundred of Willey and deanery of Clopham, which lies five miles weft of Bedford, on the road to Newport-Pagnell, belonged to the family of Jemys from the year 1311 to 1428 [z], and paffed afterwards, by heirs female, to the families of Ravenhall and Finaunce [a]. It is now the property of Lord Vifcount Hampden, by inheritance from his anceftors, the Trevors. The great tithes, which were appropriated to the priory of Newenham, are now vefted in the Mafter and Scholars of Trinity College, Cambridge. Lord Hampden is patron of the vicarage.

LITTLE STAUGHTON, in the hundred of Stodden and deanery of Eaton, about four miles from Kimbolton, was fo called to diftinguifh it from the adjoining parifh of Great Staughton, in the county of Huntingdon. The manor was formerly in the families of Peyvre [b] and Dayrell [c]. In 1700 it was purchafed of John Spicer, *alias* Hilder, by Henry Kingfley efq. whofe grand-daughter brought it in marriage

[z] Efch. Edw. II.—Hen. VI.   [a] See Efch. 6 Hen. VI. and 37 Hen. VI.   [b] Cart. Hen. III.
[c] Cl. Rot. Hen. VI.

to William Pym esq. of Radwell in Herts, father of the present proprietor, Francis Pym esq. of the Hasells, in the parish of Sandy.

In the parish church are some memorials of the family of Gery of Bushmead. The rectory is in the patronage of Christ-Church College, in Oxford. It formerly belonged to the Knights Templars. Certain common fields in this parish, containing about 1000 acres, have been inclosed by an Act of Parliament passed in 1801, when an allotment was made to the rector in lieu of tithes.

STEPINGLEY, in the hundred of Redbornstoke and deanery of Flitt, lies about three miles south-west of Ampthill. The manor passed through the same hands as Ampthill, being parcel of that honor, till the exchange between the late Duke of Bedford and the Earl of Ossory, when the lease of this manor was reserved by the former, and is now vested in his brother, the present Duke, who is patron of the rectory. The family of Abbot of Stepingley Park served the office of sheriff in 1681 and 1722. The advowson was, in ancient times, given to the priory of Dunstaple by Robert de Stepingley [d].

STEVENTON, or STEVINGTON, in the hundred of Willey and deanery of Clopham, lies about six miles from Bedford, to the north of the road to Olney. The manor was the property of Roger de Quincy, Earl of Winchester, who died in 1264 [e], and passed, by the marriage of a co-heiress of his brother Robert, to Baldwin Wake [f], who in 1281 had the king's licence to build a castle in Steventon Marsh [g]. After the death of Thomas Lord Wake, it came by marriage to the Plantagenets, Earls of Kent and Huntingdon, and Dukes of Exeter. Joan Plantagenet, the fair maid of Kent, whose second husband was Edward the Black Prince, died seised of it in 1386 [h], when it descended to the son of her first husband, Thomas Holland, Earl of Kent, who became Duke of Exeter. Anne, Duchess of Exeter, sister of King Henry IV. died seised of it in 1476 [i]. It is probable that Steventon Castle, of which there are now no remains, was the residence of some of the above-mentioned noble and illustrious persons. The manor of Steventon has been for a considerable time in the Alston family, and is now the property of Thomas Alston esq. The church of Steventon was given, in the reign of King John [k], to the nuns of Harold, to whom the great tithes were appropriated: they are now the property of Earl Spencer. The Duke of Bedford is patron of the vicarage. Upon the inclosure of the parish of Pavingham under an Act of Parliament passed in 1769, the vicar of Steventon, being entitled to the great and small tithes of copyhold tything in

[d] Chron. Dunst. [e] Esch. Hen. III. [f] Dugdale's Baronage. [g] Pat. 9 Edw. I.
[h] Esch. Rich. II. [i] Esch. Edw. IV. [k] Cart. 7 John.

that

that parifh, had an allotment of land affigned him in lieu of them. Seven acres of land were given to the church of Steventon, before the Reformation, for a *drinking* or church ale. In the centre of the village is an ancient crofs, confifting of a tall fhaft, with a capital, placed on an afcent of fteps.

STONDON, in the hundred of Clifton, lies three miles fouth-eaft of Shefford, on the borders of Hertfordfhire. The manor belonged anciently to the Mepperfhalls[1], afterwards to Lord Wenlock and the Rotherams[m], and at a later period to the noble family of Grey. It is now the property of their reprefentative, the Right Hon. Lady Lucas. The prefent incumbent, the Rev. Thomas Leach, is patron of the rectory, which is in the deanery of Shefford. *Lower* or *Nether-Stondon* is a hamlet of this parifh.

STOTFOLD, in the hundred of Clifton, lies about five miles fouth-eaft of Shefford, on the borders of Hertfordfhire, near the road to Baldock. A manor in Stotfold, which was parcel of the barony of Bedford, and defcended by female heirs to the Mowbrays and Berkeleys, was given by the Marquis of Berkeley to Sir Reginald Bray[n]. This, by the name of Lord Bray's manor, is the property of Ifaac Hindley efq. who purchafed it, in 1786, of the Dentons, whofe anceftor acquired it in like manner of the Anfells in the year 1617. Another manor in Stotfold was given by one of the Beauchamps, Barons of Bedford, to the priory of Newenham; and, after the Reformation, was granted, in 1546, to Richard Kyrke. After having been for a fhort time in the families of Butler and Anfell, it paffed to the Lyttons, of whofe defcendants it was purchafed, in 1795, by the prefent proprietor, Mr. John Williamfon. The Mafter and Scholars of Trinity College are patrons of the vicarage, and impropriators of the great tithes, which, with the rectorial manor now vefted in the College, was given by Simon de Beauchamp to the priory of Chickfand.

STRETLY, in the hundred of Flitt and deanery of Dunftaple, lies about fix miles from Luton, a little to the weft of the road to Ampthill. In the reign of Edward I. the manor was in the Gobions[o], from whom it paffed by a female heir to the Botelers. In 1637 John Lord Boteler died feifed of the manors of Stretly and Sharpenhoe, leaving an only fon, William, who had been an ideot from his birth[p]. At his deceafe the title became extinct. This manor was afterwards in the family of Nodes, from whom it paffed by inheritance to the Goldfmiths. It was lately the property of Mr. Marfhall, and is at prefent the fubject of a fuit in Chancery.

[1] Efch. Edw. II. & III.   [m] Cl. Edw. IV.   [n] Rot. Parl. VI. 529.   [o] Efch.
[p] Efch. Car. I.

The

The family of Wingate had a feat at *Sharpenhoe*, a hamlet of this parifh, for feveral generations [q]; and here it was that Edmund Wingate, the arithmetician, is faid to have been born. The manor is now the property of the Rev. John Smyth, in whofe family it has been for feveral years. James de Cauz had a chantry in his chapel at Sharpenhoe in 1235 [r]. At this hamlet is a charity-fchool for eight chil-dren, founded in 1686 by Richard Norton, and endowed with a rent-charge of 10l. *per annum.*

The great tithes of Stretly were appropriated to the priory of the Holy Trinity *de Bofco*, commonly called Markate. They are now the property of J. R. Cuthbert efq. who is patron of the vicarage.

STUDHAM, in the hundred of Manfhead, lies about fix miles fouth of Dun-ftaple, on the borders of Hertfordfhire, in which county a confiderable part of the parifh is fituated. The manor is fuppofed to have been anciently in the Wahuls, who had a feat at Shortgrave in this parifh. It was afterwards in the De la Poles. John De la Pole, Duke of Suffolk, and Elizabeth his wife, gave it to the church of Windfor [s], under which it is now held on leafe by George Goodwin efq. Robert, Earl of Carnarvon, who fell at the battle of Newbury, is faid to have died feifed of the manor of Studham in Bedfordfhire [t]. It is probable that this was fome other eftate in the parifh.

The manor of *Humberfhoe*, a hamlet partly in this parifh and partly in Cad-dington, formerly written Humbriceftho or Humbrilifhoe, lies partly in Hertford-fhire. In the 13th century it belonged to the family of Young, who founded a chantry in their chapel there [u]. At a later period it belonged to the families of Ferrers [w] and Coppin. It is now the property of Mr. William Shone by a late pur-chafe from Mr. Lambert, who bought it of the Coppins.

Barworth, a hamlet of this parifh, lying wholly in Hertfordfhire, had a chapel of eafe, long ago dilapidated. William Eldefdone founded a chantry in this chapel in 1236 [x]. The manor, of which nothing is now known, was given by King Henry II. to the priory of Dunftaple. Shortgrave in this parifh, formerly a feat of the Wahuls [y], is now the joint property of Jofeph Vandermeulen, Wortham Hitch, and John Hitch, efqrs.

The parifh church was dedicated in 1220 [z]. The great tithes and rectorial manor of Studham belonged to the priory of Dunftaple. They are now the joint property of Edward Nicolls efq. the Rev. John Wheeldon, and the reprefentatives of the late Thomas Vaux efq. The vicarage, which is in the deanery of Dunftaple, is in

[q] Bedfordfhire Pedigrees, in the Britifh Mufeum. [r] Chron. Dunft. [s] Hift. of Windfor, p. 110. [t] Efch. Car. I. [u] Chron. Dunft. [w] Efch. Car. I. [x] Chron. Dunft. [y] Ibid. [z] Ibid.

the gift of the crown. Three acres of land were given to the church before the Reformation, for the purpose of buying frankincenfe.

SUNDON, anciently SONINGDON, in the hundred of Flitt, lies about five miles north-eaft of Dunftaple. It had formerly a weekly market on Fridays, and a fair granted by the crown in 1316 [z]. The manor was anciently in the Clares, earls of Gloucefter. Richard, Earl of Cornwall, and king of the Romans, poffeffed it 40 years, in right of his wife Ifabel, widow of Gilbert Clare, Earl of Gloucefter. It had fcarcely reverted to the Clares, when Edmund, Earl of Cornwall, became pof-feffed of it, in 1272, by marrying the fifter of Gilbert, then Earl of Gloucefter, grandfon of his father's wife [a]. The manor paffed afterwards, by conveyance, to Bartholomew de Baddlefmere and Margaret his wife [b], and by marriage from the Baddlefmeres to the Tiptofts [c]. It was afterwards fucceffively in the Scroops of Bolton [d], and the Cheynes; the latter of whom continued to poffefs it fo lately as the beginning of the laft century [e]: about which time it became the property of William Clayton efq. who was created an Irifh peer by the title of Lord Sundon, in 1735. It was lately the property of Sir John Buchanan Riddell bart. by inhe-ritance from his uncle, Mr. Buchanan, who purchafed it of Lord Sundon's heirs. The prefent proprietor, J. R. Cuthbert efq. bought it of Sir J. B. Riddell in 1803. In the church are fome tombs of the Cheynes. The great tithes, which were appropriated to the priory of Margate or Markate, are now the property of Mr. Cuthbert. He is alfo patron of the vicarage, which is in the deanery of Dunftaple. This parifh has been inclofed by an Act of Parliament paffed in 1768. *Upper Sundon* is a hamlet in this parifh.

SUTTON, in the hundred of Bigglefwade and deanery of Shefford, lies about three miles north-eaft of Bigglefwade, and about a mile and a half fouth of Potton. In the reign of King Henry II. Robert Foliot, a baron, married Margaret, daughter and fole heir of Richard de Reincourt, lord of Sutton in Bedfordfhire [f]; which paffed in like manner, by heirs female, to the baronial families of Ledet, Braybroke, and Latimer [g]. There is a current tradition [h], that it belonged afterwards to John of Gaunt, Duke of Lancafter, who gave it by a rhyming grant to Roger Burgoyne, anceftor of the prefent poffeffor; and a moated fite in the park is known by the name of John of Gaunt's Caftle. The tradition, as far as relates to the grant, appears to be totally deftitute of foundation; and there is no pofitive evidence that

---

[z] Cart. Edw. II. [a] Chron. Dunft. [b] Rot. Parl. II. 430. [c] Dugdale's Baronage, vol. ii.
[d] Dugdale. [e] Magna Britannia. [f] Dugdale. [g] See the Matches in Dugdale.
[h] See Coke's Copyholder.

it

it was ever poffeffed by the Duke of Lancafter. It appears, that he claimed the manor in 1366, as being entitled to it under a deed, by which it was entailed on the heirs of Thomas, Earl of Lancafter. The manor was then in the poffeffion of Elizabeth Latimer, widow[i]; the verdict is not recorded. It is probable, that a compromife took place; for the manor of Potton, which was entailed alfo, by the fame deed, on the heirs of the Earl of Lancafter, defcended to the Nevilles, as heirs of the Latimer family: but Sutton appears to have been, in 1433, the property of Sir Thomas Swinford[k], probably a fon of John of Gaunt's wife, by her firft hufband. It was afterwards in the families of Enderby and Powley[l]; the Powleys appear to have continued in poffeffion as late as the year 1568.

The Burgoynes, who had been fettled at a more remote period in Cambridge-fhire, firft appear on record as poffeffed of lands in this county about the year 1456; when William Burgoyne died feifed of part of the manor of Wootton[m]. Richard Burgoyne, who died in 1463, had the manor of Bofoms in Wootton, and other lands, but none in Sutton[n]. Thomas Burgoyne, who died in 1516, and was buried at Sutton, is the firft who appears to have been connected with this parifh; and the family feems not to have been poffeffed of the manor till after the year 1568, probably by purchafe from the Powleys. John Burgoyne efq. was created a baronet in 1641. His immediate defcendant, Sir Montague Burgoyne bart., is the prefent proprietor.

In the parifh church are fome handfome monuments of the Burgoyne family. The learned Bifhop Stillingfleet was prefented to the rectory of Sutton by Sir Roger Burgoyne, the fecond baronet. Here he is faid to have written his *Origines Sacræ*. He refigned the living in 1665. The rectory is now, by purchafe from the Burgoynes, in the patronage of St. John's College, Oxford. An Act of Parliament paffed, in 1742, for facilitating the inclofure of this parifh, and fecuring an equivalent to the rector in lieu of tithes.

TEMPSFORD, in the hundred of Bigglefwade and deanery of Shefford, is fituated on the great northern road, between Bigglefwade and Eaton-Socon, near the confluence of the Oufe and the Ivel. Our ancient hiftorians fpeak of this place as a Danifh town, which was taken by King Edward in 921[o]. In 1010, being then in poffeffion of the Englifh, it was burnt by an army of Danes[p]. The manor was anciently in the families of Brettville[q] and Blundell[r], it was purchafed of the

---

[i] Placit. &c. de terris in Turr. Lond. (Co. Bedford, N° 20.) under the name of Harpeden.   [l] Efch. Hen. VII. and Eliz.   [k] See Efch. 12 Hen. VI.   [m] Efch. Hen. VI.   [n] Efch. Edw. IV.   [o] Sax. Chron.   [p] Ibid.   [q] Papers communicated by William Bray efq.   [r] Ibid.

latter

latter by Roger de la Leye, and paſſed, by marriage with his daughter and heir, to Hugh de Bray[s]. This manor was the property and ſeat of the late Sir John Payne bart.; it was purchaſed by his father, Sir Gillias Payne bart. in 1772, of Meſſrs. Berners and Hagar, who married the co-heireſſes of the Bendiſh family.

In the church are memorials of the families of Chetwode and Payne. The rectory is in the gift of the crown; the advowſon belonged formerly to the priory of St. Neot's[t]. The pariſh has been incloſed by an Act of Parliament paſſed in 1777, when an allotment of land was aſſigned to the rector in lieu of tithes, and a rent for the tithes of old incloſures.

THURLEY, or THURLEIGH, in the hundred of Willey and deanery of Eaton, lies about eight miles north of Bedford. John de Hervey, anceſtor of the Earl of Briſtol, became poſſeſſed of a manor in Thurleigh by marriage with the heireſs of John Harman or Hammon[u]; he made Thurleigh his principal ſeat, and died about the year 1292; his family were ſeveral times knights of the ſhire. Sir George Hervey, who was knighted by King Henry VIII. for his bravery at the ſiege of Tournay, died in 1526, leaving his manor of Thurleigh to Gerard, his illegitimate ſon by Margaret Smart, who was knighted, and took the name of Hervey[w]: his deſcendants continued at Thurleigh till the death of John Hervey eſq. in 1715: but this manor had been alienated at an earlier period, and was, in 1708, the property of Sir John Holt, of whoſe deſcendant, Thomas Holt eſq. it was purchaſed, in 1790, by the late Duke of Bedford. Another manor was in the St. Johns, as early as the year 1391[x], and was purchaſed of the Earl of Bolingbroke by the anceſtor of the preſent proprietor, John Crawley eſq. of Stockwood in Luton.

Blackburn-Hall, *alias* Black-Bull-Hall, now a farm-houſe, in this pariſh, within a moated ſite, had been the property of the Fitz-jefferys, of Creakers, in Barford, for a conſiderable time preceding the year 1651, when it paſſed out of that family by mortgage, and was purchaſed in 1707, of the repreſentatives of the mortgagees, by Sir Nathan Wright bart. In 1733, it was ſold by the Wrights to Robert Bell eſq. maternal grandfather of the late William Gery eſq.; it is now the property of his ſon-in-law the Rev. Hugh Wade Gery.

The Franklyns had a ſeat at Thurleigh for ſeveral generations[y].

Mr. Crawley is leſſee of the impropriate tithes under Trinity-College, Cambridge, and is patron of the vicarage. Near the church-yard is a circular mount, with an

[s] Mr. Bray's Papers.   [t] Plac. &c. de terris in com. Bed. in Turr. Lond.   [u] Collins's Peerage.
[w] Ibid.   [x] Ibid.   [y] Bedfordſhire Pedigrees in the Britiſh Muſeum.

entrench-

entrenchment, called Bury Hill, which appears to have been the site of an ancient mansion, perhaps that of John de Hervey before-mentioned.

TILBROOK, in the hundred of Stodden and deanery of Eaton, lies on the borders of Huntingdonshire, about a mile and a half from Kimbolton, on the road from Wellingborough to that town. The manor belonged to the Clares, Earls of Gloucester, from whom it descended to Humphrey Stafford, Duke of Buckingham, who died in 1460 [y]. In 1485 it was confirmed to Catharine, widow of Jasper, Duke of Bedford [z], and was afterwards the property of Sir James Fitzgarret, who was attainted in 1538 [a]. It is now the property of the Right Honourable Lord St. John, in whose family it has been for a considerable time. His Lordship is also patron of the rectory. The parish has been inclosed by an Act of Parliament, passed in 1800, when a small allotment of land was given to the rector, who was farther compensated by a corn-rent. The parish contains about 1380 acres.

TILSWORTH, in the hundred of Manshead, lies about four miles north-west of Dunstaple, near the Watling-Street. The manor was anciently in the family of Morteye [b], from whom it passed by marriage to the Chamberleynes. In the 16th century it was in the family of Fowler [c]. It is now the property of Charles Chester esq. whose father, a younger brother of the late Lord Bagot, took the name of Chester on succeeding to the estates of Sir Charles Bagot Chester bart. the last heir male of the Chesters, of Chichley, in Buckinghamshire and of Tilsworth. Sir Anthony Chester, their ancestor, was created a baronet in 1619. The old mansion, which was a seat of the Fowlers, and afterwards of the Chesters, is in a state of dilapidation.

In the parish church are monuments of Sir Henry Chester K.B. who died in 1666, and some of the Fowler family. There is also an altar-tomb with the effigies of an ecclesiastic under a Gothic arch, and a slab, with an ancient French inscription, in memory of Adam de Tullesworth. The great tithes were appropriated to the priory of Beachwood. The manor was inclosed by an Act of Parliament passed in 1767, when an allotment of land was given to Mr. Chester, in lieu of the great tithes, and the annual sum of 31l. 10s. was settled in lieu of small tithes on the vicar. Mr. Chester is patron of the vicarage, which is in the deanery of Dunstaple.

TINGRITH, in the hundred of Manshead and deanery of Flitt, lies about four miles east of Woburn, about two miles and a half north of Toddington, and about

[y] Esch. Hen. VI.   [z] Rot. Parl. VI. 284.   [a] Records in the Augmentation Office.
[b] Nomina Villarum in the British Museum. N° 6281. Harl. MSS.   [c] Esch. Eliz.

five

five miles nearly to the fouth of Ampthill. The manor, which had been the property of Lord Fanhope, was afterwards fucceffively in the families of Grey and Cheyne [d]. Robert Hodgfon, whofe monument is in the parifh church, died feifed of it in 1611. After this it was in the family of Charnock, of whom it was purchafed, about 1710, by the anceftor of Charles Dymoke Willaume efq. the prefent proprietor, who is patron of the rectory, and has a feat here. Part of Tingrith is within Sir John Everett's manor of Weftoning.

TODDINGTON, in the hundred of Manfhead, feven miles from Ampthill, and five from Dunftaple, was, till of late years, a confiderable market town. The market was originally held on Thurfdays, by grant from King Henry III. in 1218 [e]. It was changed to Saturday, by a charter of King Edward II. in 1316, which charter was confirmed by King Richard II. in 1385 [f]. In 1681, the market at Toddington was fo confiderable, that fixteen butchers rented ftalls in the market-place [g]. It declined by degrees, and has been of late wholly difcontinued. The market-houfe was pulled down in 1799, and the materials fold. It is probable, that it had been before difcontinued, and afterwards revived, as Leland does not include Toddington in his lift of the market towns in Bedfordfhire. A fair on the feftival of St. George, was granted by the charters of 1218 and 1316. The prefent fairs are five in number; April 25th, the firft Monday in June, September 4th, November 2d, and December 16th. The number of houfes, as returned to Parliament, in 1801, purfuant to the Population Act, was 360; that of inhabitants, 1143.

The manor of Toddington was given by William the Conqueror, to Ernulfus de Hefdin, anceftor of the Earls of Perch; on the death of Thomas, the laft earl, in 1216, his heir, the bifhop of Chalons fold it to William Marefhall, Earl of Pembroke [h]. Eleanor, widow of William Marefhall, Earl of Pembroke, (fifter of King Henry III.) held it in dower in 1231 [i]. Contemporary with this was another fmaller manor, of which William Longefpée, Earl of Salifbury, was feifed, in 1217 [k]. It was then valued at 5l. per annum.

In the early part of Henry III.'s reign, Paulinus Peyvre had the manor of Toddington, which, at firft, it is probable, he held under the Marefhalls, and in 1224, he acquired, of Hugh Wadlowe, all his eftate in Wadlowe, probably the fame which is now called the manor of Wadloes, on condition of providing him with clothes and maintenance during his life [l]. This Paulinus Peyvre, fteward of the houfehold to King Henry III. was a man of mean origin, and when he went to court,

[d] Efch. Eliz. [e] Cl. Rot. Hen. III. [f] Pat. 9 Ric. II. [g] Papers in the poffeffion of the rector. [h] See the Account of Newbury, in Berkfhire. [i] Chron. Dunft. [k] Cl. 1 Hen. III. [l] Chron. Dunft.

was

was not poffeffed of two carucates of land ; but by means, lawful and unlawful, as Matthew Paris obferves, acquired fuch wealth, that he foon became poffeffed of more than 500 carucates : a moft infatiable purchafer of lands, fays the hiftorian, and a moft incomparable builder. Not to fpeak of thofe in other places, his houfe at Toddington was like a palace, with a chapel, chambers, and other buildings, covered with lead, which raifed the admiration of the beholders. His workmen are faid to have received 100 s. and more than 10 marks a week for their wages. The fite of this noble manfion is not known. The Chronicle of Dunftaple mentions, that Paulinus Peyvre built the chamber over his gate at Wadlowe, in 1244. It is not improbable, that he might have had a houfe at Toddington, and another at Wadlowe, then a confiderable hamlet, about a mile diftant from Toddington, of which not a fingle houfe remains, but there are confiderable traces of buildings in a field which goes by the fame name. Near the church at Toddington, is a mount called Conger-Hill, which feems to have been the keep of a caftellated manfion, and there are confiderable earth-works near it. This might have been the fite of Sir Paulinus Peyvre's manfion. This favourite of fortune died in 1251. John Lord Grey married his widow, and having purchafed of the King the marriage of his fon, then a minor, married him to his own daughter, at his manor of Water-Eaton, in Buckinghamfhire. Queen Eleanor, the confort of King Edward I., had the cuftody of this manor during John Peyvre's minority [m].

Mary, daughter and heir of Thomas Peyvre, the fixth in defcent from Sir Paulinus, married Sir John Broughton, whofe daughter and co-heir, Anne, brought this manor in marriage to Sir Thomas Cheney K. G. Lord Warden of the Cinque Ports. His fon Henry was knighted by Queen Elizabeth, in 1563, fhe being then on a vifit to him at Toddington. In 1572, he was created Lord Cheney, of Toddington. Dying in 1587, without iffue, his eftates devolved to his wife, who was daughter of Thomas Lord Wentworth, of Nettlefted, and were inherited by her relations. In the month of July, 1608, Toddington was honoured with a vifit by King James I. [n]

On the death of Thomas, Earl of Cleveland, in 1667, the barony of Wentworth, and this eftate, paffed to his grand-daughter and fole heir, Henrietta, who became Baronefs Wentworth in her own right, and refided at Toddington, with an illuftrious inmate, the unfortunate Duke of Monmouth. In an ancient plan of the manor-houfe, two adjoining rooms are called the Duke of Monmouth's parlour, and my Lady's parlour. The Duke's attachment to Lady Wentworth continued to his death. On the fcaffold, he fpoke in vindication of her honour, although it was fufficiently notorious, nor did he deny it to the divines who attended him,

[m] Chron. Dunft.   [n] Mr. Archer's notes in the Regifter of Houghton-Conqueft.

that

that they lived together as man and wife, after he had forſaken the Ducheſs [o]. Lady Wentworth is ſaid to have died broken-hearted, in conſequence of his untimely end. It is certain that ſhe ſurvived his execution but a few months. Upon her death the barony of Wentworth, and this eſtate, paſſed to Lady Anne, wife of John Lord Lovelace, and were inherited by their daughter Martha, who attended at the coronation of Queen Anne, as Baroneſs Wentworth. She married Sir Henry Johnſon, a rich ſhip-builder at Poplar, who reſided at Toddington with his lady, and was buried there in 1719. His only daughter, by a former wife, married Thomas, Earl of Strafford, who became poſſeſſed of this eſtate, which is now veſted in the truſtees of the late Right Honourable Thomas Conolly, who was ſon of his daughter, Lady Anne. The manor of Youngs, in this pariſh, ſeems to have paſſed by the ſame title, and is now veſted in Mr. Conolly's truſtees.

Lord Cheney built a noble manſion at Toddington, about half a mile from the church, of which nothing now remains but the kitchen, which is remarkably ſpacious, having two fire-places, each 12 feet in width, and a few rooms fitted up as a farm-houſe. The greater part of the building was pulled down by the Earl of Strafford, about the year 1745. It appears by an ancient plan of the houſe [p], that it occupied four ſides of a quadrangle, at each corner of which was a turret: the north and ſouth fronts were 210 feet in length; the chapel was 30 feet by 24; the tennis-court 65 feet in length, and a marble gallery, 58.

The manor of Wadloes before-mentioned, did not paſs to the Wentworths. Early in the 17th century it was in the family of Aſtrey [q], of whom it was inherited by the preſent proprietor, Francis Penyſton eſq. who, reſerving the manor, has ſold the farm to John Wingate Jennings eſq. of Harlington. The manor of *Charlton*, a hamlet in this pariſh, now belongs to Mr. Cox, who purchaſed it of the preſent Viſcount Howe. It has of late years paſſed through ſeveral hands.

The pariſh church is a handſome Gothic ſtructure; the frieze, on the outſide, is decorated with various groteſque figures of animals. The north and ſouth tranſepts, belonging to the lord of the manor, are in a moſt ſhameful ſtate of dilapidation. In the ſouth tranſept are ſome ancient monuments of the Peyvres; as appears by the arms: one of them was a cruſader. In the ſame tranſept are monuments of Anne, wife of Sir Thomas Cheney, K.G. 1561, Henry Lord Cheney, 1587, and his widow, Jane Lady Cheney, 1614. On each of theſe were the effigies of the deceaſed, now much mutilated, and lying on the ground, mingled with the broken ornaments of the tombs, and the dung of birds and bats. The

[o] Granger's Biographical Hiſtory.

[p] It was, in 1802, on a fire-ſcreen at the Farm.

[q] Eſch. Car. I.

north

north tranfept, which was the burial place of the Wentworths, is not in a much better condition. The coftly monument of Henrietta, Lady Wentworth, the Duke of Monmouth's miftrefs, who died in 1686, on which her mother, who furvived her ten years, directed the large fum of 2000l. to be expended, and another monument, which appears to have been no lefs coftly, in memory of Lady Maria Wentwort h who died at the premature age of 18, in 1632, are in a ftate little better than thofe of the Cheneys. The windows of the aifle being without glafs, and the roof much decayed, they are daily receiving frefh injury, by being expofed to the ravages of the weather, and the depredations of children. In the epitaph on Lady Maria Wentworth, the following paffage, alluding to her early death, affords a curious fpecimen of the extravagant mode of expreffion in that age. The writer tells us that

> ————" Her foul grew fo faft within,
> " It broke the outward fhell of Sin,
> " And fo was hatch'd a cherubim."

In a more fober ftrain, he defcribes her character as very amiable, by faying that fhe was

> " Good to the poor, to kindred dear,
> " To fervants kind, to friendfhip clear,
> " To nothing but herfelf fevere."

In the chancel is a monument in memory of Giles Bruce, eldeft fon of Sir John Bruce, of Winham, in Suffolk, who died at Toddington, in 1595, being on a vifit to his fifter Alice, then *attending on* the Lady Cheney. Mr. Conolly is patron of the rectory, which is in the deanery of Dunftaple. The parifh has been inclofed by an Act of Parliament, paffed in 1797, when an allotment of land was made to Mr. Conolly, as entitled to a moiety of the great tithes ; and an allotment not to exceed 150 acres was made to the rector, who was alfo to have a corn-rent, equivalent to his farther intereft in the other moiety. The number of acres in the parifh, was then computed at 2800.

Abraham Hartwell, a learned writer of the 17th century, was rector of Toddington, where he founded a library for the ufe of his fucceffors [r].

John Reinolds, the epigrammatift, is faid, by Anthony Wood, to have been a native of this place.

In the year 1443, a hofpital was founded at Toddington, in honour of St. John the Baptift, by Sir John Broughton, for three poor men, and a mafter, or chaplain,

---

[r] Harwood's Alumni Etonenfes, p. 173.

who were to pray for the fouls of Thomas Peyvre, and Margaret his wife, and their anceftors. Sir John Milner was the laft mafter of this hofpital, which was diffolved by the lord warden Cheney, without the king's licence. It was feized, in confequence, by the crown, but afterwards granted to the Cheney family [s]. There are, now, no traces of the hofpital; the ftones were ufed in building the market-houfe which has been lately pulled down. Its fite was near the fpot which is called Conger-Hill.

TOTERNHOE, in the hundred of Manfhead, lies about two miles to the weft of Dunftaple. It belonged formerly to the families of Cantilupe and Zouche [t]. Sir Reginald Bray became poffeffed of it by a grant from the crown, in 1513. It has fince paffed with Eaton-Bray, and is now the property of William Beckford efq. The church was given by Walter de Wahul, of Shortgrave, to the priory and convent of Dunftaple, who endowed the vicarage in 1220 [u]. The late Alderman Wilkes was poffeffed of the rectory and advowfon, in right of his wife, who was a defcendant of the celebrated phyfician, Dr. Mead. Since the death of Mifs Wilkes, they are become the property of his nephew. Toternhoe is in the deanery of Dunftaple.

TURVEY, in the hundred of Willey and deanery of Clopham, lies on the borders of Buckinghamfhire, eight miles from Bedford, in the road to Olney. Euftace le Mordaunt, grandfon of Sir Ofbert le Mordaunt, who lived in the reign of William the Conqueror, became poffeffed of the manor of Turvey, by marriage with the heirefs of Sir William de Alneto, or Dawney [w]. William Mordaunt, in 1297, had the king's licence to inclofe a park at Turvey [x], which became the chief feat of that ancient family. Sir John Mordaunt was created Baron Mordaunt of Turvey, in 1532. His defcendant, John, Lord Mordaunt, was created Earl of Peterborough, in 1628. Turvey-Hall, having been long deferted by its noble owners, and occupied as a farm, was fold by the prefent Earl of Peterborough, to the late William Fuller efq. a banker in London, and is now the property of his daughters. The manor was fold to Charles Higgins efq. whofe nephew, John Higgins, jun. is the prefent proprietor. Mr. Higgins's feat is called (for what reafon does not appear) Turvey-Abbey. There is no record or trace of a religious houfe here, nor does any part of the parifh appear to have been monaftic property, excepting a fmall manor which belonged to the *Priory* of St. Neot's. It is probable that Mr. Higgins's houfe might have been the fite of that manor.

[s] Papers in the poffeffion of Mr. Dixon, the rector.　　[t] Efch. Rich. II—Edw. IV.
[u] Chron. Dunft.　　[w] Hiftory of the Houfe of Mordaunt.　　[x] Collins's Peerage.

Edward

Edward Dudley efq. who died in 1641, was feifed of an eftate in this parifh, called the manor of *Turveys*, held under the Earl of Peterborough's manor of Turvey. He left three daughters, co-heireffes [y]. This eftate came afterwards to the Mordaunts, who poffeffed the whole landed property of the parifh. Its name has been long forgotten.

In the parifh church are monuments of Sir John Mordaunt, and the three firft barons. Sir John was chancellor of the duchy of Lancafter, and father of the firft Lord Mordaunt. He died in 1504, having, by his will, founded a chantry in the parifh church of Turvey, and endowed it with lands for the fupport of two chaplains, to pray for the fouls of himfelf, his kindred, and his anceftors. His effigies is reprefented in armour, over which is a robe with a collar of S. S. His lady is in a robe, with a rich coif. The monument of John, the firft Lord Mordaunt, who died in 1562, has the effigies of himfelf and his lady. He is reprefented in armour with a robe. She is in a robe with puckered fleeves, and has the angular head drefs, which was worn in the reign of Henry VIII. The monument of Henry, the fecond Lord Mordaunt, is in the north chancel, and has his effigies, in armour, between thofe of his two wives, under an open canopy fupported by columns of the Doric order. In the fame chancel is a plain altar-tomb to the memory of Lewis, the third Lord Mordaunt. Charles, earl of Peterborough, who diftinguifhed himfelf in the reign of George II. both as a foldier and ftatefman, was buried in the vault under this chancel, without any memorial. The monuments above-mentioned, have been all engraved for the hiftory of the houfe of Mordaunt, a very rare work, one of the few copies of which is in the college of arms. Over the altar at Turvey is a picture of our Saviour and his difciples on the road to Emmaus, given to the parifh by the prefent rector. Upon the fale of Lord Peterborough's eftates, the late Mr. Fuller purchafed a moiety of the great tithes, which had been appropriated to the foreign priory of St. Neot's [z], and afterwards to that of Newenham. It is now the property of his daughters, who are patroneffes of the rectory. The other moiety belongs to the rector. The parifh has been inclofed by an Act of Parliament, paffed in 1783: the lands were not exonerated from tithes.

WARDEN, in the hundred of Wixamtree and deanery of Shefford, lies about three miles weft of Bigglefwade, and about nine from Bedford. It had, formerly, a market on Tuefdays, granted in 1218, to Henry de Braybroke, one of the king's juftices itinerant, together with a fair at the feftival of St. Peter and St. Paul [a]. The

---

[y] Efch. Car. I.   [z] Placit. &c. de Terris in Com. Bed. in Turr. Lond.   [a] Fin. Rot. 2 Hen. III.

market

market was confirmed in 1307, to John de Bocles, together with a fair on the feſtival of St. Leonard[b].

At this place was a monaſtery, called the Abbey of Warden, or *De Sartis*, founded in 1135 by Walter D'Eſpec, for Ciſtercian monks from Rievaux, and dedicated to the Virgin Mary[c]. In the year 1217 Fulk de Brent, a powerful baron, whoſe enormous outrages ſeem to have rendered him the terror of the country, treated the monks of this convent with much cruelty, on account of a diſpute about a wood, and carried thirty of them priſoners to Bedford Caſtle. Yet ſuch was the aſcendancy of the church at that period, that he who ſet the civil power at defiance, was glad to make his peace by ſubmitting to receive manual diſcipline from the monks in the chapter-houſe at Warden, at the ſame time confirming to them the wood about which the diſpute had ariſen, and promiſing them his protection ever after[d]. The revenues of Warden Abbey, at the time of its ſuppreſſion, were eſtimated at 389l. 16s. 6¼d. clear yearly value[e]. The ſmall remains which are to be ſeen of the conventual buildings are of brick, of no great antiquity. A conſiderable part of what is repreſented in Buck's View, was pulled down about the year 1790. The ſite of Warden Abbey, now the property of Mr. Whitbread, is nearly two miles from the pariſh church. In 1669, it was a ſeat of Sir Ralph Bovey[f].

The manor of Warden belonged, in 1250, to Adeliza Wake[g], afterwards to the St. Amands, who, in 1343, gave a moiety of it to the abbot and convent, in exchange for lands in Milbrook[h]. The manor, which was of late years in the Palmers of Warwickſhire, is now the property of Samuel Whitbread eſq. M.P. whoſe father purchaſed it of Mr. Charles Palmer, in 1773. The eſtate is tithe-free.

Lord Ongley has a ſeat in this pariſh. His father was created an Iriſh peer in 1776, by the title of Lord Ongley, of Old Warden. The late Lord Ongley's name was Henley. He took the name of Ongley as heir of Samuel Ongley, of Warden, the firſt of the family who ſettled at this place, about the year 1690. He was a merchant in London, one of the directors of the Eaſt-India Company, and the firſt deputy-governor of the South-Sea Company. He ſerved the office of ſheriff for the county in 1702, and was afterwards knighted.

In the window of the pariſh church is the figure of an abbot of Warden. The only monument of any note is that of Sir Samuel Ongley, who died in 1726, with a ſtatue of the deceaſed in a Roman dreſs. In the church-yard is the mauſoleum of the late Lord Ongley, erected by his widow. Mr. Whitbread is patron of the vicarage, which is conſolidated with Southill.

[b] Cart. 1 Edw. II.　　　[c] Tanner.　　[d] Chron. Dunſt.　　[e] Tanner.　　[f] Liſt of Sheriffs.
[g] Chron Dunſt.　　[h] Pat. Edw. III.

WESTON-ING, in the hundred of Manfhead and deanery of Flitt, lies about four miles from Ampthill, on the road to Toddington. It had formerly a market on Monday, granted in 1304, by King Edward I. with an annual fair on the feftival of the tranflation of St. Thomas the Martyr[i]. It was anciently, by the name of Wefton-Tregoz, the property of the Clares, earls of Gloucefter[k]. Early in the fourteenth century, it was purchafed of Juliana de Sandwich, daughter and heir of Matilda de Averenches (who married Hamon Crevequer, a Kentifh baron,) by William Inge[l], the fame, it is fuppofed, who was appointed Chief Juftice of the King's-Bench in 1317. From him this place acquired the name of Wefton-Inge, which it ftill retains. After the death of William Inge, fon, it is probable, of the Chief Juftice, in 1370, this manor devolved on William Lord Zouche, who had married his grand-daughter[m]. In 1542, George Zouche furrendered the manor to the crown[n]. Queen Mary gave it to her god-daughter, Mary Curzon, who was one of her maids of honour. She married Sir George Fermor, anceftor of the Earl of Pomfret[o]. It is now the property of Sir John Everitt, whofe father pur-chafed it of the Pomfret family in 1767. Worth-End and part of Tingrith belong to this manor. The church was given by Gilbert Clare, earl of Gloucefter, to the knights-templars[p], and afterwards belonged to the abbefs and convent of Elftow, to whom the great tithes were appropriated. They are now vefted in Francis Penyfton efq. by inheritance from the Aftreys. Sir John Everitt is patron of the vicarage

WHIPSNADE, in the hundred of Manfhead, lies about four miles nearly fouth of Dunftaple, on the borders of Hertfordfhire. The principal manor, now the pro-perty of William Beckford efq. appears to have paffed with Eaton-Bray. Another manor is claimed by the reprefentatives of the late Thomas Vaux efq. The rectory, which is in the deanery of Dunftaple, is in the gift of the crown. Shortgrave is partly in this parifh, and partly in Studham. In 1798, Mr. Beckford procured an Act of Parliament for inclofing certain woods and grounds, containing 232 acres, when a rent-charge of 30l. per annum was fecured to be paid to the parifh in aid of the poor rate.

WILDEN, in the hundred of Barford and deanery of Eaton, lies about five miles north-eaft of Bedford. The manor was anciently in the Pabenhams, who conti-nued to poffefs it for a confiderable time[r]. The Duchefs of Bedford died feifed of it in 1473[s]. It was afterwards for many years in the Goftwicks, of whom it was

---

[i] Cart. 32 Edw. I. [k] Dugdale's Baronage. [l] Harl. MSS. Brit. Muf. 6073. [m] Dugdale.
[n] Records in the Augmentation Office. [o] Collins's Peerage. [p] Dugdale's Baronage.
[r] Efch. Hen. III.—Ed. III. [s] Efch. Ed. IV.

purchafed

purchaſed by Sarah, Ducheſs of Marlborough. It is now the property of the Duke of Bedford, whoſe grandfather purchaſed it of the Marlborough family. Mr. Wag-ſtaffe has a ſmall manor in this pariſh, called Sextons, which has been for a conſi-derable time in his family. The Duke of Bedford is patron of the rectory. Francis Dillingham, one of the tranſlators of the Bible, was rector of this pariſh.

WILHAMSTED, in the hundred of Bedbornſtoke, lies about four miles ſouth of Bedford. The manor was granted to John de Grey in 1483. John Warner, M. D. died ſeiſed of it in 1565 [s], when it was inherited by his nephew, Thomas Norwood. It is now the property of the Right Hon. Lord Carteret. A manor in this pariſh was given to Elſtow abbey, in 1078 [t]. This is ſuppoſed to be the manor of Maid-Berry, in Wilhamſted and Elſtow, of which Richard Fitzhugh died ſeiſed in 1557 [u].

The great tithes were appropriated to Elſtow abbey: the vicar has now one-third, and the remainder is divided between two lay impropriators. Lord Carteret is pa-tron of the vicarage, in conſequence of an exchange with Sidney-Suſſex College, Cambridge. Wilhamſted is in the deanery of Bedford.

WILLINGTON, in the hundred of Wixamtree, lies nearly five miles eaſt of Bed-ford, near the road to St. Neot's. It was parcel of the barony of Bedford, and deſcended by a co-heireſs of the Beauchamps, to the Mowbrays, earls and dukes of Norfolk, who, as Leland informs us, had an old manor-place there, where they ſometimes " lay for a ſtarte [w]". From the Mowbrays it paſſed by inheritance, to John Howard, duke of Norfolk, who fell at Boſworth-field. On his attainder, it was granted, in 1485, to John, Earl of Oxford : but it is probable, that it was ſoon after reſtored to the Howards ; for Leland, who viſited this county not long after-wards, ſays, " Mr. Goſtewik beyng borne in Willingtoun, boute this lordſhip of the Duke of Northfolk, now lyving, and hath made a ſumptuus new building of brike and tymbre *a fundamentis*, in it, with a conduct of water derivid in leade pipes."

An Act of Parliament paſſed in 1541, to ſecure the manor of Willington to Mr. Goſtwick, who was ſon of Sir John Goſtwick, Maſter of the Horſe to King Henry VIII. William Goſtwick, of Willington, was created a baronet in 1612 ; his deſcendant Sir William Goſtwick, repreſented the county of Bedford in Parliament, during a great part of the reigns of King William and Queen Anne. Having impoveriſhed his eſtate by frequent election-conteſts, this manor, among others, was ſold in 1731,

---

[s] Eſch. Eliz. [t] Kennet's Parochial Antiquities, p. 62. [u] Eſch. Ph. and Mar.
[w] Itin. vol. i.

Published by T.Cadell & W.Davies, Strand, 9 Mar.1801.

SOUTH-EAST VIEW OF WIMINGTON CHURCH, BEDFORDSHIRE.

to Sarah, Duchefs of Marlborough. It is now the property of the Duke of Bedford, whofe grandfather purchafed it of the Marlborough family, in 1774.

In the parifh church, which is a handfome Gothic ftructure, are feveral monuments of the family of Goftwick : the earlieft is a brafs plate, in memory of Robert Goftwick efq. who died in 1315[x]. The monument of Sir John Goftwick, Mafter of the Horfe to King Henry VIII. was put up in 1541, by his fon, foon after his purchafe of the manor. The arms on Sir John's monument differ from others of the Goftwick family ; having, on the chief, three horfes' heads couped, in allufion to his office, inftead of three mullets. The monument of Sir William Goftwick, the firft baronet, who died in the year 1615, has his effigies in alabafter, in armour. That of Sir Edward Goftwick, who died in 1632, is a mural monument, with the effigies of himfelf and his lady, in kneeling attitudes. The title is extinct. The great tithes of Willington, which is in the deanery of Bedford, were appropriated to the priory of Newenham. They are now the property of the Duke of Bedford, who is patron of the vicarage.

WIMINGTON, in the hundred of Willey and deanery of Clopham, lies on the borders of Northamptonfhire, about three miles from Higham-Ferrers. The manor continued, for fome time, in the defcendants of Alured de Lincoln, who held it when the furvey of doomfday was taken[y]. In 1222 it belonged to Peter de Suevia. Soon afterwards it reverted to the Crown, and was granted to Robert de la Bruere. About the year 1260, it paffed from the family of Welton to that of Nowers, by marriage. Hugh Curteys purchafed it about the year 1351. About 1397 it feems to have been conveyed by his reprefentatives to the baronial family of Bromflete. In 1555 it was the property of Henry, Earl of Derby, whofe wife, Lady Margaret Clifford, was a lineal defcendant of one of the co-heireffes of Henry Lord Bromflete. In 1621 this manor was in the family of Bletfoe, from whofe reprefentatives it paffed in 1708, to John Sawyer. In 1713 it became the property of Major General Livefey, and is now, in feveralties, amongft his reprefentatives.

The parifh church, a very elegant Gothic ftructure, was built by John Curteys, lord of the manor, and mayor of the Staple at Calais, who died in 1391, as appears by the infcription on his tomb. The braffes of himfelf and his wife Albreda, are remarkably well preferved. They are on a flab of black marble, under Gothic canopies. In the chancel are braffes, of Sir Thomas Bromflete, cupbearer to King Henry V. who died in 1430, and his wife Margaret, daughter of

---

[x] The family of Goftwick was fettled at Willington as early as the year 1209, as appears by fome Bedfordfhire Pedigrees in the Britifh Mufeum.   [y] Cooper's Hiftory of Wimington, in the Bibl. Top. Brit. from whence the fubfequent dates are taken.

Sir

Sir Edward St. John, and heirefs of the Lord de Vefci, who died in 1407. The Rev. Wm. Bromwich was, in Feb. 1803, patron of the rectory; the advowfon was then on fale.

WOBURN, in the hundred of Manfhead and deanery of Flitt, is a market town fituated on the great road to Manchefter and Leeds, 42 miles from London. The market, which is held on Fridays, was granted, in 1242, to the abbot of Woburn [z]. There are four annual fairs; January 1, March 23, July 13, and September 25. The town of Woburn fuffered feverely by fire in the year 1595 [a], and in 1724 [b]; the laft time about 50 houfes were confumed. The number of houfes in Woburn parifh, according to the return made to Parliament in 1801, purfuant to the Population Act, was 277; the number of inhabitants 1563. Queen Elizabeth vifited Woburn in 1572 [c]. King Charles I. halted at this town the 26th of Auguft 1645, on his route from Wales to Oxford, and flept at the houfe of the Earl of Bedford [d], who was then in the fervice of the Parliament.

Hugh de Bolebec, in 1145, founded an abbey of Ciftercian monks at Woburn [e]. In 1234, this monaftery was fo poor that the eftablifhment was for a time broken up, and the monks difperfed into different convents till their debts were difcharged [f]. By various benefactions their revenues were fo much improved, that, at the general diffolution of monafteries in the reign of Henry VIII. they were eftimated at 391l. 18s. 2d. clear yearly value [g]. The laft abbot was hanged at Woburn for denying the king's fupremacy. The fite of the abbey was granted, in 1547, to John Lord Ruffel, afterwards Earl of Bedford, and has been ever fince the chief feat of that noble family. There are no remains of the conventual buildings.

Woburn houfe, a magnificent manfion occupying four fides of a quadrangle, was almoft wholly rebuilt by Flitcroft, for John Duke of Bedford, about the middle of the laft century. The ftate apartments are fitted up in that ftyle of coftly magnificence which then prevailed. The gallery exhibits a large and moft interefting collection of portraits, among which are to be feen thofe of many illuftrious characters of the houfe of Ruffel, and other families allied to them by marriage. Some curious portraits alfo are difperfed in other rooms; among the moft remarkable are thofe of Philip of Spain and Queen Mary, by Sir Antonio More. A *catalogue raifonné* of the pictures at Woburn was drawn up by the late Earl of

[z] Cart. 26 Henry III.   [a] A pamplet was publifhed on the fubject bearing that date.
[b] Hiftorical Regifter.   [c] Queen Elizabeth's Progreffes.   [d] Symonds's MSS. in the Britifh Mufeum.   [e] Tanner.   [f] Chron. Dunft.   [g] Tanner.

Orford,

Orford, at the Duke of Bedford's requeſt, not long before his death. Among the portraits lately added, is a fine picture of Thomas Kellegrew, the celebrated wit in Charles the Second's reign. The collection of pictures by the old maſters is large and valuable. Several of thoſe deſcribed by Pennant have been exchanged for others. Among the more recent additions (by the late Duke) are a choice cabinet collection, in a ſmall room at the end of the library, fitted up in the Etruſcan ſtyle. It conſiſts of ſome very valuable pictures by Cuyp, Teniers, Berghem, and Rubens, and a celebrated cattle piece by Paul Potter. The library (57 feet by 24) was fitted up by the late Duke. Over the book caſes are portraits of artiſts; Titian, Rembrandt, Rubens, Tintoret, Teniers, and Kneller, by themſelves; the others principally by Vandyke. The great ſtables, mentioned by Pennant as part of the cloiſters of the abbey, were pulled down by the late Duke, and their ſite is occupied by a ſuite of rooms. The preſent ſtables form the wings of a very handſome building, the centre of which is occupied by the tennis court and riding houſe. The former is 108 feet in length; the riding-houſe, including a gallery at the end for ſpectators, 130. A colonnade, a quarter of a mile in length, leads from the Duke's private apartments to the ſtables, tennis court, and other buildings.

Large ſums have been expended in altering the level of the ground near the houſe, which ſtands about the centre of an extenſive park. Numerous plantations were made, both in the park, and on the neighbouring hills, by the Duke's grandfather; others have been more recently laid out, to the great improvement of the ſcenery; but its character is more that of grandeur, than of picturefque beauty.

The late Duke's favourite purſuits are well known to have been experimental agriculture and the breeding of cattle. For this purpoſe he kept ſeveral farms in his own hands. The principal farm-yard is in the park, about half a mile from the houſe. The buildings of every kind, for the uſes of the farm, are upon the moſt extenſive ſcale, and abound with every convenience that could be deviſed; one of the moſt remarkable is the room conſtructed for ſhewing the ſheep at the annual ſhearing, which has been kept for ſeveral years paſt with great hoſpitality. The preſent Duke follows the ſteps of his late brother in patronizing agricultural improvement, and keeps up all the eſtabliſhments which he formed with a view to that purpoſe. On the farm at Woburn is a mill for malting, threſhing, winnowing, &c. and other conveniencies for the abridging and expediting of labour, moſt of which were conſtructed under the direction of Mr. Salmon, the Duke's clerk of the works, the ingenious inventor of ſeveral uſeful improvements in agricultural implements.

VOL. I.   X   The

The manor of Woburn was given to the abbey by the founder [h], and was granted to the Duke of Bedford's anceftor, together with the conventual fite.

The manor of Birchmore, in this parifh, belonged to Woburn abbey, and, after the reformation, was, for a confiderable time in the family of Stanton, from whom it paffed, by a female heir, to the Pickerings. It is now the property of the Duke of Bedford, whofe grandfather purchafed it of Sir Edward Pickering bart. in 1747.

It appears by the *Liber Regis* that Birchmore had formerly a church, to which the chapel of Woburn, called, in moft records, Old Woburn, was annexed. In a furvey of the parifh, made by Sir Jonas Moore in 1661, a garden, about 200 yards weft of Birchmore houfe, is called the church-yard. This fufficiently denotes the fite of the old church. Woburn chapel, now the parifh church, was given to the abbot and convent in 1242. The great tithes, by the name of the rectory of Birchmore, were appropriated to the monaftery in 1308 [k]. They are now the property of the Duke of Bedford. The benefice is a donative in his Grace's patronage.

In the chancel of the parifh church is the monument of Sir Francis Stanton, fheriff of the county, who died in 1635. His fon Edward was an eminent divine among the Puritans. In the fouth aifle is the tomb of John Morton, fon of John Morton, lord of the manor of Lovels-bury, in Potefgrave, who died in 1394. The tower ftands detached from the reft of the building, at the north-weft corner. The church was undergoing a thorough repair, which it feemed much to need, in the month of Auguft 1800.

Adjoining the church-yard is a free fchool, founded by Francis Earl of Bedford, who died in 1582. Francis Lord Ruffel, in 1622, gave a falary of 10l. *per annum* to the mafter, which has been fince increafed to 35l. A copy of the ftatutes is in the Duke of Bedford's muniment room in London.

There is an alms-houfe in this parifh for 12 poor perfons, founded by the Bedford family. It is endowed with 30l. *per annum*, and the endowment was confirmed by an act of Parliament in 1761.

WOOTTON, in the hundred of Redbornftoke, is a very pleafant village, lying about 5 miles fouth-weft of Bedford. The manor belonged to the Beauchamps, barons of Bedford, and defcended by female heirs to the Botetorts, Latimers, and Nevilles [l]. John Neville, Lord Latimer, died feifed of it in 1543 [m]. Early in the 17th cen-

---

[h] Dugdale's Monafticon.　　[i] Duke of Bedford's Records.　　[k] See Tanner.
[l] See Cardington.　　[m] Efch. Henry VIII.

tury,

tury, it became the property of the Monoux family. Humphrey Monoux, of Wootton, was created a baronet in 1660. It is now the property of his defcendant, Sir Philip Monoux bart. who refides at Sandy. The manor houfe at Wootton is, or was lately, in the occupation of Col. Lake. The manor of Hoe, in this parifh, was formerly in the Archer family [n], afterwards in the Botelers, and is now the property of Admiral Cornifh, whofe uncle, Sir Samuel Cornifh, bought it, about the year 1765, of Sir Philip Boteler bart. The manor of Pillinge, in Wootton, or Wootton Pillinge, was part of Lord Fanhope's property [o], and was afterwards in the family of Long [p]. Sir Francis Clerke, who died feifed of it in 1632, bequeathed it to Sidney Suffex College, in Cambridge [q]. Richard Burgoyne efq. who died in 1464, was feifed of a manor called Bofoms, in this parifh [r].

In the parifh church are feveral tombs of the Monoux family, among which are thofe of all the baronets, and of Lieut. Monoux, who was flain in the action with the Duke of Monmouth's army in 1685; he was buried at Chard in Somerfetfhire, and his body afterwards removed hither. Wootton lies in the deanery of Bedford. The great tithes, which were appropriated to the priory of Newenham, are now the property of Sir Philip Monoux, who is patron of the vicarage.

WRESTLINGWORTH, in the hundred of Bigglefwade and deanery of Shefford, lies on the borders of Cambridgefhire, about three miles from Potton, and about five from Bigglefwade. King Henry III. in 1218, gave the manor to Ifabella de Dover, till fuch time as he fhould pleafe to reftore it to the heirs of Reginald Damartin, Earl of Boulogne, whofe property it had been, promifing in that cafe to give her a penfion in lieu of it [s]. After this it was fucceffively in the families of Huntercombe [t] and Raghton; from the latter it paffed by a female heir to the Afplions [u]. In 1475, it was granted to Anthony Lord Grey, of Ruthin [x]; in 1485, to Margaret Countefs of Richmond [y], who fettled it on Thomas Earl of Derby. Of late years it was in the family of Downing, and is now the property of Jacob Whittington efq. An eftate in Wreftlingworth, which belonged alfo to the Downings, forms part of the endowment of the college, which is to be built in Cambridge, purfuant to the will of Sir Jacob Downing. The rectory of Wreftlingworth is in the gift of the crown. The parifh has been inclofed by an act of Parliament, paffed in 1801, when allotments of land were affigned to the rector, and to the rector of Cockayne Hatley, Thomas Ryder, efq. and others who had portions of tithes in Wreftlingworth; under the fame act, part of Hartley field was allotted

[n] Efch. Edw. IV.   [o] Efch. Hen. VI.   [p] Efch. Hen. VIII. and Eliz.   [q] See his will.
[r] Efch. Edw. IV.   [s] C. 11 Henry III.   [t] Efch. Edw. III.   [u] Efch. Hen. V. and VI.
[x] Pat. 14 Edw. IV.   [y] Rot. Parl. vol. vi.

and

and added to the parifh of Wreftlingworth, which was computed to contain about 1860 acres.

YIELDEN, in the hundred of Stodden and deanery of Eaton, lies on the borders of Northamptonfhire, about 14 miles from Bedford. It was anciently called Ivelden, or Givelden, and was the feat and property of the barons Traylly, who poffeffed this and other manors in the county when the furvey of Doomfday was taken. They were not fummoned to Parliament after the reign of King John [z], but their defcendants in the male line continued in poffeffion of this manor till the year 1360, or later. The caftle of Yielden is reprefented in the inquifition of that date, as having fallen entirely to decay [a]. Its fite is called the Caftle-field, where the prefent appearance of the earth-works fhews it to have been a place of great ftrength. What became of the manor of Yielden does not appear on record. It is not improbable that it formed part of the endowment of Northill college, founded by the executors of Sir John Traylly, the laft heir male of the family. It is certain that it was, at a fubfequent period, for a confiderable time, in the family of St. John. It is now the property of John Crawley efq. of Stockwood, near Luton, one of the reprefentatives of Sir Jeremy Vanacker Sambroke, whofe family purchafed it of the Earl of Bolingbroke in 1706. The advowfon of the rectory was given by Geffrey Traylly, in the reign of Henry I. to the monks of Thorney [b]. It was afterwards in the St. John family, and was fold by the Earl of Bolingbroke, in 1706, to the then bifhop of Peterborough, of whofe fon, Robert Clavering efq. it was purchafed by the Rev. Edward Bunting, the prefent patron and incumbent.

John Pocklington, rector of Yielden, was author of a fermon, entitled, " Sunday no Sabbath," preached at the bifhop of Lincoln's vifitation at Ampthill, in 1635 [c]. It gave fuch offence to the puritans, that, in the year 1640, an order of Parliament was iffued, condemning it to be burnt by the hands of the common hangman in London and in the two Univerfities.

---

[z] Dugdale. 　　[a] Efch. 34 Edw. III. 　　[b] Dugdale's Baronage, vol. i. 　　[c] Ant. Wood.

MAGNA BRITANNIA;

BEING

A CONCISE TOPOGRAPHICAL ACCOUNT

OF

THE SEVERAL COUNTIES

OF

GREAT BRITAIN.

By the Rev. DANIEL LYSONS, A.M. F.R.S. F.A. and L.S.
RECTOR OF RODMARTON IN GLOUCESTERSHIRE;
And SAMUEL LYSONS, Esq. F.R.S. and F.A.S.
KEEPER OF HIS MAJESTY'S RECORDS IN THE TOWER OF LONDON.

VOL. I.—PART I.

CONTAINING

BEDFORDSHIRE.

LONDON:

PRINTED FOR T. CADELL AND W. DAVIES, IN THE STRAND.

1813.

ADDITIONS AND CORRECTIONS.

GENERAL INTRODUCTION.

P. 15. Mr. Whitaker[a], on the authority of Richard of Cirencester, makes the ancient division of Britain to consist of six parts, adding to those mentioned in this page, *Vespasiana*; but it is not stated what this district comprised.

P. 17. l. 7. Chester has been here inadvertently inserted; it did not form part of the kingdom of Mercia, and is not in Camden's list.

P. 19. In some copies of Vol. I. the See of Gloucester (comprising the whole of Gloucestershire, except a few parishes which are in the diocese of Bristol,) is omitted in this page.

P. 20. l. 10. *After* Gloucester, *add* Peterborough.

BEDFORDSHIRE.

P. 3. A petition was presented to Parliament in the month of June 1644, from the inhabitants of Bedford, praying that the works and fortifications of that garrison, which had been in part slighted, might be repaired for the better defence and safety of the county[b]. A diurnal of the 24th of the same month states, that Parliament had received information that the King's forces had made incursions into Bedfordshire, and that on "the last Lord's day" the King passed through Hockley-in-the-Hole towards Bedford, and in the way plundered Leighton, and sent another party to Dunstaple, who plundered that town and committed great outrages in the church during the time of divine service, shooting at the minister in the pulpit and wounding several of the congregation; committing the like outrages at other towns and villages, and at Woburn, the seat of the Earl of Bedford[c]. On the 26th of August 1645, the King marched with his army from Huntingdon to Bedford, and passed on the same night to Woburn, where he slept; the next day his army halted at Dunstaple, and he took up his quarters at

---

[a] See his History of Manchester. [b] Perfect Diurnal, June 3—10, 1644.
[c] Perfect Diurnal, June 24—July 1, 1644.

the Red Lion in that town.   A diurnal of that time relates a victory gained by Lieutenant-Colonel Corkan, againſt ſome forces of the King's at Goldington, and his defence of Bedford-bridge againſt the King's approach, while the parliamentary forces in that town effected their retreat [d].

The Marquis of Bute is lord of the hundred of Flitt; and Lord St. John of thoſe of Barford and Stodden.

P. 4.   Lalega, ſometimes called Lega in the Survey of Domeſday, is ſuppoſed to have been Thurleigh.

P. 6.   Ampthill and Luton are alſo conſiderable corn-markets.

P. 13.   It was only the elder branch of the Gery's that became extinct by the death of William Gery, Eſq.; his younger brother, the Rev. Charles Gery, is now living at Grantham.

The families of Becher and Cater are not extinct, but they have no longer any property or reſidence in the county of Bedford.

P. 14.   The Earl of Upper Oſſory was created a Britiſh peer in 1794, by the ſtyle of Lord Upper Oſſory of Ampthill.

——   Bromham-houſe has been enlarged, and is inhabited by the Right Hon. John Trevor, only brother of Lord Hampden.

——   Cople, a ſeat belonging to the Duke of Bedford, was occupied by the late Earl Ludlow, who died in 1811, and now by his brother the preſent Earl.

P. 15.   Since 1801 the title of Baronet has paſſed from Sir Philip Monoux to a son of the ſame name; and at his death, in 1809, to his couſin the Rev. Philip Monoux, rector of Sandy.   Dame Judith Monoux, relict of Sir Philip, who died in 1805, reſides at Everſholt.

P. 16.   To the liſt of gentlemen's ſeats in this page, may be added,

Aſpley Guiſe	-	The Rev. Edward Orlebar Smith.
Cardington	-	The ſeat of the late John Howard, Eſq. now belonging to John Howard Channing, Eſq. occupied by George Curtis, Eſq.
Eaſt Hide	-	Robert Hibbert, Eſq.
Harlington	-	The widow of the late John Wingate Jennings, Eſq.
The Haſells	-	Francis Pym, Eſq. M.P.
Kempſton-Bury	-	William Long, Eſq.
Milton Erneſt	-	Mrs. Mary Boyden.
Roxton	-	Chas. James Metcalf, Eſq.
Sharnbrook	-	John Gibbard, Eſq.
Steppingley	-	John Parker, Eſq.
Stratton	-	Charles Barnett, Eſq.

Tingrith is the property of Robert Trevor, Eſq.

Moggerhanger is now the ſeat of Stephen Thornton, Eſq.

[d] Perfect Occurrences, Aug. 22—29, 1645.

P. 18.

P. 18. Colmworth fhould have been mentioned among the confpicuous fpires. See p. 70.

P. 19. 146. There are very extenfive quarries of an excellent freeftone at Toternhoe, of which moft of the public buildings, and the principal houfes of the nobility and gentry in Bedfordfhire and the adjacent counties, have been erected for many centuries.

P. 21. We are told by Walfingham, that in the year 1399, the courfe of the Oufe, between Harold in Bedfordfhire and Snelfon in Buckinghamfhire, was fuddenly changed, and a dry channel left for the length of three miles.

—— l. 21. Another hiftorian places the inundation here mentioned in 1256, and fays that the greater part of Bedfordfhire was overflown, many villages laid under water, and an innumerable quantity of men, women and children drowned[e].

P. 22, 23. The road from London to Higham Ferrers, &c. is now the mail-coach road to Nottingham. The turnpike-road from Staughton is completed, through Pertenhall, Swinefhead, and Rifely to Bletfoe, where it enters the London road, and paffing along it northward about half a mile, branches off through Sharnbrook, Odell, and Harold to Lavendon, Bucks, and enters the turnpike-road from Wellingborough to London near Olney. Another new turnpike-road has been made from Aylefbury in Buckinghamfhire, through Leighton-Bufard, to Hockcliffe.

P. 22 and 109. There are two fources of the Lea, one at Houghton Regis, and the other at Leagrave, in the parifh of Luton.

P. 23. l. 14. We are informed that the road from Bedford to Eaton-Socon, on the north fide of the Oufe, is not a turnpike-road, and that the two roads meet at the foot of Roxton-hill beyond Great Barford.

P. 36. Ampthill has a confiderable corn-market. There is a fair alfo on St. Andrew's day. The May fair is now held on the 4th.

P. 37. It appears by the preamble of the Act for erecting Ampthill into an honour, that it was the King's intention " to erect, build, and edifie, upon His Grace's manor of Ampthill, fumptuous, ftately, beautiful and princely buildings[f]." King Henry VIII. refided at Ampthill during the greater part of the month of September 1540, and was there again in 1541. At a council held at Grafton on the 30th of Auguft, in the former year, " att the fute of Mr. Treaforour and Mr. Coferer, of the houfehold, two placards of one tenor were paffed under the ftampe for the authorifinge one Gurley as well to make provifion of fwanns, partriches, capons, chicken, &c. for the King's highnes

[e] Annal. Mon. Burton. Rer. Ang. Scrip. vol. i. p. 333.
[f] Raftall's Statutes, 33 Hen. VIII.

[A 2]

upon refonable prices, as alfoe to take the fame by engynes, fnares, netts, or otherwife duringe the King's abode at this tyme at Grafton and Ampthill, foe that he fhall not medle within 6 miles of the courte, nor in places where reftrainte is made [g]."

P. 39.   It appears that Col. Okey was not only an inhabitant of this county, but that he poffeffed fo much influence in it as to have been appointed *Cuftos Rotulorum*, in which office he was fucceeded by the Earl of Bedford, on the 6th of March 1660   See Mercurius Politicus, publifhed by order of Parliament, March 1—8, 1660.

————— The parifh of Ampthill has been inclofed purfuant to an Act of Parliament paffed in 1806.   An allotment of lands has been given to the rector in lieu of tithes.

P. 40, 41.   Acts of Parliament for inclofing the parifhes of Arlefey and Aftwick, paffed in 1804, after thefe pages were printed off.   John Jackfon Efq., who appears to have made a recent purchafe, is defcribed in the Acts as lord of the manor of both parifhes, and impropriator of Arlefey: allotments of land were affigned in lieu of tithes.

P. 41.   The rectory of Great-Barford belonged to the prior and convent of Newenham [h].

P. 42.   An Act of Parliament for inclofing the parifh of Barton paffed in 1809, under which land was to be allotted in lieu of tithes, or otherwife a compenfation to be made.   Strype, in his Annals of the Reformation [i], (March 14, 1559,) fays, " One Duncombe, Gent. and company, had committed a great robbery in Bedfordfhire.   They were examined before the council.   After being found guilty they were carried down thither by the fheriff of the county, and were hanged in a place where the faid Duncombe might fee two or three lordfhips that fhould have been his, had he behaved himfelf as he ought."   By Strype's account it feems that this muft have been the eldeft fon of William Duncombe, the firft poffeffor of Battlefden, Potfgrave, &c.   Sir John Duncombe of Battlefden was feveral years one of the Lords of the Treafury, and in 1672, Chancellor of the Exchequer.

P. 44, 45.   De Breaute appears to have been the right name of Faukes, the warlike baron who held the caftle of Bedford againft King Henry III.   Moft of our hiftorians erroneoufly call him De Brent.   Carte, the only hiftorian who writes it Breaute, is fupported by coeval records.   His Chriftian name in Latin was Falcafius, which is varioufly written by Englifh hiftorians, Falk, Foulke, Foulkes, and Faukes.

P. 46.   A fmall part of the caftle wall remains, in a lane in the parifh of St. Paul's, called Caftle-lane.

---

[g] Council Books in the Marquis of Buckingham's library at Stowe.
[h] Dugdale's Monafticon, ii. 239.   [i] Vol. i. p. 195.

P. 46, 47. John Nevil, Lord Latimer, died feifed of one-fourth of the barony of Bedford, 34 Henry VIII. William Goftwick died feifed of half the barony in 1547; this paffed to the Marlborough family, and was purchafed by John, Duke of Bedford. Thomas Snagg, Efq. died feifed of the fcite of the caftle of Bedford, and one-third of the barony in 1642. His fon, of the fame name, in the year 1658 fold the fite of Bedford caftle, comprifing two clofes, on one of which is the Caftle-hill, where the bowling-green now is, to Mr. John Hutchinfon, then pro-prietor of the Swan inn. From this perfon, by divers intermediate purchafes and defcents, it paffed to John Staines, Efq. of whom it was purchafed by the late Duke of Bedford [k].

P. 48. After the Gardiners, Newenham-Priory was in the family of Garnault, and was purchafed of the devifees of the late Aimé Garnault Efq. by Mr. Livius.

P. 49. In the year 1803, an Act of Parliament was obtained for paving, lighting, and improving the town of Bedford; and for taking down and rebuilding the bridge, and a fecond Act in 1810, for enlarging the powers of the former. Under thefe Acts the town has been greatly improved. The antient bridge has been taken down and a new one built in its place, of Portland ftone, of five arches. Some Roman coins, and feveral rofe nobles of King Edward III. were found on taking down the old bridge; the piers of which were driven through a bed of clay to a rock of folid ftone, lying below the bed of the river, and many wrought ftones were found under the foundations of the piers. Several horfe-fhoes and a fpur were found in the fame fituation and under a caufeway on the South fide of the river near the fhore, which was pitched with fmall pebbles [l].

—— The Gothic building mentioned in this page is now unoccupied. The affizes were formerly held in it.

P. 50. The evidence of the charter of King Henry II. to the burgeffes of Bed-ford, is to be found on the Great Roll of the Exchequer. See Madox's Hiftory of the Exchequer, p. 273.

—— " Anno 17 Henry VI. the ftairs of the common hall fell on a fhire day, killed eighteen perfons and hurted many others [m]. "

P. 51. l. 17. After coals, *add* corn, timber, iron, falt and other commodities: Bedford has no communication with the port of Yarmouth.

—— A market was formerly held on Tuefday, in St. Mary's-Square, in the void fpace mentioned in p. 52.; but it has been difcontinued many years.

P. 52. The figure of King Charles, mentioned in this page, which was painted in water-colours, has been lately obliterated, when the church was newly plaiftered.

[k] From information obligingly communicated by Meffrs. Browne and Gotobed, of Norfolk-ftreet. From the information of Theed Pearfe, Efq. [m] Leland's Collectan. i. p. 492.

P. 53. There is no houfe occupied by the fingle brethren. There has been for many years a meeting-houfe for the Methodifts in Mr. Wefley's connection, and they have a chapel lately built; there is a Jews fynagogue alfo at Bedford.

P. 54. The prefent mafter of the grammar fchool, in the room of Mr. Hook, deceafed, is the Rev. John Brereton, B. C. L. The truftees of Sir William Harper's charity, though not ftrictly fpeaking, a body corporate, have, under the Act of 1764, all the privileges of a corporation, and are ftyled the Mafters, Governors, and Truftees of the Bedford charity. The prefent rental of the eftates is 6,723*l.* 18*s.* 6*d.* per ann.

P. 55. The provifions for giving the over-plus, if any, of the money appropriated for marriage portions, as defcribed in this page, is not inferted in the exifting Act.

The corporation of the borough of Leicefter, as truftees under a fettlement made by Alderman Gabriel Newton of that town, of his real eftates, to charitable ufes, pay to the corporation of Bedford, the fum of 26*l.* per annum for the purpofe of clothing and inftructing 25 poor boys.

A lunatic afylum is now erecting at Bedford, under the powers of an Act of Parliament, paffed in 1808. It is conftructed upon the plan of St. Luke's hofpital, in Middlefex; is calculated to contain 40 patients, and is intended to be opened during the prefent year (1812).

P. 56. William Botiler, Efq. was of Biddenham in 1673 [n].

—— Lord Hampden has the fmall, as well as the great tithes of Biddenham. The benefice was a ftipendiary cure of only 8*l.* per ann. till Lord Trevor, by his will, bearing date 1723, gave a rent-charge of 12*l.* per ann. to the minifter for the time being, whenever the Governors of Queen Anne's bounty fhould have fettled on the cure a further augmentation of not lefs then 10*l.* per ann.

P. 57. The leafe of the manor of Bigglefwade is now, by purchafe from Lord Carteret, vefted in Sir Alexander Dick, Bart. Bigglefwade is a peculiar.

The February fair is now held on the 14th. The third fair is on *Whit-Monday*.

P. 59. By the death of Henry Beauchamp lord St.-John, which happened December 18, 1805, the title and eftates of that noble family have devolved to his only brother, the honourable St. Andrew St.-John.

P. 60. It was Robert Thornton, Efq. who inherited Mogger-hanger, under the will of Mr. Aftell, and fold it to the late Godfrey Thornton, Efq. It now belongs to Stephen Thornton, Efq. fon of Godfrey.

[n] Blome's Britannia.

P. 60.

P. 60. George Wyan, Efq. is defcribed as of Moggerhanger, and Sir William Fleetwood of Bolnhurft, in 1673.

P. 61. The feveralties of the manor of Bolnhurft have all paffed into different hands, fince 1801. The prefent proprietors are Sir James Duberley, Knight, the fifters and devifees of the late William Campion, Efq. of Bedford, and Meffrs. Charles and Johnfon. The advowfons of Bolnhurst and Colmworth are now vefted in the truftees of Mrs. Watts, wife of the Rev. Mr. Watts, the prefent incumbent.

—— On a partition of the Mowbray property, Bromham was allotted, among other eftates, to William, Earl of Nottingham, afterwards Marquis of Berkley °. Bromham-houfe has, of late, been the occafional refidence of the Right Hon. John Trevor; Flitwick is the feat of Robert Trevor, Efq. See p. 87.

P. 62. The grave-ftone on the chancel-floor of Bromham church, with the figure of a knight between thofe of two ladies, under elegant Gothic canopies, engraved on brafs plates, fhould have been more particularly noticed. The infcription under the figures certainly refers to Sir John Dyve, whofe father became poffeffed of the manor of Bromham by marriage, and the arms over the knight's head are thofe of Dyve; neverthelefs it is equally certain that no part of thefe plates except the arms and infcription relate to the family of Dyve, but to that of Woodville. Two fhields with the arms of Woodville, having different empalements, appear, one on each fide of the knight's figure; and the armour of the knight and the drefs of the ladies are in the ftyle of the fifteenth century, whereas the family of Dyve did not become poffeffed of Bromham until the fixteenth, by the marriage of Henry, fon and heir of John Dyve of Harlfton, in the county of Northampton, with Elizabeth, daughter and heir of Thomas Wilde of Bromham. The maternal grandfather of this Henry Dyve married Elizabeth, fifter and heir of Thomas Woodville of Grafton, in the county of Northampton; whence one might be led to conjecture that the brafs-plates had been brought from that county and had not been originally placed at Bromham, with which place the Woodvilles do not appear to have had any connexion.

P. 64. The chapel at Shefford has been repaired and fitted up, at the voluntary and fole expence of the Rev. Edmund Williamfon, the prefent rector of Campton. The market has been revived; a confiderable traffic is carried on here in ftraw-plat. The fairs are now held on the 23d of January, Old Lady-Day, May 19, and October 11.

° Rot. Parl. VI. 412.

P. 65.

P. 65. The manor of Fenlake-Barnes belonged to the priory of New-enham [p].

P. 66. 69. The parifhes of Carlton and Chillington, the rectories of which are confolidated, have been inclofed, under an Act of Parliament, paffed in 1805.

P. 67. The Manor, &c. of Chickfand appear to have been mortgaged by the Snows, to Peter Ofborne and William Clarck, in the reign of Queen Elizabeth. Edward Snow, as brother and heir of Daniel, filed a bill in Chancery in 1578, againft Peter Ofborne, William Clarck, and others, for the production of the mortgage and laft will of the faid Daniel Snow, left in the hands of the defend-ants before the teftator went to fea [q].

P. 69. The monks of Ramfey feem to have had a manor at Clapham, before the Conqueft [r]. Wentworth Taylor Efq. was of Clapham in 1673.

—— A churchyard has been lately confecrated at Clapham, for the burial of the dead.

P. 70. The co-heirs of the barony of Albini (21 Hen. III.) were William de Houton, Ralph de St. Amand and Geffry de Beauchamp [s].

—— Certain open and common fields, paftures, meadows, and waftes in the parifh of Clophill have been inclofed under an Act of Parliament paffed in 1808, by which certain portions of land are allotted in part of fatisfaction for tithes, and corn-rents in lieu of the remainder.

P. 71. William Dyer, Efq. is defcribed as of Colmworth in 1673. The manors in Cople mentioned in this page, the manor of Goldington (fee p. 88.), and the manor of Willington (fee p. 151.), were purchafed of truftees acting under the will of John, Duke of Bedford.

P. 71. The Duke of Bedford's houfe at Cople was lately occupied by Earl Ludlow, who died there in 1811, and now by his brother the prefent Earl.

P. 72. We are informed that fome of the Luke family are ftill extant; although not of the rank of gentry, and refident in or near Potton.

P. 74. King Henry VIII. was at Dunftaple in October 1540, and in July 1541 [t]. King Charles flept at the Red-Lion in that town, Auguft 27, 1645 [u].

P. 78. A church at Melnho is fpoken of in ancient records as belonging to the monks of Waltham [w].

P. 79. Sir John Huxley is defcribed as of Eaton Bray, in 1673 [x]. The church of Eaton Bray was given to Merton priory by Stephen, Earl of Moreton [y].

---

[p] Dugdale's Monaft. vol. ii. 240.   [q] Chancery Proceedings in the Tower of London, S. S. 6. 32.   [r] Dugdale's Monafticon, i. 231.   [s] Madox's Hiftory of the Exchequer, p.917.   [t] Council Books in the Marquis of Buckingham's library at Stowe. Perfect Occurrences, Auguft 22—29, 1645.   [w] Dugdale's Monafticon, ii. p.11.

[x] Blome's Britannia.   [y] Dugdale's Monafticon, ii. 139.

P. 80.

P. 80. Mr. Brickwood's manor of Goldington's has been purchased by Mr. Becket, a coachmaker at Huntingdon.

—— There is a manor in the parish of Eaton-Socon, adjoining to Bush-mead, called Kings-wood, otherwise Chamois-Park, now the property of James Dyson, Esq.

P. 81. The Hales are described as of Edworth in 1673 [z].

—— In a close, about a quarter of a mile south from Elstow church, on the opposite side of the road, is the burial-place of a family of the name of Ballard, with five inscribed grave-stones, the oldest is that of Samuel Ballard, Gent., who died in 1695.

P. 82. Mr. Whitbread has the small as well as the great tithes of Elstow, which is more properly a curacy or donative, although called a *vicarage* in the *Liber Regis*.

—— The patronage of the rectory of Eversholt is vested in the Marchioness of Downshire, who has the power of appointment to either of her sons. The parish of Eversholt has been inclosed, under an Act of Parliament, passed in 1806.

P. 85. Jemima, Countess of Hardwicke, was daughter of John Viscount Glenorchy (afterwards Earl of Breadalbane), and wife of Philip, the second Earl of Hardwicke, son of the Lord Chancellor.

P. 87. An Act of Parliament for inclosing the parish of Flitton-*cum*-Silsoe passed in 1809, under which allotments of land were given in lieu of tithes. The Marchioness of Downshire has a manor in Silsoe.

—— The parish of Flitwick has been inclosed under an Act of Parliament, passed in 1806. Allotments of land were given in lieu of tithes.

P. 88. Sir Thomas Allen, Bart. is described as of Goldington, in 1673 [a].

P. 89. The church of Upper-Gravenhurst belonged to the Priory of New-enham [b].

P. 90, 91. John Cooper Esq. is now Lord of the manor of Harlington, impropriator of the rectory, and patron of the vicarage. An Act of Parliament passed in 1808, for the inclosure of this parish, by which an allotment of land in lieu of tithes was given to the impropriator, and to the vicar a small allotment, and a corn-rent. Harlington-Grange, which had been given by Ralph Pyrot to the monks of Woburn, in the reign of King Henry II., was granted by Queen Elizabeth, in the sixth year of her reign, to John Lee. This estate, which is now

[z] Blome's Britannia.   [a] Ibid.   [b] Dugdale's Monasticon, ii. 239.

the property of Sir John Everett, Knt., was proved to be tithe-free at the Bedford affizes (Aug. 1810).

P. 91. There are three fairs at Harold, on the Tuefdays before May 13, July 6, and October 11.

P. 92. Thomas Farrer Efq. is defcribed of Harold, Edmund Wylde Efq. of Houghton-Conqueft, (fee p. 97.) Richard Dennis Efq. of Kempfton (fee p. 101.) and Sir Henry Wright, Bart. of Knotting, in 1673.[c] (See p. 102.)

—— The Bedfordfhire branch of the Cockayne family became extinct by the death of Samuel Cockayne Efq. in 1746. A periodical paper[d] of that date affirms that the reprefentative of the family at that time was George, Count Cockayne, an officer in the Polifh fervice, grandfon of Scipio Cockayne of Shengay, in Cambridgefhire: Lord Cullen is faid to be defcended from a younger branch of the family. By the death of Mrs. Lucy Cockayne Cuft, which happened in February 1804, the manor of Cockayne-Hatley devolved on her nephew Lord Brownlow, who made it his occafional refidence.

P. 95. Mrs. Elizabeth Edwards, and George Edwards Efq. are both deceafed. The Henlow eftates have paffed under the will of the latter to his nephew, George Nigell Raynsford Efq., who has taken the name of Edwards.

P. 98. The parifh of Houghton-Conqueft has been inclofed, under an Act of Parliament paffed in 1806; the lands are not exonerated from tithes.

P. 101. The Monks of Ramfey appear to have had, in ancient times, a manor in Kempfton[e].

—— Mr. Dennis's manor at Kempfton has been fold to the Rev. Edward Williamfon of Campton.

P. 103. The December fair at Leighton-Bufard has been difcontinued.

P. 103. 105. Leighton-Bufard is a peculiar, under the jurifdiction of the prebendary.

P. 105. In the reign of Queen Elizabeth, the inhabitants of Stanbridge filed a bill in Chancery againft Gabriel Fowler, to recover poffeffion of a meffuage called the Town-houfe, ufed as fuch by the inhabitants beyond the memory of man, and for the ufe of a minifter by appointment of the vicar of Leighton, to fay divine fervice in; the defendant is ftated to occupy the

[c] Blome's Britannia.
[e] Dugdale's Monafticon, ii. 231.

[d] The Daily Advertifer.

faid

said house to the exclusion of the inhabitants, who aver that unless relief be had, they must be at the charge of building a new house for the like purposes [f].

P. 108. Archbishop Rotheram by his will, bearing date 1498 (printed in Hearne's Lib. Niger Scacc. vol. ii. p. 667, second edit.) gave the manors of Someries, Luton *cum Hundredo*, and Houghton, &c. to Sir Thomas Rotheram, his brother's eldest son in tail male.

P. 109. The manor of East-Hide is now, by a late purchase, the property and residence of Robert Hibbert Esq.

P. 113. It appears by Archbishop Rotheram's will above mentioned, that his mother and brother were interred in Luton church.

———— A partial inclosure Act, chiefly for confirming some old inclosures at Luton, passed in 1808.

P. 116. The greater part of the Melchborn estate was inherited by the St.-John family from the Pavelys. The St.-Johns had a seat at Melchborn before they became possessed of the Preceptory estate, as appears by the date of 1575 on the old part of Lord St.-John's house. The manor and advowson of Melchborn, which had belonged to the Knights Hospitallers, continued in the Russell family till after the death of Francis Earl of Bedford in 1583 [g].

———— John Boteler Lord of Meppershall and Polehanger, married Joan, daughter and heir of John Meppershall and Katherine his wife, who was daughter and heir of John Estricke. Joan, daughter and heir of John Boteler the younger, married John Leventhorpe [h].

P. 117. Thomas Salmon, rector of Meppershall, was author of " A Proposal to perform Music in perfect and mathematical Proportion," 1688; his sons, Nathaniel and Thomas, both natives of Meppershall, were writers of some eminence. Nathaniel published histories of Hertfordshire, Essex, and Surrey; the Lives of the English Bishops since the Reformation; a Survey of the Roman Stations in Britain, and of Roman antiquities in the midland counties; Thomas was author of several historical and geographical works.

P. 123. The manors of Pertenhall-How and Bells have been purchased of Mr. Pagett's heirs by Mr. William Bricheno.

[f] Chancery Proceedings in the Tower of London, Temp. Eliz. S. S. 17 — 17.
[g] Dugdale's Baronage, ii. 379.　　　[h] Cole's MSS. Brit. Mus. vol. xi. f. 172. b.

P. 124. The fairs at Potton are now held on the second of February, the last Tuesday in April, the first Tuesday in July, and the Tuesday before October 29th.

P. 126. In the year 1809, an Act of Parliament passed for inclosing the Parish of Pulloxhill, by which a small allotment of land and a corn-rent were given to the vicar in lieu of tithes.

———— The Rev. Robert Holt Butcher is now lord of the manor of Ravensden, and John Forbes Esq. of Ravensden-Grange. An Act of Parliament passed in 1809 for inclosing this parish, by which an allotment of land was given to the rector in lieu of tithes.

P. 127. There was an Act of Parliament in 1725, to enable Lord Ashburnham to sell Brogborough and Bickering parks to Ralph Radcliffe Esq. Lady Frances Radcliffe died in 1808, and was succeeded in her estates by Æmilius Henry Delmé Radcliffe Esq.

P. 127, 128. The Duke of Bedford and Mr. Radcliffe both appoint game-keepers for Brogborough.

P. 129. The present possessor of Roxton is Charles James Metcalfe, Esq. who has a seat there.

———— The parish of Roxton is now under inclosure, pursuant to an Act of Parliament passed in 1810. Allotments of land have been given in lieu of tithes.

———— In 1807, an Act of Parliament passed for inclosing the parish of Salford. It appears by the preamble to the Act, that the *manor* of Salford is vested in the warden and fellows of All-Souls'-college in Oxford, and that it is the impropriation only which is vested in the co-heiresses of the Hervey family (Mrs. Barbara Hervey; Mary Adams, widow; Edward Orlebar Smith, and Charlotte his wife; and the Rev. John Burton Watkin, and Barbara his wife). By the Act above-mentioned allotments of land were given in lieu of tithes.

P. 130. An annual show of cattle for sale has been held of late years at Beeston, in lieu of one before held at Ickwell-Green, in the parish of Northill.

P. 130. 155. Sir Philip Monoux, Bart. died in 1805, and was succeeded in his title and estates by his only son, of the same name, who dying without issue in 1809, the title devolved on his cousin the Rev. Philip Monoux, Rector of Sandy; and his estates were divided between his four sisters and co-heirs; when Wootton was assigned to his eldest sister Mary, widow of Sir J. Payne of Tempsford, and now wife of Lieutenant-Colonel Buckworth, of the Cheshire militia; and Sandy to his second sister Frances, wife of the Honourable Samuel Ongley.

P. 131.

P. 131.   Sir Oliver Boteler, Bart. and William Cobb, Efq. are defcribed as of Sharnbrook in 1673[i]. The rectory of Sharnbrook was given to the priory of St. Mary at Leicefter, by William Triket[k].

———— We were mifinformed as to the manor of Oufe or Ouze. It belonged formerly to the Cobbs, as did the manors of Laughtons and Parentines, but was feparated from thofe manors in the year 1700, on the partition of the eftates of George Cobb between his fifters. The manor of Ouze then paffed to Jofeph Godfrey, who married his fifter Rebecca. It was fold by them to Charles Dymoke Willaume Efq. and by him to the father of the Rev. Charles Tanqueray, of whom it has been lately purchafed by Mr. Thomas Gell the prefent proprietor[l]. The parifh of Sharnbrook, containing 2,340 acres, has been inclofed under an Act of Parliament paffed in 1809, by which allotments of land were given to the impropriator and the vicar in lieu of tithes: by this Act, John Gibbard Efq. the impropriator, was exonerated from keeping a bull and a boar for the ufe of the parifh. In the preamble to the Act, Admiral Cornifh's manor is called Loring's Toft, or Temple.

P. 133.   The church of Souldrop was given to the Knights Hofpitallers by Walter Harle, and confirmed by Richard Clare, Earl of Hereford[m].

John Keeling, Efq. is defcribed as of Southill, in 1673[n]. The date of the Southill inclofure Act was 1799.

P. 134.   The manor of Little-Staughton was granted by King Henry VIII., in the year 1547, to Anthony Cockett, and by him fold in 1552, together with Bufhmead, to William Gery Efq. Little Staughton was alienated from the Gery family by Charles Gery, grandfather of the late William Gery Efq. of Bufhmead[o].

P. 135.   The Marchionefs of Downfhire has a manor in Stepingley.

———— The parifh of Steventon has been inclofed under an Act of Parliament paffed in 1805.

P. 136, 138, 140.   Sir Rowland Lytton, Knt. is defcribed of Stotfold, William Cheney, Efq. of Sundon, and George Fitz-Jeffery, Efq. of Thurleigh, in 1673[p].

P. 137. l. 3.   For John *read* Laurence. The manor of Sharpenhoe, as being late the eftate of Laurence Smyth, Clerk, deceafed, was advertifed for fale in

---

[i] Blome's Britannia.
[l] From the information of Theed Pearfe, Efq.
[n] Blome's Britannia.
[p] Blome's Britannia.

[k] Dugdale's Monafticon, ii. 312.
[m] Dugdale's Monafticon, ii. 507. 546.
[o] From the information of the Rev. Hugh Wade Gery.

1805,

1805, under a Decree of the Court of Chancery. It is now the property of Mr. James Smyth.

P. 137, 138. The advowſon of Stretley and the manor of Sundon were ſold in 1802, to Robert Hopkins Eſq. of Tidmarſh in Berkſhire.

P. 140. Robert Bell was grandfather of the *wife* of the late William Gery Eſq.

―――――― The pariſh of Thurleigh has been incloſed under an Act of Parliament paſſed in 1805. Allotments of land were given in lieu of tithes.

P. 142. The manor, eſtates, and advowſon of Tingrith have been purchaſed by Robert Trevor Eſq., of John Williams Willaume Eſq., brother of C. D. Willaume Eſq.

P. 144, 145. The manors of Toddington and Youngs, with the advowſon of the rectory, were purchaſed of Mr. Conolly's truſtees, in 1806, by John Cooper Eſq.

P. 145. l. 29. A few words were here accidentally omitted in the printed copy. The open fields, meadows, commons, and waſtes, intended to be incloſed under the Act, were computed at 2,800 acres; the total number of acres in the pariſh, which was ſurveyed at the time of the incloſure, is 5,437.

P. 147, 148, 149. Sir William Dudley, Knt. is deſcribed of Turvey, Sir William Palmer, Knt. of Warden ; and John Vaux Eſq. of Whipſnade, in 1673 [q].

P. 147. In the eleventh year of Henry III. the biſhop of Lincoln gave 20 marks to the King that the charter for a market at Warden might be ſet aſide, it being prejudicial to the biſhop's manor of Biggleſwade [r].

P. 150. The church of Wilden belonged to Newenham-Priory [s]: the pariſh of Wilden is now under incloſure purſuant to an Act of Parliament paſſed in 1811. An allotment of land was given to the rector in lieu of tithes.

―――――― The manor of Weſt Cotton, in Wilhamſted, belongs to Samuel Whitbread, Eſq. by purchaſe from the Bakers. This pariſh, containing 3,060 acres, has been incloſed under an Act of Parliament paſſed in 1809, when allotments of land were given in lieu of tithes to the vicar, to Thomas Hind, clerk, in right of Anne his wife, and John Croſs Clarke Eſq. joint impropriators of three-fourths of the great tithes, who were thereby exonerated from keeping a bull and a boar for the uſe of the pariſh.

―――――― King Henry VIII. was at Mr. Goſtwick's at Willington on the 21ſt of October 1541, on which day he held a council there [t].

[q] Blome's Britannia.
[s] Dugdale's Monaſticon, ii. 239. ham's library at Stowe.
[r] Madox's Hiſtory of the Exchequer, p. 287.
[t] Council Books in the Marquis of Buckingham's library at Stowe.

P. 152.

P. 152. The parifh of Wimington is now under inclofure, purfuant to an Act of Parliament paffed in 1811.

——— It appears, by a narrative of the fire at Woburn in 1595 (among the late Mr. Gough's pamphlets, now in the Bodleian library), that 130 houfes and " baies of buildings" were deftroyed.

——— In the month of November 1642, the King's forces burnt part of the town of Woburn ".

——— Robert Hobbs, the laft Abbot of Woburn, who was hanged in that town with the vicar of Podington and others, for denying the King's fupremacy, is faid to have rebuilt the parifh-church.

P. 155. Richard Archer died feifed of the manor of Hoe only as tenant by the courtefy : the fee was in the family of Lucy, who held it of the Todenhams as of their part of the barony of Bedford. The Lucys had alfo a manor in Carleton, which had belonged to the Pabenhams, and a manor in Ravenfdon formerly belonging to the Trayllys, and held under the Mowbray family ˣ.

" Whitlock's Memorials, p. 188.
ˣ See Efch. 11 Edw. IV.

ERRATA.

ERRATA.

(BEDFORDSHIRE.)

Page 2 line 15, *dele* " on the fite, it is probable, of King Edward's fortrefs."
      5 correct by p. 80, Wybofton being in Eaton Socon.
  12 — 8 *dele* St.
  15 — *penult. for* Sheriffs, *read* Sheriff.
  16 in the lift of feats, *for* the Rt. Hon. John, *read* Robert.
  18 — 1, *for* rove, *read* over.
  29 — 34, *for* Albrena, *read* Albreda.
  32 — 4, *for* dodecagon, *read* dodecagonal.
  — — 12, *for* Wheatenhurft, *read* Whethamfted.
  50 — 11, *after* alderman, *read* two bailiffs.
  — — 16, *for* the firft of September, *read* the firft Monday in September.
  — — 28, *for* town-hall, *read* fhire-hall.
  — — 34, *for* Kettering, *read* Newport Pagnell.
  51 — 5, *for* Seffions-houfe, *read* Guildhall.
  — — 14, *for* freeman, *read* freemen.
  57 — 8, *for* Trinity-Monday, *read* Whit-Monday.
  — — —, *in the notes, for* Stratton *read* Barnett.
  61 — *penult. for* Placetage, *read* Plâs-Tâg.
  62 — 15, *for* Manfhead, *read* Flitt.
  75 — 19. and p. 81. l. 26. *for* Norman, *read* Saxon.
  77 — 1, *for* Henry II. *read* Edward II.
  80 — 9, *for* Bathonian, *read* Bathonia.
  83 — 32, *for* North Eaft, *read* N.W. by N.
  85 — 7, *for* Polworth, *read* Polwarth.
  — — 3 and 7. *for* Amabel, *read* Annabella.
  89 — *penult. for* 1672, *read* 1671.
  92 — 1, *for* Grove Spurgeon Farrer, *read* Farrer Grove Spurgeon Farrer.
 100 — 27, *for* North Weft *read* N. N. E.
 108 — 29, *for* Farmer, *read* Fermor.
 134 — 3, *for* built, *read* altered and newly fronted.
 135 — 4, *for* Chrift Church, *read* Corpus Chrifti.
 141 — 16, *for* Morteye, *read* Morteyne.
 147 — 26, *for* foreign, *read* alien.
 150 — 6, *for* Bedbornftoke, *read* Redbornftoke.
 153 — 2, *for* Kellegrew, *read* Killegrew.
 155 — 20, *for* Ifabella, *read* Ifolda.

BEDFORDSHIRE.

P. 48. Mr. Theed Pearce has communicated to us, from the records of the corporation at Bedford, two ancient deeds without date, but evidently, by the hand-writing, confiderably earlier than 1280, granting lands to the hofpital of St. John in Bedford, which prove that the eftablifhment founded by Robert de Paris in that year was not the original foundation of the hofpital.

P. 113. When we afferted that Sir Thomas Rotheram married the only child of Anthony Lord Grey of Ruthin, we were not aware of the mal-practices of George Rotherham and Dethick Garter King of Arms, in the reign of Queen Elizabeth, which are recorded in Collins's " Proceedings concerning Baronies by Writ, &c." The monumental evidence which we referred to is in a manufcript in the Britifh Mufeum, in the hand-writing of Monday the herald, and had every appearance of authenticity; indeed the facts there ftated are to be found in the pedigree of Rotheram, among Vincent's Bedfordfhire Pedigrees, in the Heralds' college, though they are contradicted by other evidence of better authority there preferved. The fact appears to have been, that Sir Thomas Rotheram married Catherine a daughter of John Lord Grey of Wilton[a], by Anne daughter of Edmund Lord Grey of Ruthyn. A fuit was inftituted in the Earl Marfhal's court by Henry Earl of Kent againft George Rotheram Efq. and William Dethick Garter, in the year 1597, complaining that the faid Dethick, at the inftigation of Rotheram, had made a falfe pedigree, the object of which was to defraud the faid Earl of the baronies of Haftings, Waisford, and Ruthyn, and divers manors, &c. Lord Burleigh and Lord Howard of Effingham, then jointly exercifing the office of Earl-Marfhal, declared by their judgment in this caufe, " that they did revoke and difannul the bearing of the arms of the Earl of Kent as quartered by George Rotherham, and did judge them to be unlawfully borne ; and did determine *that* part of the pedigree made by Garter to be unlawful, by which the faid Rotheram was made the coufin and heir general of Edmund Earl of Kent by the faid Anthony eldeft fon of the faid Edmund Earl of Kent, and did will that their judgment to be obeyed and continued without any contradiction until they had better proof made before them by the faid George Rotheram and Garter to alter the fame in any part."

In the courfe of thefe proceedings it was ftated, " that George Rotheram had fuggefted falfely that Edward IV. had granted the manors of Dunton and Goyfes

[a] Vincent's Baronage in the Heralds' college.

(fee p. 78. of this vol.) as efcheated to the crown by the attainder of Sir John Manningham, heir to Anthony Lord Grey, whereas he knew that both the attainder againft Manningham was reverfed by act of Parliament, and Manningham reftored to his lands, and by him conveyed, by fine, to Archbifhop Rotheram, and fo defcended to his grandfather Thomas;" this ftatement was no doubt correct as to the defcent of Dunton and Goyfes from Manningham to the Rotherhams, yet the grant to Anthony Lord Grey, of the manors of Wreftlingworth, Dunton and Goyfes, and other lands; was not among George Rotheram's falfifications, as will appear by a reference to Pat. 14 Edw. IV. part 2. m. 5.

INDEX

OF

NAMES AND TITLES.

BEDFORDSHIRE.

The Titles of the Nobility and the Names of Kings or Princes are printed in Italics.

[C]

GENERAL INDEX.

BEDFORDSHIRE.

VOL. I.

[D]

10

THE END.

Strahan and Prefton,
Printers-Street, London.